Gonzo Republic

Gonzo Republic

Hunter S. Thompson's America

William Stephenson

Continuum International Publishing Group
The Tower Building   80 Maiden Lane
11 York Road   Suite 704
London SE1 7NX   New York NY 10038

www.continuumbooks.com

© 2012 William Stephenson

All rights reserved. No part of this book may be reproduced, stored in a retrieval system, or transmitted, in any form or by any means, electronic, mechanical, photocopying, recording, or otherwise, without the permission of the publishers.

Library of Congress Cataloging-in-Publication Data
Stephenson, William, 1965–
Gonzo Republic : Hunter S. Thompson's America/by William Stephenson.
   p.   cm.
Includes bibliographical references and index.
ISBN-13: 978-1-4411-5922-9 (pbk.)
ISBN-10: 1-4411-5922-3 (pbk.)
ISBN-13: 978-1-4411-6827-6 (hardcover)
ISBN-10: 1-4411-6827-3 (hardcover) 1. Thompson, Hunter S. I. Title.
PS3570.H62Z87 2011
813'.54--dc23 [B]   2011021588

ISBN: 978-1-4411-6827-6 (hardcover)
      978-1-4411-5922-9 (paperback)

To Richard Arnold, Bill Bevan, Sarah Lee, Deb Lowe, Alison Raven, Alyson Telfer, Sally Tottle and all those at Lake Terrace 1986–87, especially Dave 'Boy' Greene for giving me my first copy of *Fear and Loathing in Las Vegas*.

'At the top of the mountain, we are all Snow Leopards.', *Kingdom of Fear*, p. 272

Contents

Acknowledgement		viii
Glossary		ix
1	Stepping into History: Values, Contexts, Influences	1
2	Riding with the Angels, Tripping in the Haight: Drugs, Authorities, Countercultures	42
3	Gonzo Fists, Guinea Worms and Freaks: The Political Circus	70
4	The Elusive American Dream; the Edge, the Lodge and the Frontier; Gonzo Sex and Gender	97
5	'Bash the Buggers Silly; Bomb the Insane': Thompson and the American Empire	124
6	Conclusion: 'The Place of Definitions'	152
Appendix I. Thompson on Film		158
Appendix II. The Gonzo Net		170
Bibliography		172
Index		183

Acknowledgement

I would like to express my thanks to the following: Haaris Naqvi at Continuum, New York, for commissioning this study and seeing it through the editorial process; Will Kaufman and William McKeen, who were kind enough to read the early drafts of the manuscript and made several invaluable suggestions; the Hunter S. Thompson Estate and especially its literary executor, Douglas Brinkley, for his enthusiastic response to the manuscript and for his help in seeing the project through; my students on the module EN6007 Literature and Addiction, who were the catalyst for this book, as they suggested that a new academic study of Thompson needed to be done.

A part of Chapter 2 is to appear, in longer form, as 'Fear and Loathing Versus the Guru Trip: the Anti-Mystical Altered States of Hunter S. Thompson's *Fear and Loathing in Las Vegas*', in *Altered States: Reflections on Induced Transcendence in Popular Culture*, ed. Steven Knowles and Christopher Partridge. A part of Chapter 5 has appeared, in longer form, as 'A Fool lies here who tried to hustle the East: Neo-Colonialism and Self-Fashioning in Hunter S. Thompson's *The Curse of Lono*', in *Critique: Studies in Contemporary Fiction* 52:2 (January 2011). I thank the editors for granting permission to reproduce this material here. A number of the journal articles cited were sourced from the JSTOR archive, under the University of Chester licence.

Glossary of Abbreviations for Works by Hunter S. Thompson

For full details of works, see bibliography.

i. Books

Better than Sex (BS)
Conversations with Hunter S. Thompson (C)
The Curse of Lono (CL)
Fear and Loathing in America (FLA)
Fear and Loathing in Las Vegas (LV)
Fear and Loathing on the Campaign Trail '72 (CT)
Generation of Swine (GS)
The Great Shark Hunt (GSH)
Hell's Angels (HA)
Hey Rube (HR)
Interviews with Hunter S. Thompson: Ancient Gonzo Wisdom (AGW)
Kingdom of Fear (KF)
The Proud Highway (PH)
The Rum Diary (RD)
Songs of the Doomed (SD)

ii. Articles

'Dance of the doomed' (*DD*)
'The fun-hogs in the passing lane: fear and loathing campaign 2004' (*FH*)
'Hey rube! I love you. Eerie reflections on fuel, madness & music' (*LY*)
'Polo is my life: fear and loathing in horse country' (*PL*)
'The shootist: a short tale of extreme precision and no fear' (*TS*)
'Why boys will be girls' (*WB*)

When referred to in citations, *Rolling Stone* magazine is abbreviated to *RS*.

1 Stepping into History: Values, Contexts, Influences

> I clearly recall thinking: *Well, this is it. These are G-Men ...*
>
> WHACK! Like a flash of nearby lightning that lights up the sky for three or four terrifying split seconds before you hear the thunder – a matter of *zepto-seconds* in real time – [...]. They had me, dead to rights. I was Guilty. Why deny it? Confess now, and throw myself on their mercy, or –
>
> What? What if I *didn't* confess? That was the question. (*KF*, p. 5: emphasis in original)

One summer day in 1946, two FBI agents knocked on the door of the Thompson family home in Louisville, Kentucky. They accused the eldest son of the house, Hunter Stockton Thompson, aged nine, of damaging a federal mailbox, an offence that carried a 5-year prison sentence. They urged Hunter to confess; they already had witnesses, they said, because his friends had squealed on him. Indeed, the boy was guilty. But, acting on impulse, he decided to turn the tables on the G-Men by asking *them* a question: exactly what witnesses did they have? They had none, and had been lying, and he never saw them again.

With the hindsight of nearly 60 years, writing in his late memoir *Kingdom of Fear* (2003), Thompson recalled his escape from the agents as 'a magic moment in my life, a defining instant for me or any other nine-year-old boy growing up in the 1940s after World War II' (*KF*, p. 5). Unlike the many hardened gangsters, let alone children, who had cracked under such pressure, Thompson had triumphed over his historical context by refusing to believe the popular myth that the Bureau always got its man: 'I learned that the FBI was not *unbeatable*, and that is a very important lesson to learn at the age of nine in America' (p. 8: emphasis in original).

Thompson then moves his memoir forward with a marvellously detailed piece of self-irony. Without that youthful victory over the FBI, he says, he would not be 'sitting alone at this goddamn typewriter at 4:23 a.m.

with an empty drink beside me and an unlit cigarette in my mouth and a naked woman singing "Porgy and Bess" on TV across the room' (p. 8). Thompson's humour arises from the ludicrously specific description of his situation. He does not say 'without defying the FBI I would not have become a writer' but implies it through depicting the consequence of his decision: entry into a world of desperate late night deadline pressure, heavy drinking and jaded soft porn consumption that mocks the received idea of a literary life.

Thompson is interrupted when his wife Anita bursts into the room, saying she has just read an online report that the USA has threatened to invade Saudi Arabia if the Saudis do not become allies in the War on Terror (p. 9). When President George W. Bush's Defence Secretary Donald Rumsfeld appears on TV to denounce this as a malicious rumour, Thompson again makes clear the duplicity and evasiveness of the state. In the 1940s, the G-Men's lies about their non-existent evidence, along with the popular legend of the invincible FBI, had threatened to ruin the young Thompson's life by sending him to jail for what was, with the benefit of hindsight, a trivial offence: likewise, in the 2000s, the Bush administration is spreading disinformation and cultivating the myth that it is fundamentally benevolent and morally sound to conceal its own ruthless pragmatism. Rumsfeld rants that he will 'track down and eliminate' the source of the rumour, while paradoxically urging sweet reasonableness, assuring viewers that the US would never invade such a close ally: 'That would be insane' (p. 9).

Thompson concludes, with heavy irony, that he would not dare to question the decisions of a president about to send the US to war against the Muslim world, as 'That would make me a traitor and a dangerous Security Risk' (p. 9). Instead, he passes to his audience the responsibility to turn the tables on the system, as the 9-year-old Thompson had done to the FBI: to interrogate Bush's foreign policy and see through the smokescreen laid down by Rumsfeld. The nation, as Thompson saw it, was at a moment of decision: 'We are coming to a big fork in the road for this country' (p. 9).

In 2001, just as in 1946, Thompson had to use his liberty or lose it. He did not want the status of a writer to protect him from urgent national questions, from the responsibility to participate in and change history. His response to 9/11 and the subsequent wars was to hit back at Bush, his backers and his hirelings, but not through 'sudden outbursts of frustrated violence' such as the childish vandalism that had first brought the FBI to his door (*PH*, p. 70). Instead, he struck at the government through texts such as *Kingdom of Fear*, which demonstrate how ideology influences the private sphere, and how everyone must try to respond to history, or even to shape it, in response to their own feelings: 'Trust thyself: every heart vibrates to that iron string' (Emerson, 1984, p. 31).

Throughout his life, Thompson followed this prompt. He was an individualist. Although he participated keenly in the American political scene as a reporter, activist and candidate, he subscribed to Henry David Thoreau's construction of the individual 'as a higher and independent power, from which all [… the state's] power and authority are derived' (Thoreau, 1992, p. 245). His life and work affirmed Ralph Waldo Emerson's repudiation of authority, whereby each person must 'not suffer himself to be bullied by kings or empires, but know that he is greater than all the geography and all the government of the world' (Emerson, 1984, p. 10).

In a letter written in 1957, when he was only 20 years old and still in military service, Thompson tentatively articulated his ideal of personal autonomy based on 'a freedom and mobility of thought that few people are able – or even have the courage – to achieve' (*PH*, p. 70). At this time, he was strongly influenced by Ayn Rand's *The Fountainhead* – a novel that had 'really impressed' him as a high school student (*AGW*, p. 156). Rand's narrative is about a maverick architect's fight against a corrupt and oppressive system. Its protagonist, Howard Roark, sets himself up as a non-conformer even in youth, just as Thompson did. Roark is told by his teachers that a life of self-sacrifice is 'beautiful and inspiring. Only he had not felt inspired. He had felt nothing at all' (Rand, 2007, p. 528). *The Fountainhead* formed an extended metaphor for Rand's belief that people should aim to be 'man-worshipers, [who] in my sense of the term, are those who see man's highest potential and strive to actualize it', as opposed to the mediocre, conformist 'man-haters' who work to stifle human self-realization (Rand, 2007, p. xii).

Thompson found such libertarian rhetoric attractive as it articulated his intuitive sense of himself as a unique individual whose lifelong quest would be to create himself on his own terms. As a relative youth, he had difficulty expressing his principles clearly, but he had faith in his future development as a writer, which would eventually enable him to crystallize his ideas: 'That will come later [… because the lack] lies not in the ability, but in the scope of perception of one's own creative ability' (*PH*, p. 70).

Throughout his life, Thompson strove to create and develop an authentic, autonomous identity; but he also understood that there was a power structure to which every individual had to adapt, and that history could mould the subject far more easily than the subject could mould itself. Indeed, history did its best to crush Thompson. His quest to reach his full potential was hindered by such outside forces as poverty and the lack of a college degree and social connections; but his strongest opponent was the state. After his brush with the FBI over the mailbox affair in 1946, he spent a month in jail as a teenager in 1955; a cop clubbed him when he showed his press pass at an anti-Vietnam War demonstration in 1968; the police raided his home in 1990 and he was charged with sexual assault and the possession of illicit drugs. He weathered all this and consistently refused to accept that historical forces, personified by state institutions, could or should determine his life. Like Emerson, he:

> internalized or subjectified history so as to be able to use it, to make it part of his own fiber. He did not step out of history but into it, deciding to make it rather than be made by it. (Porte, 1999, p. 4)[1]

Thompson's belief that the individual subject should realize itself and shape its own place in history was typified by his definition of politics as 'the art of controlling your environment' to which he added the anti-establishment caveat, 'If you don't get into politics, somebody else controls your environment, your world' (*AGW*, p. 156).

The environment Thompson controlled was, first and foremost, his dwelling place. He created his own version of Thoreau's Walden Pond at Owl Farm – the isolated ranch in Woody Creek, near Aspen, Colorado, where he lived from 1967 to the end of his life. There, relatively unhindered by officialdom, he could, in the tradition of a transcendentalist hermit, 'transact some private business with the fewest obstacles' (Thoreau, 1992, p. 13). In Thompson's case, this meant taking drugs, shooting guns, detonating explosives and driving dangerously – but above all else, it meant writing. Thompson's constant phone calls and correspondence with friends, editors, creditors and others, as well as his tastes for intoxicants and for printed and televised information, meant that he was in some respects the opposite of Thoreau, who 'would fain keep sober always' (Thoreau, 1992, p. 145) and despised letters and news as a waste of time and gossip (p. 63–4); but like his nineteenth-century ancestors, Thompson knew the value of freedom in solitude. Owl Farm was an environment that he fought tenaciously to preserve; he resisted all

---

1 'All history become subjective; in other words, there is properly no History; only Biography' (Emerson, 1984, p. 11). Emerson further privileges the individual by locating him/her as an instance of the universal: 'If the whole of history is in one man, it is all to be explained from individual experience. […] Of the universal mind each individual man is one more incarnation. All its properties consist in him. Every step in his private experience flashes a light on what great bodies of men have done, and the crises of his life refer to national crises' (Emerson, 1984, p. 8).

attempts to build on the land around it, as he struggled to keep Aspen uncontaminated by real-estate developers and businessmen hunting a fast buck.

Thompson did not share the spiritual focus of Emerson and Thoreau. He was a humanist in several senses: he celebrated humane values over cruelty and greed; he championed the individual against the system; although staunchly anti-Republican and loosely pro-Democrat, he never actively campaigned for any political party except his own Freak Power movement (see Chapter 3), as he preferred a sceptical, non-aligned stance that allowed free thought; and he was not a religious believer.[2] He subscribed to the 1960s counterculture's distrust of grand abstractions and shared its preference for 'The lively consciousness of men and women *as they are* in their vital daily reality' (Roszak, 1971, p. 54: emphasis in original).

And yet he was equally ready to criticize the emerging institutions of the counterculture. He despised the fashionable fusion of drugs and Eastern religion, exemplified by the pseudo-Buddhist doctrines of the Harvard psychologist-turned LSD guru Timothy Leary. He used hallucinogenic substances regularly, but did so in order to achieve a secular form of transcendence of the mental restrictions imposed by law and government. For Thompson, acid was not a spiritual drug but it was, in his own sense, political, as it became a medium through which he could control his sensory environment and mental state and change both for the better. Unlike Leary, Thompson did not get high to abandon his ego. He did so to *fashion* that ego (see Chapter 2); to follow his own idiosyncratic interpretation of Thomas Jefferson's creed of life, liberty and the pursuit of happiness.

The decade of the hippies, LSD, Vietnam and the Civil Rights Movement offered many opportunities to live out this ideal. The 1960s were a pivotal time in Thompson's life: he published his first book, found his lifelong enemy in Richard M. Nixon, discovered hallucinogenics, married and raised a child and founded Owl Farm. Like the 1830s context of Emerson's transcendentalist movement, the 1960s were a fine time to be a rebel: 'a moment in history containing both expansive hope and a sense of strife and embattlement, and marked by [...] new ethical and political imperatives' (Robinson, 1999, p. 13). Arthur Marwick has argued that during the decade, 'various countercultural movements and

---

2 As an adult he never attended church or professed belief, though in 2002, he wrote, with a fair dose of irony: 'I secretly worship God, folks. He had the good judgment to leave me alone to write a few genuine black-on-white pages by myself, for a change' (*KF*, p. 275).

subcultures' engaged with mainstream society and 'did not *confront* that society but *permeated* and *transformed* it' (Marwick, 1999, p. 13: emphasis in original): Thompson, though, not only confronted the establishment through his subversive, satirical writing and political activism, but also scorned the counterculture's naïve belief that it could transform society through an infusion of peace, love and dope.

Thompson was a patriot. He sought to rebel against the corrupt establishment, but only in order to return the US to its neglected core values – those of the Constitution and Declaration of Independence – that promised individual fulfilment founded on the principle that all human beings are created equal.[3] Like the Founding Fathers, Thompson had inherited from the eighteenth-century radical Thomas Paine the ideal of inalienable human rights, founded on the binary opposition between the individual and government: 'man, were he not corrupted by governments, is naturally the friend of man […] human nature is not of itself vicious' (Paine, 1969, p. 230).

Thompson believed in acting like a human being, and in treating others as such, by defying whatever degrading cruelty convention might demand. The word "human" always carries positive connotations in his writing, and usually also suggests a value under threat from hostile forces. In a 1965 letter to Lyndon B. Johnson, he exhorted the president to start 'acting like a thinking human instead of a senile political beast' (*PH*, p. 497). In 1970, he explained his search for a house and land in Aspen, Colorado, as a quest for a refuge from the brutal modernity of Johnson and Nixon, for a place where he could live 'like a human being' (*FLA*, p. 273). In a 1973 letter to the right-wing Republican ideologue Pat Buchanan, then one of Nixon's speechwriters, he said he was pleased

---

3 Thompson had faith in the *ideology* of 1776, but the historical circumstances were more problematic than the noble prose of the Declaration implies. The Founding Fathers who ratified the Declaration and the Constitution were professionals and slave-owners: 'men of substance – gentry and lawyers […]. So they tended to be conservative in social attitudes' (Reynolds, 2009. p. 75). Their families had benefited from British imperialism until the imposition of unpopular taxes in the late 1700s that led to the independence movement. The issue of slavery in the new Republic was particularly vexed: 'Jefferson's dilemma – how to throw off British "slavery" while perpetuating slaveholding at home – would be a cancer at the heart of the new nation' (Reynolds, 2009, p. 67). The Native Americans also did not seem to be entitled to the same inalienable rights as the white colonists: 'Jefferson's main object in his projected relations with Indians was to extend the fur trade and deprive the tribes, peacefully if possible, of their lands' (Bush, 1977, p. 214). Women, too, were disenfranchised: the US did not grant universal female suffrage until the 19th amendment to the Constitution became a law in 1920.

that political opponents could 'sit down at night as friends and human beings' and that he welcomed 'a human talk with you, if things work out' (*FLA*, p. 531). Later, in 1975, Thompson railed at Jann Wenner, his editor at *Rolling Stone* magazine, for betraying him over a book proposal, after having acted at first 'like a human being' (*FLA*, p. 610).

To Thompson, being or becoming human meant realizing an authentic self. Like his contemporary, the novelist Ken Kesey, whose work he greatly admired, Thompson 'began with the urge to create from within himself and to involve himself in his world, drives which suggest a need to experience fully what it means to be human' (Bredahl, 1981, pp. 76–7). 'He took it seriously – being a decent human, seriously caring about the rights of man' (Ralph Steadman, cited in Wenner and Seymour, 2007, p. 437).

In Thomson's lexicon, human beings were always opposed to the inhuman drones who served the corrupt establishment, whom he often called "pigfuckers" or "scumsuckers". Swine was another consistent term of abuse in Thompson's work, and was often linked to venality. He entitled one anthology of his newspaper columns *Generation of Swine: Tales of Shame and Degradation in the '80s*. In it, he wrote, 'Heaven will be a place where the swine will be sorted out at the gate and sent off like rats' (*GS*, p. 11). Thompson's excoriating denunciation of mindless conformity recalls Thoreau: 'The mass of men serve the State thus, not as men mainly, but as machines […]. They have the same sort of worth only as horses and dogs' (Thoreau, 1992, p. 228). In 1972, Thompson debated, with dry irony, whether Richard Nixon qualified as human: 'Is Nixon "human?" Probably so, in the technical sense. He is not a fish or a fowl. […] It is one of those ugly realities […] that we will all have to face and accept' (Wenner and Seymour, 2007, pp. 168–69).

Thompson's humanism was never self-satisfied or complacent: he was often bitterly self-critical, and did not spare the counterculture. The debauched drug abuse of Raoul Duke and Dr Gonzo in *Fear and Loathing in Las Vegas* represents an escapist, animalistic retreat from the human condition, as well as an exaggerated parody of Thompson's own drug-centred lifestyle. The novel carries the epigraph from Dr Johnson, 'He who makes a beast of himself gets rid of the pain of being a man' (*LV*, n.p.). This is amply demonstrated in the opening chapter, where the stoned protagonists bait a hapless hitchhiker, and the guilt-ridden Duke wonders, 'Had we deteriorated to the level of *dumb beasts?*' (p. 8: emphasis in original).

Thompson realized his own humanity through writing as much as through life: paradoxically, the authentic self that he wanted to create and maintain was to a great extent evolved on the page through a series of more or less autobiographical characters. Italo Calvino, the prolific

Italian fabulist and experimental novelist, once remarked that 'The preliminary condition of any work of literature is that the person who is writing has to invent that first character, who is the author of the work' (Calvino, 1989, p. 111). Calvino situates the author outside biography: the composer is no longer a flesh–and–blood person, but is as much a fiction as the protagonist.

Thompson wrote in detail about his lived experience, placing himself assertively in his texts in the first person in a way that makes him seem, on the surface, the polar opposite of the sort of author-character that Calvino proposes; and yet, much about his work suggests exactly Calvino's point that Thompson's first and most important fictional creation was himself. Over five decades of publishing journalism and novels, Thompson evolved a constantly changing persona that not only determined the direction of future writing projects, but also affected how he lived. This persona was not created overnight in a burst of inspiration, but evolved in parallel with the experiences of its real-life creator.[4]

'It Won't Fit Often, But You're Learning': The Struggles of a Self-Made Man

Thompson was born on 18 July 1937 in Louisville, Kentucky. His adolescence was a paradoxical mixture of achievement and delinquency: he was elected to the town's most prestigious literary society for teenagers, the Athenaeum Club; he distinguished himself as an athlete, writer and speaker; and yet he robbed the same gas station repeatedly, was busted for drunk driving and buying alcohol under age and served a month in Jefferson County Jail for threatening rape. The bald wording of the

---

4 For further details of Thompson's eventful life, see the large number of memoirs and biographies in print. The best of these is William McKeen's thoughtful and well researched *Outlaw Journalist: The Life & Times of Hunter S. Thompson* (2008). Also useful are: Paul Perry, *Fear and Loathing: The Strange and Terrible Saga of Hunter S. Thompson* (1992: revised 2009); Jay Cowan, *Hunter S. Thompson* (2009); Peter O. Whitmer, *When the Going Gets Weird: The Twisted Life and Times of Hunter S. Thompson* (1993); Will Bingley and Anthony Hope-Smith, *Gonzo: A Graphic Biography of Hunter S. Thompson* (2010). Thompson's friends have provided personalized biographical accounts, such as: the memoir by Thompson's artist collaborator Ralph Steadman, *The Joke's Over: Bruised Memories: Gonzo, Hunter S. Thompson and Me* (2006); Jann Wenner and Corey Seymour (eds), *Gonzo: The Life of Hunter S. Thompson* (2007); Michael Cleverly and Bob Braudis, *The Kitchen Readings: Untold Stories of Hunter S. Thompson* (2008). There have been semi-fictional memoirs that seek to imitate Thompson's Gonzo style, such as E. Jean Carroll, *Hunter: The Strange and Savage Life of Hunter S. Thompson* (1993: revised 2005).

charge simplifies the circumstances. When drunk, Thompson and two of his friends had accosted two courting couples, and Thompson had resorted to lurid intimidation in an attempt to bully the lovers into giving him money for cigarettes. After he received his custodial sentence, he began to realize the extent to which class discrimination affected American justice: his friends, who were also charged, happened to be 'sons of prominent attorneys'; they were given probation and a fine, respectively (McKeen, 2008, p. 19).

Thompson spent the day of his high school graduation in jail. For an ex-convict with no money or social connections, university was not an option. Instead, he seemed fated to be a black sheep. On completing his jail term in 1955, he realized that the law enforcement establishment in Louisville had him blacklisted: the judge at his trial had ominously warned him, 'We'll be watching you' (McKeen, 2008, p. 21). Thompson decided that his choices boiled down to military service or going back to jail (*AGW*, p. 332). He duly enlisted, and on Eglin Air Force Base, Florida, discovered not only that he could write sports journalism for the base newspaper full time, but also that sportswriting suited his literary and anti-authoritarian temperament far better than being a regular airman. Most importantly, the genre allowed him free rein to make things up: his military superiors acknowledged his talent for 'innuendo and exaggeration' (*PH*, p. 62).

After his discharge in 1958, he worked on various newspapers, and was frequently fired. All the while, he was trying to write fiction. Even this early in his life, Thompson knew that he wanted to be a writer; but to him, at this point, "writer" meant a novelist like Fitzgerald or Hemingway, whose works he literally copied, typing them word for word, to learn his craft: 'You're writing, and so were they. It won't fit often – that is, *your* hands don't want to do *their* words – but you're learning' (McKeen, 2008, p. 41: emphasis in original). He sent fiction manuscripts to publishers, but all were rejected. He thus became a journalist not out of a sense of vocation, but out of a need to make an income by writing, so that he could hone his skills and improve his novels without having his ambitions destroyed by nine-to-five drudgery.

Eventually, in 1962, he found regular work for the *National Observer* as a roving South America correspondent. On his return to the States, he continued with his unpublished novels and paying journalism. Success and money were frustratingly elusive. He found himself in San Francisco in the mid-1960s with a wife and a baby son, so poor that he lined up with alcoholics and tramps on the street seeking casual work. He was never hired, even though he looked much fitter and healthier than the competition (*C*, p. 10).

It was at this desperate moment that Thompson got the first of his many breaks: but like all the later opportunities that came his way, it was the result of applied talent and dedicated persistence as much as luck. An article he wrote for the *Nation* magazine in 1965 about the Hell's Angels Motorcycle Club of California led to his first book contract. Instead of a dry sociological report of the Angels as seen from the outside, *Hell's Angels: A Strange and Terrible Saga* (1967) was a vivid participant's tale, narrated in the first person. Thompson spent months riding with the Angels, drinking and taking drugs with them. Indeed, he lived so close to the bikers that he almost caught their parasites: 'five of the outlaws came over to my apartment for an all-night drinking bout. The next day I learned that one was an infamous carrier of vermin, a walking crab farm' (*HA*, p. 54).

Such punchy writing got Thompson noticed. On the back of the publication of *Hell's Angels*, he was hired by Random House to write a book on the death of the American Dream. However, the commission soon became a curse, as Thompson realized that he had no clear idea what the Dream was, and that the remit of the book was so vague as to make it impossible to write: 'At the moment it amounts to about 400 pages of useless swill. My need for a focus is beyond critical; it borders on paralysis and desperation' (*FLA*, p. 205).

Again, just as Thompson seemed to have walked up another blind alley, a combination of talent, hard work and good fortune came to his aid. In 1970, 'The Kentucky Derby is Decadent and Depraved', an article for the short-lived satirical magazine *Scanlan's Monthly*, led him to his "epiphany" (*AGW*, p. 270); the serendipitous discovery of his trademark style, a fusion of fiction and reportage that he named "Gonzo" journalism. Gonzo was a vehicle for outrageous semi-autobiographical narrative that did not cloak itself in any pretence of objectivity. It offered a new epistemology of satire, perfectly suited to the image-driven environment of the late twentieth century; the mediated, artificial world that Jean Baudrillard has called "hyperreality" and Guy Debord the 'society of the spectacle' (Baudrillard, 1994; Debord, 2009; see Chapter 3). Gonzo participated in, and even accelerated, the spectacle's relentless forward motion, and yet aimed to derail it. Not only was Gonzo a storehouse of hilarious, often unforgettable images, it challenged the reader to distinguish between fact and fiction when reading the Gonzo piece, and thus also to enquire what elements of the official "truth" peddled about any given situation might also be fabrications.

In 1971, Thompson wrote his first Gonzo masterpiece. He found himself enmeshed in the ethnic tensions of Los Angeles when he began working on 'Strange Rumblings in Aztlán' – a potentially explosive political article for *Rolling Stone* about the police murder of Ruben Salazar, a Hispanic investigative journalist, in August 1970: 'a perfect nightmare of a story – even for somebody with long-time blood/drug/madness ties to the radical Chicano vortex' (*FLA*, p. 359). One of Thompson's main sources was the Chicano activist, lawyer and writer Oscar Zeta Acosta. Needing time and space away from Acosta's bodyguards – who saw Thompson as biased against their movement, and wrongly suspected he was a police informer – he and Acosta decamped to Las Vegas for a weekend of pharmaceutically fuelled rest and recuperation, using the pretext of a routine assignment Thompson had been given to write 250 words about the Mint 400 motorcycle race for *Sports Illustrated*.

Thompson exceeded his word count: hugely, chaotically and brilliantly. He knew he had written a Gonzo epic that deserved to be promoted with outrageous panache, and he worked assiduously to build a myth around it. He claimed the first draft was composed 'by hand on Mint Hotel stationery during an all-night drink/drug frenzy while I waited for dawn to come up so I could flee without paying' (*FLA*, p. 375). With predictable short-sightedness, *Sports Illustrated* "aggressively rejected" (*GSH*, p. 115) what was to become *Fear and Loathing in Las Vegas*, serialized in two parts in *Rolling Stone* in November 1971. Thompson's undisputed high point, and his best-known work, *Vegas* charts the adventures of Raoul Duke and Dr Gonzo, a journalist and his attorney, in the nightmare labyrinth of the hotels, casinos and bars of Las Vegas, ostensibly on a mission to cover the Mint 400 motorcycle race and then the District Attorneys' Conference on Narcotics and Dangerous Drugs, but actually on a quest 'to find the American Dream' (*LV*, 6). The Dream turns out to be The Old Psychiatrists' Club – a burned-out nightspot in an abandoned lot full of weeds.

Thompson believed that *Vegas* was a "failed experiment" according to the strict standards of Gonzo that he had set himself (*GSH*, p. 117); he was disappointed that the novel had not been composed spontaneously and published unedited in the manner of the Kentucky Derby article, as he had intended at first. Instead, he worked on *Vegas* painstakingly over five drafts, ensuring that not a single unnecessary word went in. The result was an amphetamine-paced series of cartoon-like sketches, centred on two hapless acid abusers who come to seem like the bastard descendants of Miguel de Cervantes's Don Quixote and Sancho Panza. Duke and Gonzo's vision is a horror film of hallucinations projected from their shared subconscious. The two men stumble about in a stoned frenzy, dimly aware of the pointlessness of their mission and, indeed, of their lives. Their rootless drifting in Nixon's America comes to symbolize the failure of the 1960s counterculture: 'The big market, these days, is in Downers. [...] "Consciousness Expansion" went out with LBJ' (*LV*, p. 202).

Thompson was fast carving out a national reputation. He discovered that he had been co-opted into the emerging New Journalism movement, spearheaded by Tom Wolfe, Gay Talese and other ambitious authors dissatisfied with the tame conventions of reporting that were 'inadequate to chronicle the tremendous cultural and social changes of the era' (Weingarten, 2006, p. 6).[5] In 1973, when Wolfe put together *The New Journalism*, an anthology of the movement's work, with the stated aim of 'dethroning the novel as the number one literary genre' (Wolfe and Johnson, 1996, p. 15), Thompson was the only writer represented by two pieces: 'The Kentucky Derby is Decadent and Depraved', and an excerpt from *Hell's Angels*.

The difference between Thompson and his fellow New Journalists was that he placed himself at the centre of the story, in Wolfe's words, 'as a frantic loser, inept and half-psychotic, somewhat after the manner of Céline' (Wolfe and Johnson, 1996, p. 195). Jerome Klinkowitz has called Thompson a "SuperFictionist", or experimental novelist, on the grounds of 'the self-reflexive manner of his work. He never disguises the fact that he is a half-cranked geek journalist caught in the centre of the action' (Klinkowitz, 1977, p. 36). While developing this experimental first-person focus, Thompson was influenced by one of his literary heroes, Norman Mailer, who based his work on real events reported from the subjective viewpoint of a persona more or less modelled upon himself. Unlike Thompson, Mailer tended to adopt a position of ironic distance. In his 1968 novel *The Armies of the Night*, he made clear his peripheral role in events, and his separation from the animating passions of the central

---

5 The New Journalism evolved in tandem with the experimental fiction that sought to problematize the linear narrative and stable viewpoint of nineteenth-century realism: 'The novelist attempting to set down his world in the early 1960s found that the conventions of realistic writing shared many of the limitations of conventional journalism, since the two were based on similar assumptions about reality' (Hellmann, 1981, p. 8). This is not to say that the new novelists and New Journalists necessarily valued one another's work or ideas: Wolfe believed that avant-garde 1960s novelists, 'with their abstruse word games and dense allusiveness, were too busy with literary trickery to bother looking out of their own windows' (Weingarten, 2006, p. 10). This did not stop many literary writers of the period from trying to fuse the novel and journalism to create a new genre. Examples include Norman Mailer, *The Armies of the Night: History as a Novel; The Novel as History* (1968); Truman Capote, *In Cold Blood: A True Account of a Multiple Murder And Its Consequences* (1966).

actors: 'an eyewitness who is a participant but not a vested partisan is required, further he must be not only involved, but ambiguous in his own proportions, a comic hero' (Mailer, 1968, p. 53).[6]

In Thompson's view, his own Mailer-influenced standpoint of involvement was a more dangerous but more worthwhile position than the distance favoured by Wolfe and the other New Journalists: 'I get my interest from the adrenaline that comes from being that close. [...] It's easier to be there. Maybe it's more of a risk' (*AGW*, pp. 154–55). Thompson hugely admired Wolfe's writing, and told him 'one of the main strengths of your weird, super-detailed style is a definite dramatic tension that comes with the idea that something very brutal and final might happen to the subject on the very next page' (*FLA*, p. 338): however, he astutely took Wolfe and Mailer's techniques a stage further, and adapted them to his own personality by making the endangered, partisan subject, who is emotionally committed to events, the first-person centre of the action.

The next challenge Thompson set for himself was to become a Gonzo historian, by chronicling a significant national event in his own subjective style. After the hedonistic high jinks of *Vegas*, Thompson focused on a nominally sober theme: politics. He had already stood as the Freak Power candidate for Sheriff of Aspen in 1970, narrowly losing (see Chapter 3). Thompson's brush with activism stirred him to write a book about the political scene. He zeroed in on the 1972 campaign for the Democratic nomination, and the subsequent presidential race between George McGovern and Richard Nixon. He published each episode of his account as he wrote it, in his main outlet at the time, the fortnightly *Rolling Stone* magazine. The eventual book, *Fear and Loathing on the Campaign Trail '72*, takes on the tone of a Renaissance tragedy of hyperinflated egos and ruthless ambition warped into a comedy when seen from the cynical viewpoint of one of the peripheral participants: as if *Macbeth* had been narrated by a jaded bystander nobleman. Watching President Nixon's 'black/armoured hearse' drive past after the inauguration, 'surrounded by a trotting phalanx of Secret Service men with their hands in the air, batting away the garbage thrown out of the crowd, I found myself wondering how Lee felt at Appomattox' (*CT*, p. 82).

Thompson, who unlike the book's reader does not have the benefit of hindsight, is not aware of just how completely McGovern is going to be

---

6 Thompson had corresponded with Mailer infrequently from 1960 onwards (*PH*, p. 256). Mailer admired Thompson's writing and even made an oblique reference to *Hell's Angels* in *The Armies of the Night*: 'If the novelist had never heard of Hell's Angels or motorcycle gangs, he would still have predicted, no, rather *invented* motorcycle orgies' (Mailer, 1968, p. 82: emphasis in original).

defeated, but the realization gradually dawns before the dagger-blow of election night. In retrospect, Thompson realized that the failure of the McGovern campaign had been inevitable, as the nation remained devoted to its masochistic appetite for more of the degrading corruption, oppression and paranoia that Nixon was wantonly inflicting upon it. Thompson cites the depressingly bleak 'Conventional Wisdom' after the election, that the national mood 'was so overwhelmingly vengeful, greedy, bigoted, and blindly reactionary' that no candidate who reminded the electorate of 1960s radicalism could hope to win (*CT*, p. 439).

Thompson utterly despised Nixon: and yet, in the uncanny symbiosis with authority that often characterized his most impassioned polemics, the journalist came to depend on the egotistical, deceitful politician as a reliable source of corruption against which he could vent his spleen. Watergate, and Nixon's subsequent resignation and pardon, were occasions of political horror but literary delight, as Thompson tore into Nixon and his sidekick Gerald Ford with articles such as 'Fear and Loathing in Limbo: The Scum Also Rises' (*GSH*, p. 318–60). This culminated in his savage obituary of Nixon in *Rolling Stone* in 1994, anthologized in *Better than Sex*: 'His body should have been burned in a trash bin' (*BS*, p. 241).

Thompson's post-Watergate writing was driven by several impulses: his continuing disgust at the craven, self-serving men elected to the US presidency since the death of John F. Kennedy (the sole exception being Jimmy Carter, a man of admirable integrity who nevertheless turned out, in Thompson's view, to be incompetent); outrage at the state's treatment of minorities and dissidents; the drive to continue his jaundiced quest to expose the rottenness at the heart of America, along with his own complicity in it.

Thompson continued to produce articles that fed into the ongoing series of *Gonzo* papers, anthologized as *The Great Shark Hunt*, *Generation of Swine*, *Songs of the Doomed* and *Better than Sex*, as well as streams of letters, eventually published in three volumes, edited by Douglas Brinkley: *The Proud Highway*, *Fear and Loathing in America* and *The Mutineer*. He created semi-fictitious travelogues like *The Curse of Lono*. His most regular employment in his final years was as a columnist for the espn.com sports news website: his columns were later collected in *Hey Rube*. On espn.com, he commented on sports and the state of the Union, often powerfully blurring the two, as, for instance, when he remarked – at the time of the invasion of Iraq in 2003 – that 'Sports gambling is huge in the Army' as it represented a good distraction for those 'forever teetering on the brink of some hideous outburst of preternatural violence that could leave them all dying painfully' (*HR*, p. 184). He then went on, deadpan, to discuss the odds for the NCAA Basketball Championship.

One commonly held view of Thompson is that he peaked in the early 1970s with the two *Fear and Loathing* books and was in personal and literary decline ever since; a slow slide induced not only by the limitations of his Gonzo style and persona, but also by the staleness of repetition and the cumulative effects of his Olympian booze and drug intake. Although Thompson contributed more material to *Rolling Stone* in the early 1990s than he had since 1976, 'most of it was seen as lower-level self-imitation' (McKeen, 2008, p. 323). Around 2000, 'Hunter continued to consume enormous amounts of alcohol and drugs and became increasingly paranoid […]. Despite the paucity of fresh material, Hunter's archive helped to sustain the illusion of regular output' (Perry, 2009, p. 232). Although Thompson's later writing did not reach the heights of his superb 1970s material, this picture of decline obscures more than it reveals. Thompson always retained his sharp satirical intelligence and reflexive wit; he used his earlier Gonzo persona as a topic for irony, particularly in *The Curse of Lono*, where he was able to link his own branding as an American celebrity, or mediated product, to the soft, consumerist imperialism that had become the dominant mode of American overseas power in the last quarter of the twentieth century (see Chapter 5).

Thompson responded to 9/11, the defining event of the first decade of the new century, with uncanny prescience. Writing on the day of the atrocity, as images of the devastated World Trade Centre played across his TV screen, he warned that the US would wage a quasi-religious war in theatres such as Afghanistan and Iraq; a conflict without a clear objective and driven by a moralistic sense of superiority to a nebulous but terrifying enemy personified by the bogeyman Osama Bin Laden. In Thompson's view, America seemed poised to lash out clumsily against an adversary skilled in guerrilla tactics, just as it had done in Vietnam. The parallels were unstated but clear: 'Not even the Generals in what remains of the Pentagon or the New York papers calling for *war* seem to know who did it or where to look for them' (*HR*, p. 90: emphasis in original). Chapter 3 examines how Thompson's writing on 9/11 and on the War on Terror deepened the criticism of the establishment's manipulation of the American people that he sustained throughout his writing life.

It was a life that ended in tragic circumstances. Thompson was becoming increasingly lonely and ill as his friends died or moved on and his body deteriorated. He committed suicide at his home on 20 February 2005 at the age of 67. The details of this event have been pored over in biographies and documentaries, even to the extent that the end of Thompson's life threatens to overshadow his achievements during it.[7] Thompson appears to have been of sound mind in the period before, and to have made the decision carefully rather than in a moment of despair. As his son Juan wrote, 'He died as I knew he would someday, by his own hand, on his own terms and in his own time [...]. I know he made his decision calmly, free from despair, his judgement unclouded' (Thompson, 2005, p. 72). Jann Wenner, his editor at *Rolling Stone*, shared this belief: 'He was a careful, deliberate and calculating man, and his suicide was not careless, not an accident, and not selfish' (Wenner, 2005, p. 34). A note to his second wife Anita, written a few days before, indicates his feelings: 'Football Season is Over. No More Games. [...] 67. That is 17 years past 50. 17 more than I needed or wanted. Boring' (McKeen, 2008, pp. 350–51).

Although it is possible to read such a note, and the ensuing act, as desperate gestures born of despair, Thompson may well have been determined to follow his deepest feelings, as he always had. If so, his self-will was clear to the end, and his fatal decision was the last one in a life dedicated to personal autonomy: 'It was not so much a Hemingway death wish as a pragmatic, logical alternative to boredom and suffering. A natural-born control freak, Hunter, in all his grandiosity, disdained the thought of God determining his final outcome' (Brinkley, 2005, p. 40).

Throughout his life, Thompson's work reflected his struggle for self-determination. His writing was founded on his idiosyncratic but consistently humanist and individualist interpretation of the values that had informed the Founding Fathers of the US, which had later been adapted by their descendants like Thoreau and Emerson. As ever in Thompson, the personal and political were intimately linked: his quest for individual freedom, which involved not only egocentricity but also excoriating self-criticism, went hand in hand with his mission to criticize and even change the once-great Republic of which he found himself a part. His main tool for doing this was the genre he became famous for pioneering.

'To Play Unhinged': Gonzo Journalism

Gonzo is the first word most of Thompson's readers associate with his work, but no consensus has even been reached over the definition of the term. It was first applied to Thompson's writing in 1970 by his friend

---

7 See for instance: McKeen, 2008, pp. 352–65; Perry, 2009, pp. 236–37; Cowan, 2009, pp. 228–47; Wenner and Seymour, 2007, pp. 412–37. See also the documentaries *Hunter S. Thompson: Final 24* and *Gonzo*.

Bill Cardoso, editor of the *Boston Globe*, who had read 'The Kentucky Derby is Decadent and Depraved' and called it "totally gonzo" (McKeen, 2008, p. 149). Due to deadline pressure, Thompson had created the central 18-paragraph section of the article for *Scanlan's Monthly* by sending unedited pages of his notebook to the magazine. He had expected to be castigated for such unprofessional sloppiness and thought he had fatally harmed his career as a journalist. However, to his overjoyed astonishment, readers were excited by what they saw as a fresh approach to satire. Thompson remarked gleefully, 'It was like falling down an elevator shaft and landing in a pool full of mermaids' (*C*, p. 21). Thompson had unwittingly pulled off an audacious feat of double voicing, because he spoke not only from inside his story, 'following loopy digressions until they landed in unanticipated pools of revelation', but also as an outsider, 'chronicling systems of accepted values that really had no value at all' (Gilmore, 2005, p. 46).

With typical astuteness, Thompson turned serendipity into strategy. He immediately began to promote Gonzo as a term and to legitimize it as a technique. In the jacket copy for *Fear and Loathing in Las Vegas*, he cited as a precedent William Faulkner's claim that 'the best fiction is far more *true* than any kind of journalism – and the best journalists have always known this' (*GSH*, 114: emphasis in original). He wasted no time in applying Cardoso's adjective to himself, and twisting it into a noun that signified a style of writing. It became, in effect, Thompson's unique selling point; his brand. Considered in this light, the term is full of self-irony, especially given its origins in Thompson's desperate last-minute cutting of corners over the Kentucky Derby article: Gonzo is said to stem from 'an Americanization of [the Spanish] *ganso* "gander; lazy, slovenly person, dunce"' (Tamony, 1983, p. 75).

The main point for Thompson, though, was not the term's etymology, nor even its precise meaning, but its connotations. Gonzo suggested the capering of the holy fool, exposing the shortcomings of the society around him even as he flouted its rules of acceptable behaviour, either through the lowering of inhibitions brought on by drink and drugs, or just through not caring. Gonzo writing was born of spontaneous outrage, fuelled by chemicals and manifested in a decentred, broken-down prose of loose grammar and scattergun syntax, holed by ellipses and fractured by sudden jumps in perspective or subject matter. It allowed Thompson's quest for freedom to find expression not just in what he wrote, but in *how* he wrote it. He flouted the conventions of journalism and fiction and violated the rules of syntax in order not only to represent drugged consciousness, but also to subvert the premises of the state. Thompson's Gonzo writing, like his edgework (see Chapter 4), offered a form of resistance, a variation of the 'Chaos Linguistics' that are based on 'an aesthetics of the borderland between chaos and order, the margin, the area of "catastrophe" where the breakdown of the system can equal enlightenment' (Bey, 2003, pp. 128–9). Even when they addressed seemingly non-political topics, Thompson's fragmentary structures managed to suggest how the orthodox politics of behaviour (mores, unwritten codes, conventions) served the interests of power.

Jesse Jarnow notes how Thompson's ideal of spontaneous journalism was connected to his sceptical awareness of the power structures inherent in the status quo:

> At his best, a Gonzo journalist works not unlike an improvising musician. Just as a soloist must be able to spontaneously formulate coherent music from a knowledge of theory, form, and historical vocabulary, a Gonzo journalist should be able to parse a story in real-time. It is a way of experiencing things with open antennae, fully aware of the mechanisms grinding under a scene's surface, both subjectively and objectively.
>
> And, sure, the drugs help, too. Gonzo is a primal manifestation of what might be deemed 'the authentic American Dream.' (Jarnow, 2008, p. 199)

Jarnow goes on to explain his reference to the American Dream. He points out that by 'the pursuit of happiness', Thomas Jefferson 'meant something more classical' than 'the right to be left the fuck alone' (p. 199): one alternative is to become 'an active citizen […] aware of what's going on around him' (pp. 199–200).

Thompson put himself in this neo-Jeffersonian position of pursuing happiness through awareness rather than solipsism. Gonzo journalism depends not on self-absorption but on perception that is often all too painful. It is a form of active resistance to literary, journalistic and social convention; by abandoning nominally "objective" reporting, Thompson turned away from the "truth" determined by metropolitan editors and their establishment paymasters, and lit out for his own frontier. Jarnow's jazz simile illustrates how Gonzo requires not randomness, but spontaneity based on a thorough knowledge of craft, convention and tradition, even if the end result is to overturn the acceptable.

Douglas Brinkley has claimed that 'The Internet is full of bogus falsehoods propagated by uninformed English professors and pot-smoking fans' about the etymology of Gonzo (Wenner and Seymour, 2007, p. 125). If true, this is not surprising, because the term's *actual* etymology – meaning whatever historical source it ultimately derived from – was, even from the outset, much less important to Thompson and his readers than Gonzo's *potential* as a term that meant many things to many people. Gonzo has tapped into the zeitgeist so deeply and has been so successful as a brand that it has become an entry in *Webster's Dictionary*, framed with particular reference to its creator: '[from Hunter S. Thompson] 1. With total commitment, total concentration, and a mad sort of panache. (Thompson's original sense.) 2. More loosely: Overwhelming; outrageous; over the top' ('Gonzo').

Less formal definitions abound. Gonzo is said to be an Irish term for 'the guts and stamina of the last man left standing at the end of a marathon drinking bout' (Whitmer, 1993, p. 168). It was the title of a James Booker organ piece that Thompson had heard on the radio and liked (McKeen, 2008, p. 150). It was a Cajun musician's term that meant 'to play unhinged' (Douglas Brinkley, cited in Wenner and Seymour, 2007, p. 126). It is supposed to come from the French Canadian *gonzeaux*, meaning "shining path" (Carroll, 2005, p. 124), although this word does not appear in French dictionaries (Hirst, 2004, p. 5); *gonze*, however, is French slang for "guy" or "bloke" (Hirst, 2004, p. 7). Gonzo became the name of the turkey-beaked clown on Jim Henson's puppet programme *The Muppet Show*; it has been applied to excessively large collections of computer information; it can mean a form of pornography in which the filmmakers are directly involved, either as interviewers or participants; it has been used in a negative sense to refer to sloppy, politically motivated scholarship: 'Gonzo genealogy [...] demands only a sense of self-righteous infallibility to support its holy war against the foe' (Stempel, 2007, p. 99). Uncle Duke, the gun-toting hell-raiser, CIA agent and US diplomat of Garry Trudeau's *Washington Post* cartoon strip *Doonesbury*, a caricature closely based on Thompson, but that came to lead its own life, was introduced as 'the ex-gonzo stringer for *"Rolling Stone"*' (Tamony, 1983, p. 73). Gonzo journalism has become a generic reference point: it is defined in *Key Concepts in Journalism Studies* as: 'A style of journalism inextricably associated with the late American writer Hunter S. Thompson [...]. Contra the conventions of standard journalism practice, gonzo journalism features a bold, exaggerated, irreverent, hyperbolic and extremely subjective style of writing' (Frankin et al., 2005, p. 95).

'Writing Unfolds like a Game': Thompson's Manipulation of Authorship

Through his self-marketing as the original and ultimate Gonzo journalist, Thompson was creating and manipulating a persona and an image. First and foremost, he was a writer who wanted to sell his work through influencing what people thought and expected of him. In his 1969 essay 'What is an Author?', Michel Foucault argued that an author was not, as popularly believed, the source of the meaning of a work. Instead, the author was a socially created concept or function, a device used not to produce meaning, but to *reduce* it by restricting the range of possible readings of a text:

> the author does not precede the works; he is a certain functional principle by which, in our culture, one limits, excludes, and chooses; in short, by which one impedes the free circulation, the free manipulation, the free composition, decomposition and recomposition of fiction. [...] The author is therefore the ideological figure by which one marks the manner in which we fear the proliferation of meaning. (Foucault, 2000, pp. 221–22)

Foucault also links the construction of the author to the emergence of the Enlightenment concept of the individual as a free agent responsible for its actions. The birth of the author 'constitutes the privileged moment of individualization in the history of ideas, knowledge, literature, philosophy, and the sciences' (p. 205).

The author was identified as the originator of a text, and thus was punishable for any sedition therein. The author was primarily a role and a legal status: not a flesh-and-blood human being but an *idea* designed to channel interpretation and make sense of disparate texts by grouping them under a name. Later, the concept was debased, in Foucault's view, to become merely biographical: if a reader had a clear concept of who the author was, and how he/she had lived, then it was thought they could achieve a clearer understanding of the work and what it meant: the result was the school of 'the-man-and-his-work-criticism' (p. 205).

Foucault's tone is dismissive: he sees biographical criticism as weakened by its meek acceptance of the privileged status of the author, and by its consequent unconscious construction of the author as a hermeneutic filter, a barrier to creative and/or dissident interpretation of the text. Thompson, though, did not want his readers to accept him meekly. The complex issue of the link between Thompson and his writing makes studying both much more interesting than the disparaging label 'the-man-and-his-work' implies. Many of the events described on Thompson's pages had a basis, however loose, in events that actually happened: indeed, Thompson asserted that 'I'm a great fan of reality. Truth is easier. And weirder. And funnier. Not all the time, but you can fall back on the truth' (*AGW*, p. 153). Here, yet again, he echoes Thoreau: 'No face which we can give to a matter will stead us so well at last as the truth. This alone wears well' (Thoreau, 1992, p. 218).

Despite this, writing can never be the same as the object or event it purports to describe. On paper, Thompson produced not his life, but sequences of words; not to mention dots, dashes, ellipses, outrageous ink splashes, comic photographs, hilarious document facsimiles and splendid illustrations by Ralph Steadman and others. In doing this, he came close to achieving the creative *absence* of an author that Foucault sought in modern writing:

> today's writing has freed itself from the theme of expression. Referring only to itself, but without being restricted to the confines of its interiority, writing is identified with its own unfolded exteriority. This means that it is an interplay of signs arranged less according to its signified content than according to the very nature of the signifier. Writing unfolds like a game [*jeu*] that invariably goes beyond its own rules and transgresses its limits. In writing, the point is not to manifest or exalt the act of writing; nor is it to pin a subject within language; it is, rather, a question of creating a space into which the writing subject constantly disappears. (Foucault, 2000, p. 206)

Thompson's writing is far more challenging than a simple Gonzo autobiography. As his work evolved, it grew into a game for breaking the rules of journalism at the same time as making its creator disappear into the page, becoming translated from a real person into a complex and often self-contradictory series of words and images.

Thompson has become an author in the sense meant by Foucault. His name and the Gonzo brand are more famous than any of his works, with the possible exception of *Fear and Loathing in Las Vegas*. Thompson has become a product and even a role model. However, his writing itself, when separated from the t-shirts, badges, cartoons and other appropriations of his persona, reveals a protagonist caught between self-promotion and self-abnegation, seeking fame and oblivion at the same time.

The 'Author's Note' that introduced his 1979 anthology of essays, *The Great Shark Hunt*, is eerily prophetic of Thompson's suicide in 2005, but it also reads as a conceptual statement about the contradictory ways in which he intended to deploy his persona in his work. Thompson finds himself sitting down to type the contents table for his own collected works at the age of 40; consequently, he feels an uncanny dread of already being dead, of being his own posthumous editor. With self-mocking irony, he considers a suicidal leap off the hotel terrace, right into the fountain 28 floors down, as the only suitably conspicuous means of closure: 'Nobody could follow that act' (*GSH*, p. 21). Thompson implies a theatrical performance by a character: a public feat so bold that it cannot be followed except by a radical break. And yet, at the same time, he is willing himself to disappear: after the crazy suicidal leap, he wants to vanish into his own image, his own writing, so that he can, in a literary sense, be reborn into 'A New Life' (p. 21).

The article 'Fear and Loathing at the Super Bowl' (*RS* 28 February 1974, pp. 28–52), selected by Thompson for *The Great Shark Hunt*, develops this theme. Thompson's character is again on a hotel balcony, 20 floors up in the Hyatt Regency in Houston, Texas; he is high in both the altitudinal and pharmaceutical senses. It is the morning of the game, at the climax of the American football season. He intends to deliver from the balcony a hellfire sermon derived from a religious pamphlet he claims to have found on the floor of the men's room. He feels a giant leech crawling up his spine, and decides he just has enough time to give his sermon and write the lead to his Super Bowl story before the parasite reaches his brain.

Then, in a stroke of inspiration, he realizes that he has *already* written the required lead paragraph last year: all he has to do is substitute the name of one team for another and thus finish his lead even before the game has begun (*GSH*, p. 54). This is a satire on the mindless clichés of conventional sportswriting, and by extension, mainstream journalism as a whole. Thompson deliberately thumps out repetitive macho banalities: '*The precision-jackhammer attack of the Miami Dolphins stomped the balls off the Minnesota Vikings today by stomping and hammering with one precise jack-thrust after another*' (p. 55: emphasis in original).

'Fear and Loathing at the Super Bowl' demonstrates how, throughout his Gonzo writing, Thompson was aiming to step off the conveyor belt of objective journalism. Convention insists that reporters set out the five Ws (who, what, when, where and why) in the lead paragraph, followed by paragraphs of diminishing significance, so that even a casual reader can quickly gain a sense of the story. Another name for this principle is the "inverted pyramid", meaning that the report always gives the most important information first, allowing for the easy deletion of later paragraphs by a sub-editor (Franklin et al., 2005, p. 122): 'In a nutshell, that means putting the most important stuff at the top and proceeding in an orderly fashion until you get to the bits that could be cut out' (Fleming et al., 2006, p. 46).[8]

---

8 One textbook defines the entire genre of journalism as 'a form of communication based on asking, and answering, the questions Who? What? Where? When? Why? How?' (Harcup, 2004, p. 2). The inverted pyramid structure, 'pioneered by American journalists in the nineteenth century, replaced the older narrative style according to which journalists reported events in a chronological order: in much the same way as oral storytelling proceeds' (Franklin et al., 2005, p. 122).

Thompson knew that this approach could only lead to superficial, timid, conformist banality: 'Mastery of the pyramid lead has sustained more lame yoyos than either Congress or the peacetime army. Five generations of American journalists have clung to that petrified tit' (*GSH*, p. 304). He knew that the job of the reporter using the five Ws was merely 'to hold a mirror up to an event and show its surface' (Dennis and Rivers, 2011, p. 2). He satirized the inverted pyramid in his account of campaign reporting in 1972, where each journalist was expected to act like 'a goddamn methedrine bat: Racing from airport to airport, from one crisis to another – sucking up the news and then spewing it out by the "Five W's" in a package that makes perfect sense' (*CT*, p. 88). Even the vigorous but deliberately awful prose of his fake lead paragraph on the Super Bowl quoted above answers who, how and when: although a mere collage of gung-ho clichés, it steers close to textbook reporting.

So in order to break away from the five Ws, Thompson stands up and shouts down to the lobby restaurant 20 floors below a farrago of images from the book of Revelation, mixed with contemporary sporting and political allusions: 'General Haig has told us that the forces of darkness are now in control [...]. And Al Davis has told us that whosoever was not found written in the book of life was cast into the lake of fire!' (*GSH*, p. 57). This is the alternative to the lead paragraph about the jackhammer attack of the Miami Dolphins, in a game so predictable it can be written up before it happens: it is a rant about another kind of prediction, of four years of social and political hell under a corrupt Republican administration. By throwing General Alexander Haig and Oakland Raiders owner Al Davis into his biblical stew, Thompson conflates the religious, political and sporting forces of darkness. And yet, Thompson implies, this hotchpotch is just as pointless and ludicrous as the written-by-numbers Super Bowl lead. After ranting about Green Bay Packers coach Vince Lombardi, an idol of the football fanatic Richard Nixon, and the high value Lombardi placed on "discipline" (p. 56), Thompson encourages his audience to shout hallelujah, and naively hopes that a few of the figures 20 stories below might be shouting it back.

Thus 'Fear and Loathing at the Super Bowl' charts the despair of the politically aware journalist. Follow the clichéd formula and you are widely read, but say nothing – or worse, you reinforce the status quo – or rant about the evils of the world and you make your statement all right, but no one listens. Moreover, the statement you make may be mere rambling, as in Thompson's knowingly absurd pastiche of sports, politics and apocalypse. Thus he finds himself in the same dilemma he agonized over in the 'Author's Note'; in each case he feels the impulse to put on an outrageous act (jump over the balcony, deliver the hellfire sermon) out of a sense that all he has to offer has already been done; the collected works or the rehashed phrases of convention, respectively.

While appearing simply to chart his own experience, albeit in a comically exaggerated, Gonzo way, Thompson is posing the same question formulated by Foucault:

> How, under what conditions, and in what forms can something like a subject appear in the order of discourse? What place can it occupy in each type of discourse, what functions can it assume, and by obeying what rules? In short, it is a matter of depriving the subject (or its substitute) of its role as originator, and of analyzing the subject as a variable and complex function of discourse. (Foucault, 2000, p. 221)

In the 'Super Bowl' piece, Thompson is announcing himself as just this: not an originator but a persona – a function of the discourse itself. The persona is created through its choice of rhetoric. Both options available to it are equally derivative; the off-the-shelf gung-ho nonsense about jackhammers, or the religious harangue derived from Revelation. However, the result of *combining* the two is a remarkably original work. Through a Hegelian process in miniature, their dialectic leads to a higher synthesis – the semi-autobiographical Gonzo discourse for which Thompson was already famous.

The dilemma and resolution at the centre of this piece encapsulate how in a Gonzo text, there is not a fixed subject but the overarching *question* of how that subject can be represented and what it can do. The Thompson studied in this book, and indeed by any critic seeking to engage with his work as literature, is not the man himself but a product of text: an image based on the combination of countless paragraphs from the Thompson canon. This is why, to recall Foucault, his writing develops like a game that goes beyond its own rules and transgresses its own limits. Even as it expounds or advertises its protagonist, who is often named Hunter Thompson, it refuses to limit itself to autobiography, journalism or fiction, and never draws clear lines between experience, reportage and fantasy.

'I'm Never Sure Which One People Expect Me to Be': Celebrity and the Gonzo Persona

Thompson could not sustain the rule-breaking audacity of Gonzo forever. His once outrageous, cutting-edge style became merely fashionable. His persona became so popular that he felt trapped in it, both in everyday practical terms and in a literary sense. In 1974, the year 'Fear and Loathing at the Super Bowl' appeared, Thompson became caricatured as Uncle Duke, the gun-toting, drug-abusing journalist, CIA spy and American ambassador of Garry Trudeau's *Doonesbury* strip (McKeen, 2008, p. 231: see Trudeau, 1992).[9] By 1976, Thompson found himself unable to cover the presidential race of that year as a journalist, as he had become more famous than many of the candidates (McKeen, 2008, p. 243). By 1980, he had been further caricatured by Bill Murray in *Where the Buffalo Roam*, a weakly scripted satirical movie. In 1977, he told a BBC film crew that he could not decide whether they had come to film Duke or Thompson: 'I'm filling with hate and rage, just thinking about it. I'm never sure which one people expect me to be. Often, they conflict' (McKeen, 2008, p. 202). Thompson had become a 'Prisoner of Gonzo' (Perry, 2009, p. 169).

Thompson's problem was that a once ground-breaking motif had become a cliché: the drug-ridden reporter mired in events spiralling out of control, struggling desperately to cover the story, snorting, smoking or swallowing greater quantities of the deadly fuel required for his heinous trade. In 'The Great Shark Hunt', an article published in *Playboy* in 1974 that gave its title to Thompson's first compilation of his own work, he knowingly recycles some of the themes of *Fear and Loathing in Las Vegas*, especially the Gonzo staple of the stoned freak trying to deal with officialdom. The climax comes as Thompson and his sidekick Yail Bloor try to pass through customs while high on LSD, with several capsules of amphetamine concealed in Thompson's shoes. The speed leaks out, and the protagonists leave a trail of bright orange spansules behind them. Thompson, trying to control his hysteria, carefully picks one pill off his shoe under the gaze of the customs officer, who has just handed him his receipt for his liquor tax. The officer ignores his antics. Thompson is upset to realize that this is because the officer has rightly concluded that no serious drug smuggler would make such a fool of himself: 'I would have preferred not to understand this embarrassment so keenly, because it plunged me into a fit of depression' (*GSH*, p. 476).

Thompson is trying to come to terms with his own insignificance. He and Bloor have become pathetic parodies of outlaws. Like Duke and

---

9 Christopher Lamb has claimed that although Uncle Duke was 'a thinly disguised replica' of Thompson, 'Other characters [in Trudeau] grew from metaphors', meaning they stood for social tendencies such as the women's movement (Lamb, 1990, p. 118). Trudeau's Duke, though, was *both* types of character, in that he imitated Thompson and yet also stood for the Gonzo tendency that Thompson's work initiated. As Lamb points out, Duke 'echoed that [countercultural] voice', also echoed by *Rolling Stone*, which stood for '"sex, drugs and rock'n'roll" as more than a philosophy but as a way of life' (p. 124).

Gonzo in *Vegas*, the characters are clowns, who, although they commit blatant felonies, remain largely beneath the notice of the local law enforcement. Bloor is taking cocaine and smoking marijuana in the airport toilet when he hears his and Thompson's names called over the PA: in a fit of paranoia he flushes the cocaine away and runs out of the toilet, having forgotten to zip himself up, running down the hall 'with my joint hanging out' (p. 474). It isn't clear whether Bloor's penis is hanging out or his drugged cigarette (perhaps both), but his status as a buffoon is clear. The PA announcement turns out to be merely a warning that they may miss their plane.

The Gonzo-writer-and-sidekick-take-drugs-and-act-stupid routine had become a knowing self-parody by this stage, only 3 years after *Fear and Loathing in Las Vegas*.[10] Thompson's self-irony implies his awareness of how drug-taking and related antics, once disseminated in print, could lead to a demand for more of the same. In short, he knew the dangers of becoming trapped in his own persona.

Thompson was confronting an issue that had vexed the tradition of confessional drug literature against which he was reacting, but from which his work was in part derived. Thomas De Quincey, the originator of the tradition, had had some of the same problems when creating a suitable narrator for the *Confessions of an English Opium-Eater* in 1821. The persona had to be contrite but self-centred; abased and ashamed but interesting enough, and even positive enough about his drug experiences, to engage the reader. De Quincey declared that 'Guilt and misery shrink, by a natural instinct, from public notice', and yet he proceeded to exhibit exactly these feelings in great detail to the reader over thousands of words (De Quincey, 1971, p. 29). Thompson had become caught in a variation of this double bind; although hardly guilty or miserable, he had to narrate authentic-sounding drug stories to his readership while somehow avoiding the trap of allowing that very readership to dictate the presentation and even the nature of the drug experiences themselves.

Thompson was partly responsible for his own dilemma. He had been happy to exploit his public persona when it suited him: if the myth fitted his own interests, he deepened it. *Fear and Loathing on the Campaign Trail '72*,

---

10 Even as early as 1970, Thompson had been aware of the dangers of Gonzo cliché. In a letter to Ralph Steadman about a proposed series of articles, he enclosed a marvellous mockery of what was to become his signature style: 'As we buckled down for the approach to New Orleans I snorted the last of our cocaine. Steadman, far gone on acid, had locked himself in the men's room somewhere over St. Louis and the head stewardess was frantic. I knew I would need psychic strength and energy when we landed – to meet the press limousine and get on with our heinous work' (*FLA*, p. 320).

for instance, was cast very much in the mould of *Fear and Loathing in Las Vegas*, even though the end result was very different. Thompson set out to replicate his own successful formula, by playing the Gonzo journalist caught up in something bigger, and in the process exposing its seedy underbelly, as well as his own complicity in the nightmarish scene.

The opening pages of each book bear comparison. In both cases, Thompson 'creates a self-caricature who is extremely disoriented, both by actual events and by paranoid illusions' (Hellmann, 1981, p. 69). He positions his persona in an extreme situation: either very stoned 'on the edge of the desert', driving at 'about a hundred miles an hour' to cover a story in Las Vegas (*LV*, p. 3); or stuck in a hotel room at the edge of the Pacific Ocean, working at a figurative hundred miles an hour, but still bemoaning the lack of the powerful amphetamine he needs, while trying to finish the book through 'fifty-five consecutive hours of sleepless, foodless, high-speed editing' (*CT*, p. 11). In each case, animals play a key role. In *Vegas*, Raoul Duke is disturbed by an acid vision of predatory bats: outside Thompson's hotel room in *Campaign Trail*, the seals are barking on Seal Rock, and a colleague's dog, distracted by them, runs amok, 'scattering my book-galley pages all over the floor, knocking the phone off the hook, upsetting the gin bottles' and ruining a campaign photograph Thompson had hoped to use (p. 11).

Thus, at the beginning of each book, Thompson's persona is situated on the edge: on the border of a mysterious zone of Otherness, trying desperately to complete his assignment but harassed by strange animals whose actions he does not fully understand. The two openings share a sense of writing as theatre. The act of writing, or of journeying with intent to write, or of trying but failing to write, becomes part of the text itself. The protagonist is no mere hack struggling with a deadline, but is an antihero on a quest, confronted by powerful enemies whose symbolic representatives are the animals he has summoned up himself, either through the agency of LSD (the bats) or by his own failure to file his copy (the dog is brought by the editors who are trying to help him finish the book).

Thompson had a great deal to say about edgework, or the deliberate cultivation of danger (see Chapter 4), but here the edge symbolizes not so much a place of extreme peril as a gateway to a zone of creativity. To help pass through this gateway, an industrial quantity of licit and banned drugs is required: 'two bags of grass, seventy-five pellets of mescaline, five sheets of high-powered blotter acid, a salt shaker half full of cocaine' (*LV*, p. 4); 'two cases of Mexican beer, four quarts of gin, a dozen grapefruits, and enough speed to alter the outcome of six Super Bowls' (*CT*, p. 12).

Thompson's introduction to *Campaign Trail* self-consciously replicates the stoned, maniacal persona sketched out at the start of *Vegas*; an anti-realist self-caricature with 'virtually no complexity of thought or motivation' (Hellmann, 1981, p. 69). The persona is instead characterized by its cartoon-like brightness and vulgarity. Thompson aims for continuity of character and symbolism, even though the context of each assignment is very different. In fact, within each book, Thompson's protagonist persona – Raoul Duke in *Vegas* and Dr Hunter S. Thompson in *Campaign Trail* – comments on the *other* book's persona as if discussing an entirely different individual, thus making the two texts reflexive mirrors of each other (Hellmann, 1981, p. 73). In each case, the Gonzo journalist is facing the edge but has his trusty chemicals to help him: the important thing, as always, is the Story, for good or ill.

Libertarian *Bricolage*: Thompson as Producer and Product

In seeking the Story, Thompson became what Claude Lévi-Strauss (and later Jacques Derrida, Gilles Deleuze and Félix Guattari) would call a *"bricoleur"*, meaning an improviser, a user of ready-made materials to construct a new work. The term *bricoleur* derives from the French term for a handyman who is always ready to extemporize with found materials, thus creating *bricolage*, rather than relying on dogma or pre-set plans:

> The 'bricoleur' is adept at performing a large number of diverse tasks; but, unlike the engineer, he does not subordinate each of them to the availability of raw materials and tools conceived and procured for the purpose of the project. His universe of instruments is closed and rules of his game are always to make do with 'whatever is at hand', that is to say with a set of tools and materials which is always finite and is also heterogeneous because what it contains bears no relation to the current project, or indeed to any particular project, but is the contingent result of all the occasions there have been to renew or enrich the stock or to maintain it with the remains of previous constructions or destructions. (Lévi-Strauss, 1972, p. 17)

In his writing, Thompson liked improvising with what had been handed to him. Sometimes he used a journalistic assignment as a pretext, as in *Fear and Loathing in Las Vegas*. On other occasions, he presented the text as a pastiche of found materials, as in his later books *Songs of the Doomed* (1990) and *Better than Sex* (1994), in which the words are interspersed with photographs, telegrams and facsimiles of documents, sometimes scrawled over in Thompson's handwriting.

Stepping into History: Values, Contexts, Influences 29

In the same way as he pasted his texts together, he was composing himself, creating both a central character within the narrative and an implied author behind it. From *Fear and Loathing in Las Vegas* onwards, Thompson would take whatever signs were to hand and weave out of them a tale in which he became an elusive outlaw, maintaining his subjectivity and freedom in an ongoing conflict with a clumsy but crushingly powerful oppressor. *Vegas* has been read as 'journalism as bricolage: Thompson moved around freely in space and time [...] always searching in vain for the American dream' (Weingarten, 2006, p. 248). The adversary stopping the *bricoleur* Duke from finding the Dream was the vulgar, oppressive capitalism of the Nixon era, personified by Las Vegas itself. Thompson's response articulated one of his recurring myths: David and Goliath, with the underdog's slingshot made of words.

On the face of it, this makes Thompson's work conflict with Jacques Derrida's interpretation of *bricolage*. Derrida argues that *bricolage* is decentred, as it lacks a privileged source or origin, such as a controlling author. Derrida points out that in Lévi-Strauss the *bricoleur* is diametrically opposed to 'the engineer' – the subject who originates and controls his own discourse, producing it out of nothing (Derrida, 1978, p. 285). Thompson seems at first sight to be an engineer, producing his persona and his paragraphs out of his highly distinctive imagination.

However, the Gonzo myth was not based on self-discipline or self-organization; it required the participation of the subject in events to such an extent that control, both of events and of reporting, was lost. Hence the importance Thompson placed on first drafts and the lack of editing: before beginning *Vegas*, he had intended that 'The writing would be selective and necessarily interpretive – but once the image was written, the words would be final' (*GSH*, p. 114). In reality, 'Hunter was *always* edited, relentlessly and exhaustively, for reasons of space and potential litigation, as well as taste and coherency' (Cowan, 2009, p. 86: emphasis in original). Nevertheless, he held on to the ideal of the spontaneous first draft: a stricture intended to preserve the original chaotic impressions of the Gonzo journalist and therefore to help fashion an authentic self, however disorderly, from *bricolage*, rather than rely on the prefabricated identity of an engineer.

This did not mean that Thompson's work was egotistical. Far from it: the subject at the centre of Thompson's Gonzo work is fractured, riven by conflicts, and rarely in a state of full self-control or self-knowledge. He thus enters the orbit of self-destruction, of flirting with death, chaos and insanity. Gilles Deleuze and Félix Guattari develop Lévi-Strauss's concept to suggest that *bricolage* is in fact the epitome of schizophrenic discourse:

> The schizophrenic is the universal producer. There is no need to distinguish here between producing and its product. We need merely note that the pure 'thisness' of the object produced is carried over into a new act of producing. […] The rule of continually producing production, of grafting producing onto the product, is a characteristic of desiring-machines or of primary production: the production of production. A painting by Richard Lindner, "Boy with Machine," shows a huge, pudgy, bloated boy working one of his little desiring-machines, after having hooked it up to a vast technical social machine – which, as we shall see, is what even the very young child does.
>
> Producing, a product: a producing/product identity. It is this identity that constitutes a third term in the linear series: an enormous undifferentiated object. Everything stops dead for a moment, everything freezes in place – and then the whole process will begin all over again. (Deleuze and Guattari, 1984, p. 7)

Deleuze and Guattari interpret production and creativity in terms of flux rather than stasis; of the schizophrenic desiring-machine rather than the rational subject; of the body without organs rather than the dissected corpse.

This may seem far too abstract for a master of the gut-wrenchingly real like Thompson, who rarely philosophizes and writes instead of brutally concrete experience. However, his work is schizophrenic in the sense meant here. It offers a perpetually reporting, writing subject at its centre who manifests 'a producing/product identity'. On the page, Thompson is his own product, the perpetually evolving basis of his own myth; a subject in flux, perpetually decomposing and recomposing itself. This helps explain why his work is neither an engineer's discourse nor a decentred one.

Take, for instance, Raoul Duke's encounter with the District Attorneys' Conference on Narcotics and Dangerous Drugs that forms the pretext for the second part of *Vegas* (*LV*, pp. 137–49). Duke and Gonzo have managed to register for the conference and sit through it, stoned on mescaline. They are horrified at the misinformed gibberish they are hearing from the platform and the crowd, but are also amused that they are passing as cops, getting through this stupefyingly ignorant farce undetected. The role of Duke and Gonzo seems clear; they are countercultural covert observers and saboteurs.

In accordance with this role, Duke uses what he sees around him to begin improvising. He notices that the organizers' placement of speakers on huge poles among the audience depersonalizes the venue (p. 137). He feels further alienated from the proceedings when he realizes that the address of the keynote speaker, E. R. Bloomquist, MD, is total nonsense. Bloomquist divides the cannabis subculture into four strata: 'Cool, Groovy, Hip and Square' (p. 139). Duke is baffled by this bizarre imaginary hierarchy and assumes that Bloomquist has been deliberately misled by someone like Timothy Leary who has set out to have fun at his expense. He then begins to fantasize about a police precinct notice board, with its lurid warnings about the crazed behaviour of drug fiends, based on false assumptions taken from Bloomquist (p. 139). The narrative moves fluidly from outside Duke's head to within it; from observation to imagination. Just as in an earlier scene where Duke *remembers* a musician licking powdered LSD off his sleeve in a San Francisco nightclub and then *imagines* what might have happened had a young square come in and seen them, the novel moves from one ontological level to another with barely any warning (p. 66).

In each case, Duke is improvising on his main theme, but the ease of the transition serves to cast doubt on the distinction between reality and fantasy; the point of the exercise is to maintain the 'disturbing lack of a clear dividing line between fact and fiction' that characterizes the novel as a whole (Sickels, 2000, p. 64). Through his memories, observations and fantasies alike, Duke is fuelling his outsider persona. This process continues in the bar in the next scene, when Duke and Gonzo improvise a routine where they pretend to a hapless hick cop from Georgia that tribes of drug fiends in California have gone the way of the Manson Family, have acquired a lust for human sacrifice, and are raiding the homes of innocent suburbanites to behead men, women and children and suck their blood (p. 146). Throughout, Duke is a *bricoleur*, making his story out of ready-made materials: at the same time, he creates himself; as observer, critic, writer, comedian, fantasist, trickster and drug fiend disguised as a cop.

Fear and Loathing in Las Vegas has only the most rudimentary of plots: Duke and Gonzo go to Las Vegas on an assignment, return for another assignment, then leave. Nearly everything is episodic, rather than caused by what has happened before. The novel is an enormous undifferentiated object, to recall Deleuze and Guattari's phrase, overlaid with only the most rudimentary structure of a quest for the American Dream, where everything stops at the end of each chapter 'and then the whole process will begin all over again', in an echo of Samuel Beckett's *Waiting for Godot* (Deleuze and Guattari, 1984, p. 7). This helps explain the repetitions in the novel; the constant ingestion of drugs, the encounters with women (the reporter in the lift, Lucy, the maid, the diner waitress) or with hapless male victims (the hitchhiker, the Georgia cop) and the continual background noise of the Vietnam War that intrudes through television, radio and print reports. Some of the dreadful headlines about the war actually calm Duke down, as they help him place his situation in perspective; he feels his own offences are "pale and meaningless" by comparison (p. 74).

Duke is like Lindner's *Boy with Machine* in the example cited by Deleuze and Guattari. He is working the desiring-machine of his own brain; he agitates it with drugs and hooks it up to the great social machine of Las Vegas. The result is a nightmare thrill-ride akin to the negative vision of the schizophrenic or the drug user on a bad trip, as described by Aldous Huxley in *Heaven and Hell* (see Chapter 2). It is also *bricolage*: an improvised discourse, schizophrenic in Deleuze and Guattari's sense of being in perpetual flux, always producing itself anew. The novel's closest parallel to *Boy with Machine* occurs when Duke is accosted by a salesman in a funfair attached to the Circus-Circus casino. The man tells him that for 99 cents he can step into a booth that will project his image over downtown Las Vegas, 200 feet tall; for $1.98, he can say anything he wants and it will be broadcast with the image (p. 47). This encapsulates the function of Las Vegas as a great social apparatus to which individual desiring-machines can become attached and symbolically magnified as their specious sense of self-importance is inflated by gambling, showbiz, the sex industry, pills or booze.

A great paradox of Thompson's work is that all this *bricolage* occurs in the name of an authentic self. Thompson was working in the individualist tradition of Emerson and Thoreau, but he adapted it to his own hedonistic tastes and secular mindset, and reworked it for a postmodern, image-driven age of the spectacle. His work does not aggrandize an already formulated ego; instead it dramatizes the processes of change and breakdown that occur when someone *tries* to become or remain a free individual in the America of the mid-twentieth century and beyond. His writing represents the confrontation between the subject seeking autonomy and the historical forces – personified by Nixon and his cronies, the police, tame journalists and other establishment lackeys – that seek literally and figuratively to imprison him: 'he was a hypersensitive medium who channelled the underlying currents of truth, concealed in veils of silken lies that we have become accustomed to swallowing' (Depp, 2005, p. 49).

'These Fragments': Influences

Thompson's awareness of the fractures in America's national façade is evident not only in the content of his political writing, but also in the fragments, gaps and associative leaps of his Gonzo prose. The Gonzo style was the cracked mirror of a broken nation: 'The jagged realism of the writing struck a nerve that was directly connected to the increasing fragmentation of American culture' (Whitmer and Van Wyngarden, 2007, 83). Gonzo offered Thompson's idiosyncratic development of the high modernist project of representing a fragmented reality in fragmented form, seen most acutely in T. S. Eliot's *The Waste Land* (1922), with its sombrely reflexive conclusion, 'These fragments I have shored against my ruins' (Eliot, 1974, p. 79, l. 430).

Eliot's project was also continued by the experimental poets of the 1960s such as Thompson's friend Allen Ginsberg.[11] He, like Thompson, sought to critique US society and record his personal experience by means of the form as well as the content of his writing. Ginsberg's most famous poem 'Howl' has a distinctly 1950s Beat Generation flavour that is largely absent in Thompson's work, but its free-associative approach allows it to be compared to Gonzo prose:

> who chained themselves to subways for the endless
> ride from Battery to holy Bronx on benzedrine
> until the noise of wheels and children brought
> them down shuddering mouth-wracked and
> battered bleak of brain all drained of brilliance
> in the drear light of Zoo [...]. (Ginsberg, 1959, p. 10, l.14)

Ginsberg exaggerates and shapes his experience, creating the archetype of the Beat Generation hipster as he writes. 'Howl' offers a hallucinatory version of New York that is intended for consumption as a romantically reified, vision-transfigured product for a turned-on audience.

Part of Ginsberg's achievement is the long unpunctuated line, intended to be read in one breath and absorbed as a unit whose connotations and symbolism can suggest visions and possibilities beyond the surface content on the page. Thus the rhythm of 'Battery to holy Bronx on benzedrine'

---

11 Ginsberg had a less problematic relationship than Thompson with the nineteenth-century drug literature: he took marijuana as 'a self-conscious continuation of the tradition of Rimbaud and the European nineteenth-century literary experimenters' (Boon, 2002, p. 161; see also Miles, 2000). Ginsberg was part of a movement in poetry that sought to develop the modernist experimentation of T. S. Eliot, Ezra Pound and William Carlos Williams through the lens of radical politics in order to challenge establishment morality. As well as the Beat poets like Ginsberg, other schools such as the l=a=n=g=u=a=g=e poets and the Black Mountain poets popularized radical verse forms from the 1950s to the 1970s: see Allen (ed.), 1999 for the definitive anthology of 1950s experimental poetry.

not only sketches an amphetamine-fuelled journey on the subway through its train-bump stresses that fall on the alliterative "b" sound, but also conveys the existential battering felt by the Beat subject encountering the world around him (masculine pronoun intended) in such a direct, unmediated way that it comes as a series of shocks, overwhelming the perceptual apparatus, leaving him Beat in its dual senses of exhausted and spiritualized; beaten-down and beatific.[12]

Thompson did not reproduce such rhythms. For one thing, he was always a prose writer and his attempts at poetry were few and relatively weak.[13] In his fiction, he used a different syntax from that of Ginsberg, which nevertheless drew on the Beat sense of the possibilities of free experimentation: 'you hear yourself mumbling: "Dogs fucked the Pope, no fault of mine. Watch out! ... Why money? My name is Brinks; I was born ... born?"' (*LV*, p. 45). This is Raoul Duke's description of the effects of ether. Like Ginsberg's Beat heroes, Duke and Gonzo are 'bleak of brain all drained of brilliance', worn down into incoherence by the drugs they are using. Thompson demonstrates the brain-numbing influence of ether through a prose that accumulates clauses as Ginsberg's poetry accumulates lines, but that does so in the service of irony rather than sincerity, to expose the subject's induced vacuity rather than explore his inner vision. Ginsberg's images build up to create a higher meaning, and to celebrate as well as mourn the self-destructive talents of those rebels who were, he believed, the finest minds of his generation. Thompson, by contrast, wants to plumb the depths of the worst that his generation can offer; the slot-machine dystopia of Las Vegas, a distillation of the complacent, selfish and ruthless capitalism of the era of Spiro Agnew, which forces the protagonists, withdrawing into fear and loathing, to deaden their nerves with a cheap anaesthetic.

---

12 Jack Kerouac popularized the term "Beat", which he had borrowed from the novelist John Clellon Holmes, who meant by it simply "wiped out"; Kerouac extended its meaning to include 'the connotation of upbeat and of beatific' (Morgan, 1991, p. 154). The Beats saw themselves as literary and spiritual seekers, on a quest for personal authenticity. Opponents have read their work as elitist and fundamentally immature: 'The Beats' behaviour constituted a process of *becoming* – involving guilt, as Holmes said, but also attitudinizing – rather than anything fixed. They scorned and reviled the self-assertion of American capitalism, yet they advertised their own accumulation of experience – by drugs and other means – as a way of asserting their own elite status' (Davenport-Hines, 2002, p. 246: emphasis in original).

13 Thompson was well aware of this. See, for instance, his 1965 poem 'Collect Telegram from a Mad Dog' (*PH*, pp. 544–45), which begins: 'Not being a poet, and drunk as well' (p. 544, l.1).

Another Beat model for Thompson was Jack Kerouac, whose *On the Road* was a major inspiration for *Fear and Loathing in Las Vegas*, as well as to the impressionable adolescent Thompson: 'Between [Robert] Mitchum and [William] Burroughs and James Dean and Jack Kerouac, I got myself a serious running start before I was twenty years old, and there was no turning back. Buy the ticket, take the ride' (*LY*, p. 40). Kerouac's novel, originally presented as a long scroll without pages or paragraphs, was based on the adventures of Neal Cassady, personified as Dean Moriarty, the hip modern incarnation of an Old West frontiersman, whose innermost desire is always to travel, to seek new experience, to live life to the absolute limit:

> We all jumped to the music and agreed. The purity of the road. The white line in the middle of the highway unrolled and hugged our left front tire as if glued to our groove. [...] It was crazy; the radio was on full blast. Dean beat drums on the dashboard till a great sag developed in it; I did too. The poor Hudson [car] – the slow boat to China – was receiving her beating.
> 'Oh man, what kicks!' yelled Dean. (Kerouac, 1991, 134)

Kerouac's work retains a celebratory innocence that Thompson's almost entirely lacks. It is as if Thompson has absorbed the work of this earlier generation of dissident writers, looked around him and then, figuratively speaking, spat the work out. Although he had 'internalized Kerouac's worldview with a close reading of the books' (Weingarten, 2006, p. 246), Thompson rejected the Beat axiom that rhythm, syntax or the descriptive powers of prose should be put to the task of creating a new progressive sensibility through the relentless, manic quest of the battered but enlightened protagonist. Instead, Thompson's characters are often 'losers – dropouts, failures and malcontents' (*HA*, p. 307); they are social rejects not only because of their refusal to conform, but also because of their inadequacy.

Sal Paradise, who is Kerouac's alter ego, and Dean Moriarty are driving to San Francisco in the scene quoted above, just as Thompson would do in the early 1960s when he sought a secure space to write in as well as a clear space of freedom; later on, I refer to these spaces as "the lodge" and "the frontier", respectively (see Chapter 4). Like Kerouac's heroes, Thompson found himself deliberately seeking danger or the extremes of experience; unlike Kerouac, his main metaphor for this was not the road, an endlessly unrolling non-destination, in which – in an appropriately Zen-like way – the journey was its own goal: 'the means, the avenue, the movement and the end itself' (Brown, 1976, p. 25). Instead, Thompson chose the term "the edge", meaning a border between the mapped and the unknown, a liminal line between stifling security and fatal danger (*HA*, p. 323: see Chapter 4). So when Thompson or his characters test their machines to the maximum, as Sal and Dean do with their Hudson, they do so not in the service of travel, but as a means of courting danger in itself. Kerouac's protagonists seek perpetual motion: Thompson's prefer to exceed the speed limit and sometimes crash.

Kerouac's heroes enjoy the kick of having the radio turned up full. Duke and Gonzo in *Vegas*, though they too have the radio on loud, mix it with a tape of the Rolling Stones' song 'Sympathy for the Devil', which they play again and again, thus blending the two sound sources in a form of 'demented counterpoint' (*LV*, p. 5). The point is not a celebration of the freedom symbolized by jazz improvisation, as Kerouac intended in his writing, but an ambiguous immersion in the repetitive chaos symbolized by the random mixture of one constant loop (the tape) and another, perpetually changing sound (the radio).

Although Thompson admired much jazz, such as the music of Herbie Mann and Roland Kirk (*FLA*, p. 344), the musical analogue to *Vegas* and much of his other Gonzo prose is not the blowing of the bebop master but the distortion-fuelled intensity of the rock performer, a style based on 'outrageous side stories and guitar solos' (Cowan, 2009, p. 100). Like a Jimi Hendrix of journalism, Thompson cranks the volume up so loud that the feedback and the original signal become blurred; or put another way, the characters' trains of thought become difficult to unravel as the distortions induced by drugs and by the extremity of their situation take their toll. Thompson was conscious of the figurative links between writing and musical virtuosity; he conceived of his electric typewriter keys as 'my Instrument, my harp, my RCA glass-tube microphone, and my fine soprano saxophone all at once. That is my music, for good or ill, and on some nights it will make me feel like a god' (*KF*, p. 39).

Thompson did not aim to reflect a new generation's emerging consciousness in the manner of Kerouac and Ginsberg. He envisioned himself primarily as a protagonist-cum-reporter, someone whose intent was to enter the story with a view to participating in events and then recording them, and to structure his perceptions and experience accordingly. In his construction of himself as a journalist, he drew on the tradition of subjective reporting established by Mark Twain and continued by others such as H. L. Mencken and Ernest Hemingway. Mencken was a reporter who said more about himself than about the ostensible focus of his work and whose 'assaults on the mountebanks of his day are not dissimilar from Thompson's mad-dog tirades' (McKeen, 1991, p. 102). One of Mencken's most famous pieces, the merciless obituary of the creationist orator and failed presidential candidate William Jennings Bryan, was a direct influence on Thompson's tooth-and-claw rending of the corpse of Richard Nixon: 'What animated him from end to end of his grotesque career was simply ambition – the ambition of a common man to get his hand upon the collar of his superiors, or, failing that, to get his thumb into their eyes' (Mencken, 1925, p. 1); 'he was a smart young man on the rise – a hubris-crazed monster from the bowels of the American dream with a heart full of hate and an overweening lust to be President' (*BS*, p. 244). In neither case are we offered evidence, or even information: instead, each piece conveys something far more striking and far harder to find in any reporting, least of all obituaries; the unvarnished loathing of the journalist for his subject.

Thompson admired Hemingway's individualism, but their styles were far apart. In his fiction, especially his short stories, Hemingway is a master of minimalism who often leaves his most significant material unsaid. This, to say the least, was not Thompson's approach, especially in his Gonzo masterworks, which achieve their effects through jarring juxtapositions of brutally direct description, reportage, quoted source material and stream-of-consciousness. Hemingway's journalism was a much more direct influence on Thompson, as William McKeen has pointed out (McKeen 1991, pp. 19–20; McKeen 2008, pp. 74–5). The key link between the two authors is the way they position themselves as part of the story. Both use the ostensible subject of the report as a pretext to deliver a meditation on what matters; writing, drugs (whisky in Hemingway's case) and their core values of individual liberty and self-realization.

Hemingway's 1937 dispatch from the Spanish Civil War, 'A New Kind of War' shows how he, as an American journalist, is able to see the effects of the fighting, but is not directly involved. What strikes Hemingway in the end is how the story he hears from a severely wounded republican volunteer turns out, against first impressions, to be true: 'This is a strange new kind of war where you learn just as much as you are able to believe' (Hemingway, 1967, p. 267). As this implies, Hemingway *himself* is changing, as he is now learning, through being able to believe more than he could before. His identity is historically contingent, as it is this 'new kind of war' that has created the change. Hemingway, the evolving subject, is the centre of the piece, even though he spends much of it reporting the war stories of others.

This subjective centre had to live and report authentically. Hemingway believed that 'Good writing is true writing' (Hemingway, 1967, p. 215). William McKeen has shown how Thompson echoes this in 'The Great Shark Hunt', where he complains that he cannot write about hunting sharks because he still 'didn't have the flimsiest notion of what deep-sea fishing *felt like*' (*GSH*, p. 461, emphasis in original; cited in McKeen, 1991, p. 87). Both writers agreed that 'After you learn to write your whole object is to convey everything, every sensation, sight, feeling, place and emotion to the reader' (Hemingway, 1967, p. 216). The point of this appears, at first, to be realism; to record reality faithfully, and thus to represent it. However, both Thompson and Hemingway believed it even more important that the journalist record *himself* – 'every sensation, sight, feeling'. Thus, the reader should grasp not only the reality of the report, but also the Story, meaning the reality of the reporter's experience.

This did not prevent either writer from composing fiction. To his point about true writing, Hemingway added, 'If a man is making a story up it will be true in proportion to the amount of knowledge of life that he has and how conscientious he is' (Hemingway, 1967, p. 215). Thompson internalized this as part of his Gonzo approach.[14] 'The Great Shark Hunt' slides into fantasy just at the point when what it says *ought* to be true, or is designed to appeal to the reader's desire for bravura action: in a typical Gonzo flourish, based on Duke's hotel escape in *Fear and Loathing in Las Vegas*, Thompson claims that when stoned the previous night, he conceived the plan of 'checking out in a raving frenzy at dawn' and charging the bills to *Playboy* magazine, his sponsor for the assignment (*GSH*, p. 463). As Thompson had done when fooling the FBI over the mailbox incident all those years ago, he wanted to transgress but also live to tell the tale. Even if cheating the system remained a fantasy, it was both comically appropriate and true to his persona.

Thompson's inclusion in his work of undeveloped fantasies, or stories he alludes to but does not tell, has been compared to the minimalist metafictional techniques of Jorge Luis Borges and Kurt Vonnegut Jr.: 'those [deliberately undeveloped] books and stories and fantasies are born of the writer's own imagination. Hence the system of allusions is fully organic, completely self-contained, and expressive of the fullest dimensions of the writer's mind' (Klinkowitz, 1977, p. 39).

Such metafictional intertextuality was probably unconscious on Thompson's part. A more deliberate source for the insouciant blend of reportage, lies and invective in 'The Great Shark Hunt' and many other of Thompson's articles was Mark Twain, who concocted a nineteenth-century ancestor of Gonzo when he created comedy by contrasting surface decorum with outrageous content. As Thompson would a century later, the young Twain found that his ambitions 'lay in a still-unmapped area bounded by journalism, humour, entertainment, and popular

---

14 Thompson believed that in his best Gonzo writing he had surpassed his mentor. He once claimed that *Vegas* was as good as *The Great Gatsby*, and better than Hemingway's *The Sun Also Rises* (McKeen, 1991, p. 109).

literature' (Kaplan, 1970, p. 29). Also like Thompson, he found that many readers confused persona and author. Both writers have remained protean and controversial since their deaths: 'More fluid than a mosaic, Twain's image shimmers like endless MTV' (Budd, 1995, p. 11).

Twain's and Thompson's reflexive, ironic satires feed this fluidity endlessly. In the story 'Journalism in Tennessee', Twain's protagonist innocently signs up for work at a local newspaper, only to find that the chief editor is the victim of continual assassination attempts by rival journalists. Most of the bullets hit the hapless protagonist instead of their target. In the middle of an all-out gun battle, the chief editor shows the narrator how to write effective copy, by turning his fairly neutral draft of a local news round-up into a savage attack on another paper's editor. The chief editor thus unwittingly creates a satire on his own profession:

> The heaven-born mission of journalism is to disseminate truth – to eradicate error – to educate, refine and elevate the tone of public morals [...] – and yet this black-hearted villain, this hell-spawned miscreant, prostitutes his great office persistently to the dissemination of falsehood, calumny, vituperation and degrading vulgarity. (Twain, 2004, p. 25)

Thompson's work has many of the hallmarks of Twain; the ironic deployment of a seemingly factual narrative to tell lies and attack journalism as a genre corrupted by petty interests; the centring of the narrative on a subjective viewpoint whose reliability is, to say the least, uncertain; the gradual development of an excoriating denunciation of a victim through an accumulation of damning accusations, never relying on one insult when several will do the job better, as in the chief editor's barbed prose, that might have served as a template for Thompson's damning obituary of Richard Nixon.

Thompson inherited Twain's ability to make the Story the centre of the action and to problematize the notion of objective reporting by blurring it with subjective fiction until the two became impossible to unravel. Like Thompson, who found the Raoul Duke persona at first a benefit and then a burden, Samuel Clemens found himself restricted by his public façade, and yet dependent on it: 'For years, Samuel Langhorne Clemens struggled against the image of himself as Mark Twain the Humorist, a mere entertainer, and yet he persistently used that image to make money' (Hamill, 2004, p. xvii).

Clemens, writing as Twain, involves his own persona in the action: his first published short story, 'Jim Smiley and His Jumping Frog' relates a series of hoaxes perpetrated on a narrator who signs himself as 'Mark Twain' (Twain, 2004, p. 9). Twain, like Duke in *Fear and Loathing in*

Las Vegas, finds himself on a meaningless mission; he has tried to discover the truth about a vanished priest, Leonidas W. Smiley, only to be told a tale about someone entirely different, the notorious Jim Smiley, who has a mania for betting on the actions of bizarrely gifted and eccentric animals such as an asthmatic racehorse, a fighting dog who habitually fakes weakness early in a match in order to raise bets against himself, and the jumping frog of the title. Like Thompson's *Vegas* or 'The Kentucky Derby is Decadent and Depraved', Twain's tale is episodic; it accumulates egregious events in order to force the reader to the conclusion that it is, in effect, all lies, albeit with a core of truth buried somewhere within.

Thompson could find inspiration in texts he believed to be untrue. Although almost the polar opposite of a Christian fundamentalist, he read the book of Revelation weekly (Brinkley, 2006, p. 214). He admired it hugely: 'There are not too many things that I'm afraid to compete with; well, the Book of Revelation is one' (*AGW*, p. 284); 'I still read the Book of Revelation when I need to get cranked up about language' (*C*, p. 126). Thompson was unafraid to borrow lines and ideas from this text, 'not because I am a biblical scholar, or because of any religious faith, but because I love the wild power of the language and the purity of the madness that governs it and makes it music' (*GS*, p. 9). In fact, he adds, the Bible is at its most useful when its reader is under deadline pressure in a hotel room far from any library, as it is the book most likely to be at hand: 'If there is a God, I want to thank Him for the Gideons, whoever they are' (*GS*, p. 10).

Thompson was saved in a journalistic rather than spiritual sense. Nevertheless, his declaration of his love for the language of Revelation carries far more than the pragmatic admiration of a writer for a useful source. He saw in its apocalyptic narrative a suitably deep reservoir of images for his excoriation of leading political figures and the system as a whole. He was not above composing hilarious secular parodies of Revelation to get his points across: 'Pink is the color of stupid, and yellow is the color of dumb. There are too many whores in politics these days, but the night of the whore-hopper is coming' (*BS*, p. 67). Thompson described Satan as having seven heads and six hundred teeth, a cross between a crocodile and a hyena, and then added the punch line, 'That is what a vote for Ross Perot will get you' (*BS*, p. 69).[15]

---

15 Thompson left the reader to decide whether he meant the voter's reward would be the independent candidate Perot himself, or George Bush, who would – Thompson felt – get elected by default if Perot took too many votes away from his Democratic opponent, Bill Clinton. Jay Cowan argues that Thompson was completely wrong in this belief, as Perot's candidacy in fact ensured two election victories for Clinton by reducing the Republican vote (Cowan, 2009, p. 199).

Thompson also imitated the rhetoric of Revelation in order to castigate bogus claimants to moral authority, like the adulterous TV evangelist Jimmy Swaggart: 'How long, O Lord, how long? Are these TV preachers *all* degenerates? Are they wallowing and whooping with harlots whenever they're not on camera? Are they *all* thieves and charlatans and whoremongers?' (*GS*, p. 21: emphasis in original).[16] Thus, the high madness of Revelation could be applied to elections and scandals, and made to sound not like the thundering of a crazed Jeremiah, but like a knowing *imitation* of one: Thompson was aware his audience would not accept the eschatological gibberish of Revelation at first hand, hence his confession to having stolen from it. He positions himself as a facsimile of a prophet, a simulacrum of John of Patmos, announcing the apocalypse down the mojo wire.

Thompson saw in Revelation the rant of a stoned visionary, and thus a useful model for the rhetorical energy of his own Gonzo persona: 'Who the fuck do you think wrote the Book of Revelation? A bunch of stone-sober clerics?' (*C*, p. 151). Drugs, he thought, had motivated some of the most powerful and long-lasting writing in the world. His own relationship to chemicals was more complex. He took a huge variety of substances recreationally, but he usually let only amphetamine and alcohol influence him directly while writing. He tended to work when relatively sober, using his *recollections* of drug highs as catalysts for scenes of outrageous satire. The next chapter will address Thompson's relationships to illicit substances, especially LSD, and to the countercultural groups that embraced them in the 1960s.

---

16 See Rev. 6.10: 'And they cried with a loud voice, saying, How long, O Lord, holy and true, dost thou not judge and avenge our blood on them that dwell on the earth?'.

2 Riding with the Angels, Tripping in the Haight: Drugs, Authorities, Countercultures

Before Thompson settled in his permanent home at Owl Farm, he sought out non-conforming subcultures and lived among them: he also took illicit drugs throughout his adult life. Chemical and cultural dissidence went together as means of resisting authority and pursuing the perpetual quest for personal autonomy. In 1965–1966, at the same time as he was riding with the Hell's Angels, he lived a few streets away from another unorthodox group, the hippies of the Haight-Ashbury district of San Francisco. In the early 1960s, the Haight had been 'a small, discreet colony of Beats' (Davenport-Hines, 2002, p. 266); by the middle of the decade, it had metamorphosed into a mass experiment in communal living, fuelled by a blend of utopian ideals, Eastern religion and drugs, chiefly marijuana and LSD. However, by 1967, the San Francisco hippie honeymoon was over. The Haight had become 'a cop-magnet and a bad sideshow' (*GSH*, p. 166); it had degenerated into a chemical boot camp for disaffected youths, hustlers and rip-off artists from all over the States and became menaced by heroin-related crime (Davenport-Hines, 2002, p. 267). 'San Francisco was where the social haemorrhaging was showing up. San Francisco was where the missing children were gathering and calling themselves "hippies"' (Didion, 2006, p. 67).

The city as a whole, let alone the few already crowded blocks of the Haight-Ashbury enclave, could not adjust to the huge influx of 'hordes of wannabe hippies – penniless runaways armed only with their fantasies' (DeGroot, 2008, p. 253). Racial tensions increased: 'Black teenagers accosted white longhairs who wandered through their neighbourhood and sometimes physically attacked them' (Hoskyns, 1997, p. 145). Many of the original hippies had fled the district by 1967. Thompson left in autumn 1966. Five years later, he looked back at the dream of a new society kindled in the Haight as a chemically fuelled illusion, 'more like a speed-laced acid trip than anything real' (*FLA*, p. 364).

Thompson's published accounts of Haight-Ashbury and its downfall reveal the fundamental contradiction in reporting on, and thus publicizing, a subculture as a space for living freely but anonymously beneath the radar of authority. The Haight was a catalyst for self-realization, at least if taken on its own terms, and was thus well suited to a man of Thompson's individualist ideals. It was a temporary autonomous zone, meaning an ephemeral space of communal liberation from the dominant ideology:

> Humans seem to need the "peak experience" of autonomy shared by cohesive groups – "free freedom" as Rimbaud says – not only in imagination, but in real space / time, in order to give value and meaning to the social. [...] it sometimes appears that the TAZ [Temporary Autonomous Zone] is the last and only means of creating an Outside or true space of resistance to the totality. (Bey, 2003, pp. x–xi)

The Haight succeeded for a span of 2 years in being one of the largest and most successful temporary autonomous zones in the USA, if not the world. However, it soon became exposed to destructive outside forces, partly thanks to journalists like Thompson himself.

Thompson saw this as an instance of a universal pattern: 'a low-rent area suddenly blooms new and loose and human – and then fashionable, which attracts the press and the cops at about the same time' (*GSH*, p. 166). He argues that in any publicly visible bohemian enclave, increased press and police attention and the rise in local rents caused by media coverage eventually combine to force out the original free spirits, thus returning the area to conformity. Thompson's withering analysis of the inevitable implosion of any temporary autonomous zone in a media-driven capitalist society was published in *Rolling Stone* in 1970. He was thus reflecting on an area he had himself left not long before, without apparently being aware of the irony of his words. As a journalist, he had been partly responsible for the publicity that ended the great hippie experiment in the Haight.[1] In 1967, he had placed 'The "Hashbury" is the Capital of the Hippies' in the *New York Times Magazine*. Although at the time he considered the article 'second-rate' (*PH*, p. 611), it was a hit with *Times* readers (McKeen, 2008, p. 116): Thompson anthologized it in

---

1 'As the "Summer of Love" became a reality, the outside world moved in for the kill. *Time* put together a special issue, and *Life* ran a major feature entitled "The New Rock: Music That's Hooked the Whole Vibrating World." Hollywood churned out exploitation movies like Roger Corman's *The Trip* and Sam Katzman's *The Love-Ins*. By April [1967], the Gray Line bus company was including a "Hippie Hop" tour of the Haight among its San Francisco attractions' (Hoskyns, 1997, p. 143).

The Great Shark Hunt, and it remains a valuable document of a significant subcultural phenomenon.

Thompson's thesis on the article was to expose how close mainstream America had become to the hippie movement in certain hidden but important ways. The Haight was, in Thompson's view, merely the most obvious manifestation of a wider trend whose attractions were being efficiently and profitably disseminated by the nominally disapproving straight media such as the *New York Times Magazine* itself. He cited an interview conducted in the Haight by an establishment journalist. He sardonically concluded that the reporter 'wasn't sure if she did [dig the hippie scene] or not, but she passed on the interview for the benefit of those readers who might. Many did' (*GSH*, p. 415). The few blocks of San Francisco on which the article focused were 'only the orgiastic tip of a great psychedelic iceberg that is already drifting in the sea lanes of the great society' (p. 416).

Thompson reworks the cliché of the tip of the iceberg here by pointing out that the berg is *mobile*, in an image that connotes mercantilism and piratical danger. By floating in the sea lanes of Lyndon B. Johnson's America, the Great Society, the iceberg threatens trading ships, but is also analogous to one of those ships itself, roving in order to seek commercial opportunities. The hippies, in short, were not as distinct from ordinary, materialist Americans as they at first appeared. They, just like the suburban salarymen and their wives who despised them, were engaged in the quest for life, liberty and the pursuit of happiness. Thompson's incongruous phrase 'orgiastic tip' mixes the metaphor, but does effectively suggest how the Haight was an erogenous pleasure-zone, outstanding in several senses. Most hippies or drug-using fellow travellers, though, did not want to stand out. They kept well away from the Haight scene and the police attention it drew: 'Submerged and uncountable is the mass of intelligent, capable heads' seeking mere 'peaceful anonymity' (p. 416). Thompson concluded that in fact, 'drugs, orgies and freak-outs' were as frequent in the outwardly respectable mainstream of Bay Area society as they were among the hippies of the Haight (p. 416).

Thompson himself was neither an outwardly respectable secret doper nor a Hashbury hippie. He thus found himself awkwardly positioned outside both the non-using mainstream and the dominant tendencies of the drug subculture. He enjoyed illicit substances openly and admired the hippies' equally overt rejection of authority, but he did not agree with the cant associated with the Haight, such as the pseudo-religious rhetoric of self-styled acid gurus like Timothy Leary. This was particularly evident in *Fear and Loathing in Las Vegas*, where Thompson articulated his complex outsider position at greatest length.

Fear and Loathing versus the Guru Trip: Acid in Vegas

Thompson took hallucinogenics regularly, but never claimed that through them he had accessed a spiritual realm. On the contrary, he referred to the dubious synthesis of chemicals and religion as 'my main argument with the drug culture. I've never believed in that guru trip; you know, God, nirvana, that kind of oppressive, hipper-than-thou bullshit' (C, p. 8). *Fear and Loathing in Las Vegas* engaged in detail with the altered states of consciousness induced by psychedelic drugs, but debunked the theory that such substances can create 'a profoundly religious, yet instant, mystical experience' (Partridge, 2003, p. 101). As Charles Perry, Thompson's colleague at *Rolling Stone*, put it, the fashionable approach to psychedelics at the time 'was the Timothy Leary way, which was essentially a spiritual experience. Hunter was writing about the fact that sometimes when you're on acid, you're just totally fucked up. It was a breath of fresh air' (Wenner and Seymour, 2007, p. 133).

Thompson first took LSD in August 1965, despite warnings from psychiatrist friends that he was unsuited to the drug and might become violent under its influence. In fact, he enjoyed himself and realized that there was no monster lurking under the surface for acid to bring out: 'I've gone to the bottom of the well here and the animal's not down there' (SD, p. 114). He did concede that the drug would overpower inhibitions: 'with a head full of acid you can't pull back. You're going to do whatever you feel like doing. You can't repress anything' (SD, p.114). When her husband first used acid, Sandy Thompson recoiled in fear: 'he was *out* there. He was saying things to me that made no sense whatsoever. [...] And it was scaring me. [...] It was totally paranoid' (Carroll, 1993, p. 100: emphasis in original).

Sandy eventually learned to trip alongside Hunter, and developed a pragmatic approach to the drug: 'It was a great escape. And it was also great fun, mostly' (Wenner and Seymour, 2007, p. 99). Similarly, as Hunter became accustomed to acid, he believed himself able to manage its effects. Tripping generally made him calm: he liked listening to music and thinking. He found LSD to be a means of removing societal conditioning and internal repressions. It allowed original thought: 'heavy thinking, images coming, connections' (SD, p. 114). 'LSD allowed me to trust my instincts [...] it is nice to blow out the steam. Like a cleaning factory. All the tubes rattling. You find out what is in there when you clean it out' (Whitmer, 1993, p. 158). 'About twice a year you should blow your fucking tubes out with a tremendous hit of really good acid. Take seventy-two hours and just go completely amuck, break it all down' (C, p. 6). Jay Cowan, the writer and Owl Farm caretaker who tripped on many occasions with Thompson, remarked that it made his boss 'usually less antic than normal, more reflective, less verbal, and clearly enjoying himself instead of raving' (Cowan, 2009, p. 62).

For Thompson, then, LSD was far from being a drug for transcending the ego. On the contrary, it acted as a subjective cleansing agent, a device for maintaining and developing an individual's sense of identity. In this, as opposed to any naïve notion of dropping out, it offered subversive possibilities. David Lenson astutely points out that the potential psychedelic drugs offered for self-fashioning, rather than for ego-death, may have been a major part of the threat the authorities perceived in them:

> What if the menace of acid in the 1960s was nothing more or less than the old menace of American individualism – that rhetorical icon, that template, to which politicians pay homage, then nullify with laws and fees and paperwork? What if these drugs, instead of 'freeing Westerners from their slavery to the ego,' enabled them to master that ego, to become truly themselves? (Lenson, 1995, p. 153)

In seeking to realize rather than abandon his ego through hallucinogenic drugs, Thompson found himself at odds with Leary, who saw tripping as a catalyst for the 'transcendence of verbal concepts, of space-time dimensions, and of the ego or identity' (Leary et al., 1995, p. 11).

In fact, throughout his writing, Thompson positioned himself against the mystical tradition of drug literature in English, which began with Samuel Taylor Coleridge and Thomas De Quincey and continued into the mid-twentieth century with Aldous Huxley's experiments with mescaline, and Leary's exhortation to his followers to 'Turn On, Tune In, Drop Out' (Leary, 1990, p. 253). Although always ready to document the hellish as well as heavenly moments of drug experience, the tradition consistently positioned drugs such as opium, hashish and mescaline as catalysts for altered states, which were often, if not nearly always, worthwhile and highly desirable. These states ranged from the opium-induced 'state of cloudless serenity' promoted by De Quincey (De Quincey, 1971, p. 75) to the 'spiritual insight' created by the modification of body chemistry (Huxley, 1959, p. 121) to 'the new realities of the expanded consciousness' or 'new interior territories' that Leary claimed drugs had made accessible (Leary et al., 1995, p. 11).

Thompson would have no truck with this visionary rhetoric. He despised Leary, in particular, as a charlatan who was exploiting the credulity of large numbers of disaffected people. As early as 1969, he knew that Leary was 'still the same power-freak who tried West Point and the priesthood before he found an opening in the Acid World. He is still hustling the idle rich [...]. He's nothing but an aging PR man – for himself' (*FLA*, p. 171). Thompson accurately perceived the self-centred basis of Leary's work. Leary promoted ego-death, but his writing reveals him as the ultimate psychedelic self-fashioner. He placed himself at the centre of his texts, using his persona as 'an exemplary ego, not a dissolved one' (Lenson, 1995, p. 154).[2]

Leary thus exposed the limitations of his own theory that individuals taking acid would ultimately change Western society for the better by dropping out of it:

> He combined the model of organized religion with pseudo-Oriental cant, where what was needed was an avatar of personal revelation comprehensible within the individualistic rhetoric of Europe and America. This, even more than the rhetoric of Easternization, compromised LSD's potential for bringing about the mass societal change of which its proponents dreamed. (Lenson, 1995, p. 154)

Even Leary's dubious rhetoric of ego-death implicitly recognized that LSD was a tool whose transformative potential was limited to the *individual* taking the drug; it was this that exposed Leary's programme of *social* revolution through psychedelics as a fantasy.

In *Fear and Loathing in Las Vegas*, any such project of social change is relegated to a distant memory of a naïve past. Raoul Duke remembers how in San Francisco in the mid-1960s, the counterculture felt that its victory over the establishment was "inevitable" (*LV*, p. 68). In Las Vegas in 1971, by contrast, all that is left to gain from LSD is a hallucinatory thrill ride that rapidly decays and is difficult to distinguish from state-sanctioned pleasures such as the alcohol, showbiz and gambling enjoyed by the conformist majority. The relative permissiveness of Las Vegas allows Duke and his attorney and sidekick, Dr Gonzo – who stand metonymically for the counterculture as a whole – to degenerate faster than they could anywhere else, as the city offers 'merely the most appropriate setting for the self-destruction of the counterculture, where the death orgy can proceed with the greatest ease, rapidity, and absence of friction' (DeKoven, 2004, p. 87).

---

2   *High Priest*'s title is self-explanatory. *Flashbacks* is subtitled *A Personal and Cultural History of an Era: An Autobiography*: 'anyone who has read Leary knows that dissolution of the ego is a trick not in his repertory. In later times he became the Hugh Hefner of drug culture, interviewed in *Playboy* and dwelling as much upon his sexual conquests as his spiritual prowess' (Lenson, 1995, pp. 153–54).

Duke and Gonzo's outrageous debauchery was more a metaphor than an autobiography. Although the novel was loosely based on Thompson's two trips to Las Vegas in 1971, the relationship between the text and its author's life was a tenuous one. When Thompson visited the city with Oscar Zeta Acosta, the Chicano lawyer who became the model for Gonzo, they both took drugs, but not in the industrial quantities attributed to the protagonists. Indeed, after his time in Las Vegas, Thompson sometimes played down his involvement with illicit substances there. He claimed to Jim Silberman of Random House that he had not been high at the time: instead, the novel was 'a very conscious attempt to *simulate* drug freak-out' (*FLA*, p. 405: emphasis in original). Although he once boasted, in a piece of mythologizing hyperbole, that in Las Vegas he and Acosta 'took enough speed to keep Hitler awake in the bunker for fifty days and enough acid to make him think he was in the Austrian Alps' (Perry, 2009, p. 140), Thompson was generally coy about the origins of *Vegas*. When asked if he had really taken as many drugs as Duke in Las Vegas, he replied, 'Fiction is the truest form of journalism. [...] You figure it out' (Perry, 2009, p. 146). Whatever he did in his actual visits to the city, Thompson was not using psychedelic drugs when he wrote up the novel from his notes later on: instead, he preferred to alternate uppers and downers as an aid to his working routine. He wrote *Vegas* on 'Dexedrine and bourbon' (McKeen, 2008, p. 166) during breaks from the difficult work of composing 'Strange Rumblings in Aztlán', his political article for *Rolling Stone* on the murder of the Chicano journalist Ruben Salazar (see Chapter 5).

Vegas charts a few days in the lives of two jaded, cynical ex-hippies. Duke and Gonzo leave Los Angeles for Las Vegas on a work assignment, which turns out to be a mere pretext to take implausibly huge quantities of LSD and other drugs. Rather than transforming their consciousness by using acid in the manner of psychedelic pioneers like Aldous Huxley, as a 'chemical Door in the Wall into the world of transcendental experience' (Huxley, 1959, p. 64) or as a 'gateway to a larger, truer grasp of reality' (Partridge, 2003, p. 99), Duke and Gonzo end up signifying the drug's redundancy, because in a city offering constant technological overstimulation and strident, garish pleasure, acid visions come to seem outdated and irrelevant.

The protagonists are living anachronisms – 1960s throwbacks in the decade of Nixon. Their trips reflect their fear and anxiety about the state of the world in the 1970s and their roles within it. They drop acid compulsively, but with no clear sense of *why* they are doing so. Underlying their compulsive behaviour is nostalgia for the temporary autonomous zone of the Haight: Duke and Gonzo's journey is partly a doomed attempt to reach out to a vanished world, to bathe for one last time in the receding undertow of what Duke calls 'the Great San Francisco Acid Wave' (p. 63). But instead of immersing themselves once again in the 1960s, the protagonists find themselves washed up in a late capitalist milieu where the business establishment offers ecstasies that make LSD seem passé: 'this is not a good town for psychedelic drugs. Reality itself is too twisted' (p. 47).

Marianne DeKoven has argued that Thompson's novel embodies a key moment of transition in 1960s America, between the dominant (but increasingly residual) modernist ethic of authenticity, truth-seeking and depth, set against the emerging (but increasingly dominant) postmodernist aesthetic of artificiality, play and surface embodied by Las Vegas. She contends that Duke *appears* alienated from Las Vegas, but is, in fact, very much at home there, as the novel represents the city 'not just as the antithesis to, or in the death of, but also, contradictorily, as the intellectual, cultural, political, emotional and literary legacy of the sixties' (DeKoven, 2004, p. 88). Robert C. Sickels presents a similar argument, when he claims that the counterculture is to blame for how the whole of the USA has, since the publication of the novel, allegedly become more like Las Vegas, because the permissiveness promoted by the hippies encouraged a general tolerance of vulgarity: 'moral liberalism has played a huge role in the Las Vegasization of America' (Sickels, 2000, p. 68).[3]

Las Vegas, though, evolved as a gambling resort in the 1940s and 1950s. It had been founded on a combination of bank loans and Mob profits.[4] It was a thoroughly pre-1960s institution, rooted in organized crime, which hardly needed an upstart counterculture to teach it how to offer licentious thrills or to entertain in bad taste. By the 1950s, before the

---

3 Along with DeKoven, Sickels tends to overstate the influence of countercultural liberalism and to obscure the far greater power of the dominant capitalist mainstream, which includes the outlawed but thoroughly entrepreneurial Mafia. This is not to say that the counterculture was blameless. It was always imbued with capitalist values: 'so-called counter-cultural practices were manipulated by the usual commercial interests; the distribution of economic and political power was exactly the same in the seventies as it had been in the fifties' (Marwick, 1999, p. 4). Woodstock, a commercial festival mythologized as the counterculture's highest moment, typified this: 'Believing in Woodstock Nation was an act of faith so transcendent that all the hype miraculously vanished, along with the extortionately expensive hot dogs. [...] The stage had hardly been dismantled before exploiters invaded' (DeGroot, 2008, pp. 240–1).

4 'Yet proceeds from the drug traffic and other corruption were only one of many sources of the money that made for a Las Vegas so largely operated by and for organized crime. American capitalism was also a founding if silent partner in financing the Strip. In 1946, Phoenix and Salt Lake City banks quietly joined [the gangster Meyer] Lansky and his partners to back the Flamingo' (Denton and Morris, 2002, p. 6).

hippies existed, 'Las Vegas had become one of the most distinct and showy cities of its kind anywhere on the planet [...] a garish, vulgar place – either too greedy or too cheap, but in any case too much' (Denton and Morris, 2002, p. 128). 'Thompson continually describes Las Vegas as replete with pre-, post- and antisixties cultural phenomena, from Sinatra, Dean Martin and Debbie Reynolds to Nixon and Agnew' (DeKoven, 2004, p. 88). The city and its hotels represent an enclave of conspicuous consumption centred on the wealth and privilege of a pre-counterculture generation: 'This was Bob Hope's turf. Frank Sinatra's. Spiro Agnew's. [...] a high-class refuge for Big Spenders' (*LV*, p. 44).

DeKoven sees Duke and Gonzo's quest to discover the American Dream as essentially modernist, because it belongs to an era that cherished sincerity and sought authenticity and was, by 1971, beginning to seem naïve and out of date. She represents *Vegas* as Thompson's parody of this quest, in which Duke and Gonzo's self-destructive excess embodies the failure of modernist ethics in an increasingly postmodernist world to which Duke is, despite his professed alienation, highly suited: 'Duke's identification with Las Vegas, rather than his fear and loathing, is the book's postmodern conceit, while Thompson's underlying horror at the place is the book's deep modernist truth' (DeKoven, 2004, p. 105).

This argument, although insightful, understates the force of the dialectical conflicts between conceit and truth, surface and depth, and between fear/loathing and desire/pleasure, that fracture Duke's experience. DeKoven is right to point out that Duke fits into Las Vegas more than he would like to or would admit to, but his failure to register this is more than a symptom of 'the defeat of the sixties' (DeKoven, 2004, p. 89). Instead, it emerges from his complex inner struggle based on his muted recognition not only of how the utopian dream once chased in the Haight has become appropriated and commercialized, but also of how the counterculture itself had always been open to such corruption. The movement, including the New Journalism it spawned, was never straightforwardly 'lodged in modernity' due to its professed belief in 'truth and authenticity' (DeKoven, 2004, p. 91). Instead, the counterculture – or, at least, a significant element of it – was as riven with meaningless superficiality as the capitalism it rejected.

The term "counterculture" is a convenient simplification. It was never one thing, but is a catch-all label for a constellation of disparate individuals and subcultures whose attitudes and practices were wildly divergent and who had little in common except a strong disrespect for traditional authority figures such as parents, politicians and police. It was intellectually and sometimes literally nomadic; it was philosophically unstable, having 'something in the nature of a medieval crusade: a variegated procession constantly in flux, acquiring and losing members along the route of march' (Roszak, 1971, p. 48). Countercultural lifestyles varied: LSD, for instance, was a drug that some counterculture members took for life, others never, infrequently or just once. It offered a gateway to Inner Truth for Timothy Leary and his coterie of spiritual seekers, but was utterly different for many others: Ken Kesey's Merry Pranksters believed the tripper should simply 'go with the flow' and 'freak freely' (Stevens, 1993, p. 324); the Hell's Angels embraced the drug enthusiastically and then generally reduced their intake or moved on (Stevens, 1993, p. 334). For many 1960s users, including Thompson, acid was seen not as a gateway to a higher state but as a means to reflect and take stock, or to scramble the senses, or simply as a kick: the comedown was as inevitable, and banal, as a hangover, and the trip's content often inane. As one user put it, LSD merely led to 'gummy, Disney, meaningless shit at the tail-end hours of tripping' (Davenport-Hines, 2002, p. 268).[5] Some countercultural groups and individuals, then, were prepared to accept a degree of insincerity, meaninglessness and play: or in DeKoven's terms, to embrace postmodernism.

Hallucinogenic drugs have always been ambiguous. They can offer ecstatic quasi-spiritual states but can just as easily register on the user as merely pleasurable, vulgar or frightening. The term "ecstasy" derives from *ekstatis*, existence outside the self, a breaking with normal modes of sensing and thinking, or in Leary's definition, 'The experience of attaining freedom from limitations, either self-imposed or external; a state of exalted delight in which normal understanding is felt to be surpassed' (Leary, 1998, n.p.). Such freedom has inevitable temporal limits and begs the question of what happens when the ecstasy wears off. Lars Bang Larsen has suggested that ecstasy cannot be dissociated from corruption, a term he rescues from its negative connotations and uses in the morally neutral sense of fragmentation:

> The etymology of 'corruption' (*com* + *rumpere*, to break) connotes decomposition but could also suggest waking up from a state of ecstasy. Ecstasy and corruption are like day and night: ecstasy is mind-blowing and outside of time, while corruption is a process through which something comes undone slowly but surely. (Larsen, p. 183)

At the peak of the 1960s acid wave, corruption was often denied. The most sincere and self-righteous of the hippies were committed not just to the temporary visions of their trips, but to a permanent mystical world view in which the tripper represented a variant of the 'modernist holy

---

5 For further accounts of LSD users embracing banality and/or corruption, see: Stevens, 1993, pp. 324–45; Shapiro, 2003, 141–65; Miles, 2004, p. 36.

fool, privileged with profound insight into a deeper truth beyond the superficial perceptions of the well-adjusted and conventional' (DeKoven, 2004, p. 93). Raoul Duke, though, as DeKoven argues, is no such person (pp. 93–4). Instead, he is struggling to deal with the fallout of the moment when the truth-seekers of the Haight attempted to give their ecstasies ulterior meaning: 'The religious problem arose again: when ecstasy is given a purpose, morality comes into play. Illumination itself is easily tainted and rendered profane, and the ensuing guilt cannot be avoided' (Larsen, p. 181). The problem arose from the contradiction inherent in the truth-seeking, modernist subset of hippies' wish to transcend socially imposed rules, but in the service of a higher law or purpose. Larsen argues that these hippies were too moralistic and too spiritualized to accept that chemically generated ecstasy could be mere purposeless fun; neither did they wish to incorporate corruption into their view of it, except as a negative to be avoided.

If seen as an account of the entire 1960s acid culture, Larsen's theory is reductive, as some LSD users, like the Merry Pranksters and the Hell's Angels, *did* avoid imposing morality on ecstasy, and did embrace the link with corruption, at least some of the time. Nevertheless, Larsen's thesis is provocative, especially when he argues that after the 1960s, capitalism appropriated the dialectic of ecstasy and corruption:

> Today, pleasure is no longer antithetical to authority, as is evidenced, for example, in the level of social production and exchange controlled by the entertainment and service industries. One of the ways that the1960s politics of ecstasy persist today is through the notion that it is possible to get high, make money, and express yourself – all at the same time. This is, in different ways, inherent to most ideas of self-realization today. (Larsen, pp. 181–83)

Larsen posits a postmodernist world in which 'many ecstasies are offered for individualized mass audiences, manifold ways to forget the past and fend off the future', leading to a strong association between ecstasy and apathy (p. 183). By introducing a degree of permissiveness, the system neutralizes a potentially disruptive force and thus tightens social control: 'The individual must adapt himself to a world which does not seem to demand the denial of his innermost needs […]. The organism is thus being preconditioned for the spontaneous acceptance of what is offered' (Marcuse, 1964, p. 70). Mainstream capitalism has thus applied to ecstasy, if not yet to psychedelic drugs themselves, the efficient procedure of repressive desublimation, which it applied to sexuality in the 1960s and 1970s.[6]

Fear and Loathing in Las Vegas astutely anticipates this: Duke and Gonzo find desublimated ecstasy all around them in Las Vegas, causing their own drug experiences to be 'tainted and rendered profane' (Larsen, p. 181). The problem is not simply that Duke fits very well into the garish, postmodernist, superficial milieu of Las Vegas but does not realize it. Instead, Thompson's 'complex representational layering' of the protagonists' quest for the American Dream (DeKoven, 2004, pp. 88–9), allows Duke to demonstrate the fear and loathing he feels towards the virulent capitalist vulgarity of Las Vegas, and yet at the same time to deny utterly the validity of the spiritual claims made for hallucinogenics by dominant elements of the counterculture. *Vegas* exposes the fissures that arise from the stresses between Duke's nostalgia *and* hatred for the failed utopian visions of the past, and his enjoyment *and* fear of the world he explores. He contentedly depicts himself and Gonzo as 'Tooling along the main drag on a Saturday night in Las Vegas', then is immediately jerked back into horror by the crassly patriotic pro-Vietnam War song 'The Battle Hymn of Lieutenant Calley' on the radio (*LV*, p. 29).

'Just Chew it Up Like Baseball Gum': The Anti-Learyism of *Fear and Loathing in Las Vegas*

The protagonists enter Las Vegas only a few years after the 1965–1966 high point of the hippie subculture that Duke lived through in San Francisco; but even in that short time, the adventurous mindset of the peak psychedelic years has become superannuated, because the America of Nixon and Agnew attacks hallucinogenic drugs not only directly through the repressive state apparatus, but also indirectly through the state-sanctioned gambling and hospitality industries of Las Vegas, which promote a coarse, capitalist analogue to tripping. This indirect attack in fact pervaded the whole of the Republic: Las Vegas's brash vulgarity

---

6 'Today compared with the Puritan and Victorian periods, sexual freedom has unquestionably increased [...]. At the same time, however, the sexual relations themselves have become much more closely assimilated with social relations; sexual liberty is harmonized with profitable conformity' (Marcuse, 1969, p. 85). '*Playboy* sexuality is, ideally, casual, frolicsome, and vastly promiscuous. It is the anonymous sex of the harem. It creates no binding loyalties, no personal attachments, no distractions from one's primary responsibilities – which are to the company, to one's career and social position, and to the system generally' (Roszak, 1971, p. 15). For further accounts of repressive desublimation, see: Marcuse 1964, pp. 58–77; Roszak 1971, pp. 84–123; DeKoven, 2004, pp. 26–54.

stands metonymically for the consumerism of America as a whole, which drives its citizens into a cycle of rapidly alternating ecstasy and corruption, and thereby makes them in some ways indistinguishable from LSD users: 'In a town full of bedrock crazies, nobody even *notices* an acid freak' (*LV*, p. 24: emphasis in original). Even as early as 1975, the Union was starting to look like Las Vegas, whose garish but vigorous buildings and signs were becoming templates for designers across the States: 'Already the forms of Las Vegas pervade the American landscape. [...] They have become new American landmarks, the way Americans get their bearings' (Landreth, 1975, p. 202).

By demonstrating the metonymic significance of Las Vegas, the novel debunks the routine condemnation of the drug user as escaping reality, in which the addict 'cuts himself off from the world, in exile from reality, far from objective reality and the real life of the city and the community' (Derrida, 1995, p. 235). In *Vegas*, the city's objective material life is based on fabricating simulacra for profit. These include cheap simulations of drug culture. Icons of the psychedelic scene of the mid-to late 1960s are appropriated, debased and regurgitated as showbiz: Debbie Reynolds grinds out a clunky rendition of the Beatles' *Sergeant Pepper* while sporting 'a silver Afro wig' (p. 44). Duke imagines a 'vicious nazi drunkard' at the casino funfair booths, screaming *'Woodstock Über Alles!'* (p. 47). His paranoid vision of Woodstock as a province of Las Vegas's 'Sixth Reich' (p. 46) is highly appropriate: Las Vegas is where hippie signifiers are corrupted as part of the venal information-flow of a fascistic America bent only on inducing sensory overload as a means of making money.

Upon stumbling stoned into the Circus-Circus, which is a casino and a circus simultaneously, Duke realizes that this 'is what the whole hep world would be doing on a Saturday night if the Nazis had won the war [...] all manner of strange County-Fair/Polish Carnival madness is going on' (p. 46). This grotesque carnival is, in part, mainstream capitalism's equivalent to a countercultural happening, or multimedia show. Like a beatnik or hippie event, it is energized by its flamboyance. Duke's encounter with it resembles Thompson's account of one of Ken Kesey's acid tests at La Honda in May 1965, which he attended with no first-hand knowledge of LSD (as he would not take it for another 3 months) and indeed without using any drug other than beer. From this relatively sober viewpoint, he found Kesey's party 'one of the strangest scenes in all Christendom – a wild clanging on tin instruments on a redwood hillside, loons playing flutes in the darkness, mikes and speakers planted all over' (*PH*, p. 512).

Las Vegas is the straight world's mirror image of the hippie dream of ecstasy through sensory derangement. It is as visually and sonically vibrant as an acid test, but with all the drugs removed except alcohol and the occasional pep pill, and with gambling and prostitution added. It offers a specious ecstasy to the tourist, fuelled by booze, sex on tap and the mirage of easy money: 'house-whores for winners, hand jobs for the bad luck crowd' (*LV*, p. 41). Thompson's *Las Vegas* is the world of Larsen's "today", articulated as early as 1971. The novel shows how ecstasy, once an elusive state seemingly exclusive to religious mystics and a far-out counterculture, has degenerated into a commodity suitable for distribution by the leisure and hospitality industries.[7]

Duke has seen a number of burnt-out cases wandering around as a result: 'ugly refugee[s] from the Love Generation' (63) who cannot cope in the post-hippie world, especially when confronted by capitalism's reification of ecstasy. Duke and Gonzo are themselves such refugees. Accordingly, *Vegas* has a strong vein of nostalgia. It is partly Thompson's funeral address to Haight-Ashbury: a narrative of the great countercultural comedown of the early 1970s. Among the hallucinations, clowning and satire, Thompson included a sincere tribute to the bohemian San Francisco he lived in from 1965–66. He remarks that the energy of his generation peaked 'in a long fine flash [...]. We had all the momentum; we were riding the crest of a high and beautiful wave' (67–8). Thompson's metaphor of a flash recalls the impact of transcendentalism in the nineteenth century, which created 'a brilliant flash, and those who experienced it were changed profoundly by it' (Robinson, 1999, p. 24). But Duke extends his second, aquatic metaphor to demonstrate the transience of the experience: in 1971, he finds that in Las Vegas, looking west, he can almost see 'the high-water mark' where the wave broke (68). The book as a whole is Thompson's attempt to bury the counterculture, not to praise it, but this does not lessen the poignancy of Duke's account of an idealistic movement doomed to failure. *Vegas* was 'a vile epitaph for the drug culture of the sixties [...] a reluctant salute to that decade that started so high and then went so brutally sour' (*GSH*, p. 118).

---

7 Contemporaries of Thompson had foreseen this possibility, and had suggested the advantage the establishment might gain by legalizing hallucinogenics. As early as 1970, Theodore Roszak had asked: 'Why should not the technocratic society accept into its arsenal of social controls methods of emotional release as sophisticated as the psychedelics? An occasional turn-on, a periodic orgy, a weekend freak-out' (p. 176). Roszak cites the possible legitimization of psychedelics as an instance of repressive desublimation (p. 173): 'Marcuse is undoubtedly right in identifying denatured permissiveness as one of the key strategies of contemporary social control' (p. 111).

In Thompson's view, part of this sourness came from the hippie subculture's passive submission to its self-appointed internal authorities, the psychedelic gurus such as Timothy Leary. Thompson was one of the 1960s users of hallucinogenics who not only witnessed and participated in the drug scene of that decade, but also chronicled its decline, which was partly initiated by the fallacious attempts of Leary and others to imbue chemical ecstasies with a religious significance they did not possess.[8] Rather than creating a viable alternative to existing hierarchies, the self-proclaimed acid gurus co-opted psychedelic drugs into top-down, authoritarian power structures taken from established institutions with little adaptation. *Vegas* openly pours scorn on Leary for the damage he wrought: he created 'a generation of permanent cripples, failed seekers' (pp. 178–9).

Duke does not object to LSD, but to those who seek to claim power or status through it. He remembers when, curious about the drug, he sought advice from a guru, the mysterious Dr _____, who is clearly a fictional amalgam of Leary and others, though Duke wryly claims his name has been removed from the text 'at insistence of publisher's lawyer' (p. 63 f/n). Upon introducing himself to the doctor, Duke realizes that he is being ignored, as the doctor is desperately chanting *Om* in an attempt 'to block me out of his higher consciousness. […] Forget LSD, I thought. Look what it's done to *that* poor bastard' (p. 65: emphasis in original). Some 6 months later, Duke discovers LSD's powers when he takes it for the first time at a nightclub. After briefly describing his first trip, Duke immediately marginalizes the experience and moves on by claiming he was, at that time, 'A victim of the Drug Explosion. A natural street freak, just eating whatever came by' (p. 66).

Duke's dismissal of his LSD-using background emerges from his retrospective disillusionment. The protagonists of *Vegas* are far more jaded than Leary or Huxley. By 1971, acid had lost its halo, having been

---

8   Aldous Huxley, unlike Leary, was well aware of how problematic the role of psychedelic guru could be. He met two psychiatrists who were using LSD in therapy sessions, and saw them as vulgar and insensitive: 'To think of people made vulnerable by LSD being exposed to such people is profoundly disturbing' (Huxley, 1999, p. 161). Writing during the peak of the hippie movement, and shortly after LSD had been made illegal in the USA, Huxley's wife Laura expressed the dismay felt by the early psychedelic pioneers at the way the drugs had become popularized and thus value-laden: 'Now, in 1967, when LSD has become a household word, I realize how lucky those of us were who ten years ago approached LSD before it had either the demoniacal or paradisiacal vibrations it has now – when it had no echoes of gurus and heroes, doctors or delinquents' (Huxley, 1999, p. 74).

passed over by the vagaries of fashion. It had become a dated consumer product, 'the Studebaker of the drug market' (p. 201), although Duke and Gonzo, being stubborn Haight-Ashbury atavists, still consume it avidly. They bring with them five whole sheets of impregnated paper (p. 4), and then ingest between half a sheet and a whole one at a time: 'Your half of the sunshine blotter. Just chew it up like baseball gum' (p. 21); 'The whole blotter was chewed up' (p. 58).

In accordance with Duke and Gonzo's consumerist construction of the drug, the form of the novel is episodic, rather than subordinated to a totalizing quest for a mystery or holy vision: 'So long as psychedelics were experienced within an atheistic worldview, they produced convoluted, fragmentary, chaotic snakes of text' (Boon, 2002, p. 274). This is reflected in the sometimes incoherent dialogue. When Duke and Gonzo attempt to check into the Mint Hotel while high on acid, Duke begins spouting gibberish at the clerk, who is turning into a poisonous moray eel: 'Free lunch, final wisdom, total coverage… . why not?' (p. 23). He then sees vicious lizards fighting all over the hotel bar, where the carpet is soaked in blood.

Duke and Gonzo experience many such chaotic, visceral thrills: but in the final analysis, this makes them much the same as the more conventional tourists who go to Las Vegas to gamble, drink, see shows and have sex with prostitutes. Lindsey Michael Banco has claimed that Thompson 'becomes one of the first to question whether hippie anti-tourism and mainstream tourism were all that different' (Banco, 2010, p. 105); however, the same point was made by Tom Wolfe 6 years earlier than *Vegas*, in an article that had a significant influence on Thompson's book. This was 'Las Vegas (What?) Las Vegas (Can't hear you! Too noisy) Las Vegas!!!!', anthologized in Wolfe's first collection, *The Kandy-Kolored Tangerine-Flake Streamline Baby* in 1965 (Wolfe, 1981, pp. 17–35). Thompson enjoyed Wolfe's work immensely: he had written a favourable review of the book in the same year and had corresponded with Wolfe about journalism (*PH*, pp. 533–34, pp. 650–53).[9]

Wolfe takes the viewpoint of a detached observer. He zeroes in on Raymond, a deranged tourist at the craps table who keeps repeating the word "hernia" aloud like a mantra (Wolfe, 1981, p. 17). Wolfe discovers that Raymond has kept himself high for days by alternating amphetamine and barbiturate pills, to allow himself to gamble continuously. Wolfe then mockingly turns him into a hippie-like seeker of altered states: in effect, a forerunner of Raoul Duke. 'He was also enjoying what the prophets of

---

9 See DeKoven, 2004, p. 72–85 for an account of Wolfe's essay and its relationship with Thompson's novel.

hallucinogen call "consciousness expansion." The man was psychedelic. He was beginning to isolate the components of Las Vegas' unique bombardment of the senses' (Wolfe, 1981, pp. 18–19). Like Duke, Raymond does not create original visions but internalizes and reworks the data his senses receive from his already garishly overwrought environment. Wolfe adds that Raymond's mumbled "hernia" incantation is merely an intensified echo of the arcane nonsense spouted by the dealers, a nasal babble that 'contains next to no useful instruction. Its underlying message is, We are the initiates, riding the crest of chance' (Wolfe, 1981, p. 19).

Thompson's debt to Wolfe is clear. Both dissect the craziness of Las Vegas hilariously, both explore what it is like to engage with such a city when high on drugs, and both blur the line between stoned consciousness and the quotidian routines of the casinos. In Wolfe, though, the drugged buffoon is observed by the sober journalist. Thompson adds power to Wolfe's prototype by making the drugged fount of gibberish the centre of the action, doubling him into Duke and Gonzo and making the central couple aware of their poignant anachronism as jaded ex-hippies, once deluded by the counterculture's specious sense of hope but now disillusioned and cast adrift. In both Thompson and Wolfe, the craziness of the protagonists is less eccentric than it appears, because it echoes and redoubles what is going on around them. As has been argued by several critics, *Vegas* can be read as an exaggeration of countercultural excess, a debasement of the Haight's utopianism (see DeKoven, 2004, p. 88; Sickels, 2000, p. 68). Wolfe's image of gambling as surfing, or riding the crest of chance, was echoed, probably unconsciously, by Thompson in Duke's metaphor of 'riding the crest of a high and beautiful wave' that described the idyllic scene of Haight-Ashbury, which had long since been corrupted (*LV*, p. 68).

Like Wolfe's hapless tourist, Duke and Gonzo are customers. Their attempt to mock the square entertainment scene exposes their own complicity in it, both as consumers and as freaks (Thompson's own highly suggestive term for 1970s ex-hippies still clinging to non-conformity). Like those of Wolfe's Raymond, the stoned antics of Duke and Gonzo mean that they form *part of* the show, shocking the spectators like circus geeks, albeit without the approval of the authorities. A typical instance is when they draw up next to a car occupied by 'two hoggish-looking couples', stereotyped by Duke as provincial cops and their wives (p. 151). Gonzo pretends he is a traumatized Vietnam veteran who wants to sell them heroin. The couples ignore him, but as his sales pitch intensifies, he resorts to a string of disconnected, meaningless but outrageous epithets: 'Shoot! Fuck! Scag! Blood! Heroin! Rape! Cheap! Communist!' (p. 152). One of the men finally reacts, screaming with rage. Duke brakes hard before a stoplight and swerves to escape from the incensed rednecks. Thus, in true Gonzo fashion, the reporter becomes part of the scene he is reporting on, and affects it through his actions.

This bears comparison with Leary's theory that 'set and setting', meaning the mindset of the user and his/her environment respectively, determine the outcome of the drug experience (Leary et al., 1995, p. 11). In Thompson, though, much more than in Leary, the relationship between the user and the environment is interactive: set and setting are bound up with performance and spectacle. The Gonzo journalist and his sidekick have a role in *reshaping* the setting, as their various stoned babblings and pratfalls are performed. This altered setting, in turn, affects the protagonists' mindsets. In a vicious feedback loop, these mindsets cause further outrageous actions, thereby worsening the drug users' environment and the process continues. The dense, overloaded sensory atmosphere of Las Vegas, and its mythological status as a place of licence and danger, make the transfer of internal emotion (set) to the outside (setting) very easy: 'The neon-saturated night of Las Vegas is just as much a hallucination, a myth, a product of the imagination, as any vision triggered by LSD' (Boon, 2002, p. 266).

'The Hateful Glare of the Land of Lit-Upness': *Fear and Loathing in Las Vegas* and Negative Visionary Experience

Although *Vegas* is a satirical novel by an author who despised the 'guru trip', some of it corresponds closely to descriptions of psychedelic experience offered by Huxley and Leary – in particular, the states of resistance or arrested development, which can prevent mystical experience, or become a problematic part of it, because 'negative visionary experience may be induced by purely psychological means. Fear and anger bar the way to the heavenly Other World and plunge the mescaline taker into hell' (Huxley, 1959, p. 109). Leary develops this argument to claim that unenlightened trippers in the third bardo state are likely to encounter 'Mind-controlling manipulative figures and demons of hideous aspects'; 'the first impulse will be to flee from them in panic and terror' (Leary et al., 1995, p. 80).

Duke and Gonzo's fear and anger produce a classic third bardo experience, where the ego is most certainly not transcended, reality is felt keenly, and they are plunged into a Huxleyan hell. The two men differ in the way they react to LSD: Duke, on the whole, is more anxious, while Gonzo is more aggressive; when tripping, they personify, respectively, the fear and loathing of the title. This is suggested when Duke and Gonzo retire to their suite, having finally checked into the Mint Hotel, and cut the intensity of the acid with alcohol, a cheap, legal depressant. On seeing a neon sign outside the window, Duke cowers, complaining that the sign is an "electric snake" coming straight towards them; Gonzo advises him to shoot it (p. 27).

Here, Thompson's text comically reworks Huxley's account of the role of electricity in limiting the visionary otherness of intense colour by making it commonplace: 'Modern technology has tended to devaluate the traditional vision-inducing materials' (Huxley, 1959, p. 94); city illumination, once a special event, now occurs nightly 'and celebrates the virtues of gin, cigarettes, and toothpaste' (Huxley, 1959, p. 94). Las Vegas copies this technique but adds gambling, lounge acts and commercialized sex to Huxley's list.

It is not hard for this violently stimulating environment to provoke negative visions. Huxley refers to the threatening light of the world as experienced by schizophrenics or those on a bad trip as 'the hateful glare of the land of lit-upness' (Huxley, 1959, p. 111). This is a perfect description of the hellish otherness into which Duke and Gonzo are plunged: the hell is not one of the lonely absence of stimulation, but of its incessant overabundance through cheap technological imitations of the visionary world:

> Everything in it [the universe of the negative visionary], from the stars in the sky to the dust under their feet, is unspeakably sinister or disgusting; every event is charged with a hateful significance; every object manifests the presence of an Indwelling Horror, infinite, all-powerful, eternal. (Huxley, 1959, p. 108)

As an example of a negative visionary, Huxley cites Kafka, whose most famous short story, 'Metamorphosis', starts with a man transformed 'into a gigantic insect' (Kafka, 1961, p. 9).

In a reversal of Kafka's vision, Duke sees poisonous eels, lizards and snakes coming towards him; the world is metamorphosed instead of the protagonist. Kafka's Gregor Samsa ignores his condition and worries comically that he will be late for work (Kafka, 1961, p. 10). Duke, on the contrary, feels existentially threatened because he is having to face the horror of registering for his room and his press credentials while on acid: 'There is no way to explain the terror I felt when I finally lunged up to the clerk and began babbling' (*LV*, p. 23). Unlike Samsa, a classic salaryman, the ex-hippie Duke wants to, but cannot, reject his place in society: it is the ritual formalization of his identity as a worker and consumer that triggers his panic. For Huxley, the negative visionary is on a wrong path; for Leary, he/she is trapped in the second or third bardo; but for

Thompson, Duke's negative vision is inevitable because it arises from the inescapably awful setting of Las Vegas.

Transcendence of this setting through drugs appears impossible. The only guaranteed escape is death. Soon after Duke's paranoid outburst at the registration desk, Gonzo turns his characteristic anger against himself. While lying in the bath, high on a huge dose of LSD, Gonzo threatens Duke with a blade. He demands that Duke help him commit suicide by throwing the plugged-in cassette recorder into the water at the moment the tape reaches the peak of Jefferson Airplane's hippie anthem 'White Rabbit'.[10] The attorney's only explanation for his death wish is 'tell them I wanted to get *Higher!*' (p. 60: emphasis in original), as if the greatest and only remaining form of transcendence is dying while under the influence of acid.[11]

Thompson offers the attorney neither death nor transcendence but forces his suicide attempt to fail, as Duke throws a grapefruit into the bath instead of the cassette recorder. After thrashing about grotesquely for a few seconds, Gonzo realizes he is still alive and comes after Duke with the knife: Duke counters by brandishing a can of Mace. Outgunned, the attorney retreats to the bath to calm down. Leary's ideas are both subverted and confirmed here. Any claim of mystical insight through LSD seems nonsense after the reader encounters Gonzo's suicidal then violent tendencies, along with his clumsiness and buffoonery. However, Leary's maxim that the 'set and setting' of an acid trip are crucial is clearly relevant. In this one respect, at least, *Vegas* proves Leary right about acid. Duke and Gonzo have exactly the wrong mindset for the sort of insightful spiritual experience that Leary was aiming to promote.

They are also in precisely the wrong place, although Las Vegas is merely the most obvious evidence of a national malaise. Despite appearances, it is by no means exceptional: 'when demeaning (or celebrating) Las Vegas as a modern-day Babylon, we surreptitiously create a critical viewpoint that presupposes a mythical American Heartland' where all is

---

10 The song was a personal favourite of Thompson's. It carried powerful connotations of edgework and, by association, made him remember his time at the Haight: 'Every time I hear "White Rabbit" I am back on the greasy midnight streets of San Francisco, looking for music, riding a fast red motorcycle downhill into the Presidio, leaning desperately into the curves through the eucalyptus trees, trying to get to the Matrix in time to hear Grace Slick [Jefferson Airplane's lead singer] play the flute' (*LY*, p. 40).

11 This was the fate of Aldous Huxley, who requested, and was given, the drug on his deathbed in 1963. This was perhaps appropriate, as it was the logical conclusion of Leary's guidebook *The Psychedelic Experience*, a loose translation of Tibetan prayers intended to be read to the dying (Leary et al., 1995: see Partridge, 2003, p. 105).

healthy and normal; this illusion must be resisted (Cooper, 1992, p. 529). Instead, Thompson's Las Vegas is as corrupt and debased as the rest of Nixon and Agnew's USA, only more blatantly so: 'Las Vegas is the horrific incarnation of what the establishment would look like if only matter were malleable enough' (Cooper, 1992, p. 541).

Vegas is a political novel as well as a drug text. The demented carnival of Las Vegas personifies the state's co-option of ecstasy and thus the failure of the Leary-Huxley dream: *Vegas* implies that this was inevitable, as the fabric of the emerging acid movement was always too thin to avoid being ruptured by 'the grim meat-hook realities' of American capitalism (*LV*, p. 178). Duke notes that by 1971, psychedelic drugs have become so unpopular that volume dealers only handle them for jaded dilettantes like himself and Gonzo (p. 201). Instead, heroin and Seconal are fashionable, as drug users only want to numb their senses: 'downers came in with Nixon' (p. 202). Thompson was not the only one to notice this. In the same year (1971), Jim Morrison, the lead singer with The Doors, commented on the mass comedown after the hallucinogenic boom of the mid- to late 1960s: 'I don't think anyone really has the strength to sustain those trips forever. Then you go into narcotics, of which alcohol is one. Instead of trying to think more you try to kill thought' (Hopkins and Sugerman, 1980, p. 339). 'In London, acid euphoria cooled with the coming of winter [1967–8 ...]. Throughout 1968 violence was the new radical pose' (Shapiro, 2003, p. 163). By the 1970s, many hippies were contributing to the mainstream's co-option of ecstasy by turning themselves into businessman: Thompson's *Rolling Stone* editor, Jann Wenner, encapsulated the new sensibility in his sardonic reworking of Leary's slogan: 'Turn-on, tune-in, drop-out, make money' (Whitmer, 1993, p. 188).

Although this capitulation to the system was due in part to Nixon's 'War on Drugs', it also came about because of the internal contradictions of the counterculture: its search for individual freedom versus its tendency to seek spiritual authorities such as gurus; its rural, anti-technological ethos, which conflicted with its dependency on modern machinery to manufacture music, film, lightshows, printed matter and drugs such as acid; the earth-mother and hippie-chick stereotypes set against the emerging feminist aspirations of many women; racial tensions; and the socio-political contradictions between 'the lower/ working class biker/dropout types and the upper/middle, Berkeley/ student activists' (*LV*, p. 179). As Duke says, 'The final split came at Altamont' (p. 179), the disastrous 1969 rock festival where a black fan was murdered by the Hell's Angels, who objected to his having a white girlfriend (Shapiro, 2003, p. 164). By then, Duke argues, it had been obvious for years that 'the energies of The Movement were long since aggressively dissipated by the rush to self-preservation' (*LV*, p. 180).¹²

'The Menace is Loose Again': Thompson and the Hell's Angels

Gilles Deleuze and Félix Guattari distinguish between two forms of social organization: the hierarchical, settled State and the tribal, nomadic war machine (Deleuze and Guattari, 1988, pp. 351–423). They are not mutually exclusive but must co-exist: 'their opposition is only relative; they function as a pair, in alternation [...] antithetical and complementary, necessary to one another' (p. 351). In Thompson's writing, the Hell's Angels represent an incarnation of the war machine, a nomadic group that despite its outsider status remains thoroughly dependent on continual conflict with the State: in this case, post-frontier, twentieth-century America. Thompson describes the Angels as self-styled outsiders, renegade motorcycle enthusiasts who meet regularly to 'get drunk and naked and fall on each other like goats in the rut, until they all pass out from exhaustion' (*HA*, p. 178). They wear provocative clothing, including club insignia featuring a death's head, and Nazi regalia such as Iron Crosses and *Wehrmacht* helmets from World War II. Despite these sartorial affectations, the Angels are not literally soldiers: instead, the war machine is, in their case, a metaphor for a state of 'psychic nomadism' (Bey, 2003, p. 104), meaning the mindset of the '*apaches* (literally "enemies") of the old Consensus. [...] These nomads chart their courses by strange stars' (Bey, 2003, p. 105).

The Angels' warrior values are the exact opposite to the pacifistic ethic of the Haight-Ashbury hippies, except for a shared disrespect for authority. Their self-image and others' perception of them are based on aggression directed at straight society: 'The Menace is loose again, the Hell's Angels, the hundred-carat headline [...] show the squares some class, give 'em a whiff of those kicks they'll never know' (*HA*, p. 3). The opening paragraph of Thompson's book encapsulates the Angels' war machine mobility and their ambiguously threatening social role. They are capitalized as 'The Menace', and named as 'the hundred-carat headline': in other words, they are a media creation as much as a reality. Their existence cannot be separated from the moral panics that generate the popular image of them. This relationship is determined by the cash

---

12 The term 'The Movement' is a usually used with specific reference to the Free Speech Movement, a radical New Left student group at Berkeley in the mid-1960s: see Thompson's article 'The Nonstudent Left' (*GSH*, pp. 421–9). In this case, Thompson uses the term to apply to the whole counterculture.

nexus, and is ultimately an expression of class relations: the hundred-carat headline means profit.

Thompson compares the Angels to frontiersmen and outsiders: cowboys ('low in the saddle'), jazz musicians ('jamming crazy'), nomadic barbarian marauders ('Genghis Khan'), shape changers ('flat out through the eye of a beer can') and mythical beasts ('a monster steed with fiery anus') (*HA*, p. 3). These strands of representation combine in Thompson's expression of the display of pride and hostility with which the Angels greet the mainstream. Showing "class" to the "squares" means asserting independence and self-worth, but also represents the Angels' unconscious appropriation of Marxist dialectics; their implicit recognition of their status as working-class dropouts who act out their rejection of the nine-to-five routine of alienated labour offered by capitalism. Behind this façade, some of the Angels do hold down jobs, for instance 'on the assembly line at a nearby General Motors plant' (*HA*, p. 6) or as 'casual labourers at any work that pays quick wages and requires no allegiance' (p. 61). The point of Angelhood is not so much to drop out of society as to display one's contempt for it by asserting the right to enter the temporary autonomous zone of the club meeting, freeway run or illicit party whenever one wants. The Angels' sense of "class" depends upon *showing* that class by being observed.

Thompson mostly sidesteps the issue of what forms of class, if any, the Angels are provoked to show by his own presence. He is accepted by them at first because he tells them that – unlike earlier, biased reporters – he will give a fair account of their lives: perhaps because of this, Thompson does not tend to problematize his own role as an observer. Instead, he makes an effort to remain neutral. This is pre-Gonzo Thompson. Objectivity is still important, although difficult: his early encounters with the Angels soon reached the stage where 'I had become so involved in the outlaw scene that I was no longer sure whether I was doing research on the Hell's Angels or being slowly absorbed by them' (p. 55). Despite this admission, for the greater part of the book, Thompson treats his complicity with the Angels as a practical rather than literary or philosophical problem: 'she asked me whether "those boys" were my friends. I said yes, and four days later I received an eviction notice' (p. 55).

Thompson, though, was far from a mere camp follower or passive observer. As well as riding and partying with the Angels, he initiated a sociological experiment and tested the Angels' ability to integrate with the hippie counterculture, when he introduced them to the novelist Ken Kesey, who invited them to an acid test (or LSD party and multimedia 'happening') held at La Honda, California, in August 1965, under the aegis of his anarchic commune, the Merry Pranksters.[13] The Pranksters shared the Angels' distrust of education and hierarchy: they embraced a spontaneous approach to psychedelic drugs that was the opposite of Leary's structured, intellectualized pseudo-mysticism. In their view, the visionary world of an LSD trip 'existed only in the moment itself – *Now* – and any attempt to plan, compose[,] orchestrate, write a script, only locked you out of the moment, back in the world of conditioning and training' (Wolfe, 1996, p. 57: emphasis in original).

Thompson's account of the acid test in *Hell's Angels* bears comparison with Tom Wolfe's version in *The Electric Kool-Aid Acid Test*, published a year later in 1968. Both writers were aware of the importance of the meeting of the Angels and the Pranksters to the counterculture, but unlike Wolfe, Thompson was present at La Honda, and he is careful to cite his own participation in the LSD sessions (he is not confessing to a crime, as the drug was not made illegal in California until October 1966): 'Dropping acid with the Angels was an adventure; they were too ignorant to know what to expect, and too wild to care' (*HA*, p. 282). Wolfe's description of the same event, based on an audio tape supplied to him by Thompson, is totally different. Following the style of his early journalism, Wolfe breaks his syntax to intercalate segments of sound or dialogue: 'Mountain Girl ready – *Hey, Kesey!* – Hermit grin – Page ablaze […] about 3 P.M. they started hearing it. […] The Angels were up there somewhere weaving down the curves on Route 84, gearing down – *thraggggggh* – and winding up' (Wolfe, 1996, p. 154). Wolfe is proto-Gonzo in his style and effects: yet what is lacking is the Gonzo catalyst of the first-hand involvement of the reporter.

Thompson's main aim, unlike Wolfe's, is not to imitate the anarchy of the La Honda acid test through scrambled syntax or sound effects, but to distinguish between it and another contemporary narrative of LSD use: the pseudo-intellectual sessions of spiritual questing enabled and embodied by *The Psychedelic Experience's* cod-Buddhist rhetoric. Thompson was

---

13 Thompson had been impressed with Kesey's work even before meeting him. Of Kesey's novels, *One Flew Over the Cuckoo's Nest* (1962) and *Sometimes a Great Notion* (1964), Thompson commented: 'no other writer around had written two books like that. A real achievement' (Whitmer, 1993, p. 152). As well as for the acid tests, the Pranksters are known for their 1964 bus ride across America that led to a memorable encounter with Timothy Leary's more academic and more spiritually-orientated LSD-using group, The Castalia Foundation, at Millbrook, New York State: 'Kesey probably expected an Eastern version of La Honda and the Pranksters. What he found was a bunch of Ivy League eggheads walking around in robes and talking like comparative religion professors. Millbrook was a bore, and hostile to boot' (Stevens, 1993, p. 323). For first-hand accounts of the Pranksters, see: Wolfe, 1996; Perry and Babbs, 1990.

already preparing for the anti-Leary stance he took openly in *Fear and Loathing in Las Vegas*. The Angels, by dint of sheer naïve enthusiasm, are to him more "interesting" and "alive" than Leary and his coterie of 'well-educated truth-seekers' (*HA*, 281–2). Here Thompson distances himself from the self-conscious rationalizing of psychedelic experience. By celebrating the approaches of the Angels and the Pranksters to LSD, he positions them in the tradition of those frontier Americans who were doers, not thinkers. The La Honda trippers were carving out a new chemical frontier in a world when the literal one had vanished, and thus aspiring to a contemporary form of the American Dream of self-realization in a social order sufficiently mobile and permissive to make it possible (see Chapter 4): however, both the Angels and the Pranksters were typical of the counterculture in that they would never realize the Dream in any sustainable way.

'Exterminate All the Brutes!': Bringing the Angels Back to Earth

Like the Pranksters' acid tests, the temporary autonomous zones of the open freeway and the mass parties allowed the Angels a feeling of frontier autonomy on a few limited occasions: but if the Angels or their educated admirers thought a bunch of down-at-heel bikers were truly free, Thompson knew they were being naïve. A look at the Angels' crude political thinking was enough to show this. Rather than having a coherent ideology, the Angels wallowed in the same reactionary stew as the John Birch Society and other fringe groups. These right-wing organizations would have persecuted the Angels ruthlessly if given any power. Consequently, the Angels remained 'blind to the irony of their role […] knight errants of a faith from which they have already been excommunicated' (*HA*, p. 295).

Thompson's allusion to knight-errantry accurately placed the Angels as protagonists in their own atavistic myth, living a quest which – even on its own terms – was doomed. The Angel's ingenuous attitude towards the American establishment was encapsulated in a letter sent by the club's president, Sonny Barger, to the then US president, Lyndon B. Johnson, offering the Angels' services to the Vietnam War in a Special Forces role, as 'a crack group of trained gorrillas [sic]' (*HA*, p. 303). Johnson mysteriously declined Barger's offer, perhaps because most of the Angels, as convicted felons, would have been ineligible for the draft anyway.

Therefore, to Thompson, the Angels represented a dead end. He could party with them, and he learned to enjoy the edgework of dangerous motorcycle riding (see Chapter 4): but the Angels' worldview was fatally limited as far as he was concerned. Although he admired their commitment to mutual aid and their take-no-bullshit stance, as well as their penchant for fast riding, alcohol and drugs, he saw that their subculture was ultimately a failure due to its lack of a credible social and political vision. He compares them to another outlaw group, the left-wing activists of Industrial Workers of the World, a.k.a. the Wobblies. Although the Angels, unlike the Wobblies, had no programme for changing society, they shared 'the same feeling of constant warfare with an unjust world. The Wobblies were losers, and so are the Angels' (p. 313).

Thompson explains that the outlaw is a special subset of loser, as the outlaw actively resists the dominant ideology, albeit without hope of lasting success, whereas the loser is merely passive. The Angels exert a fascination over vast numbers of ordinary losers who would dearly like 'to be transformed – even for a day – into hairy, hard-fisted brutes who walk over cops' (p. 313). Even to the mainstream non-losers who would like them disbanded, the Angels 'command a fascination, however reluctant, that borders on psychic masturbation' (p. 313).

By denouncing the mainstream's fascination with the Angels, Thompson was implicitly denouncing his own; he wanted to cut himself off from them. The final break came on Labour Day, 1966, when he was viciously beaten up by a group of Angels after an argument.[14] Even if this had never happened, Thompson would still have parted ways: first, as the Angels were a job – he had been paid to write a book, and the work was finished – and secondly, because his individualist humanism would not accept the kind of mindlessly violent group ethic that held them together. In the postscript to *Hell's Angels*, added after the beating, Thompson compared the whole experience of riding with the Angels to a bad LSD trip: 'fast and wild in some moments, slow and dirty in others, but on balance it looked like a bummer' (*HA*, p. 325). His final comment alluded to Joseph Conrad's 1899 novella of colonial depravity, *Heart of Darkness* (Conrad, 1990): 'there was no escaping the echo of Mistah Kurtz's comment from the heart of the darkness: "The horror! The horror! ... Exterminate all the brutes!"' (*HA*, pp. 325–26).

Thompson's attempts at objectivity, sustained through most of the book, have disappeared. His meaning is clear; angry after being severely assaulted, Thompson feels instinctively that he wants the Angels killed. However, he is selective in his quotation. 'Exterminate all the brutes' is a scrawled postscript at the end of Kurtz's report on the 'Suppression of Savage Customs'; Conrad's narrator Marlow keeps this note concealed from Kurtz's backers and his fiancée (Conrad, 1990, p. 208, p. 243). 'The

---

14 Accounts and interpretations of the incident vary. See for instance: *HA*, pp. 324–26; *PH*, pp. 585–86; Barger, 2001, pp. 125–7; McKeen, 2008, p. 111.

horror! The horror!' by contrast, is Kurtz's dying utterance, overheard on a separate occasion by Marlow (Conrad, 1990, p. 239). On his deathbed, Kurtz realizes that the horror does not simply inhere within the primitive civilization of the "brutes", but that it lies as much, or more, within himself. Thompson's juxtaposition conceals this realization, but it is there within his work nevertheless. Like Kurtz, he has been complicit in the violence of the alien world, and has done much to stir it up: he has confronted the dark, violent heart of Angel culture, and found it lying within.

There is, accordingly, an existential anxiety at the centre of *Hell's Angels* that has less to do with The Menace, that is, the bikers themselves, than with what Thompson discovers about himself after riding with them. He inherits 'the legacy of the big machine' (p. 321); his motorbike comes to stand as a symbol for what he has carried with him from his time with the Angels. The bike – a metonym of the war-machine ethos of the nomadic, macho Angels – exerts its own addictive pressure on Thompson, as, although he has nearly lost his driving licence, he goes out and speeds: 'Tail-lights far up ahead coming closer, faster, and suddenly – zaaapppp – going past' (p. 322).

Here Thompson's prose anticipates his later Gonzo work, and reflects Wolfe's livewire syntax in *The Electric Kool-Aid Acid Test*. In 1990, Thompson remarked that the description of illegal speed-riding that concludes *Hell's Angels* was written in true Gonzo fashion, in a single draft put down immediately after such a drive, with the tears caused by the high wind still on his face: even a quarter of a century after the writing, it remained one of his favourite pieces (*SD*, p. 109). Thompson had learned to defy authority on his bike, and to seek out danger through acid and fast riding, both forms of edgework (see Chapter 4), but his text implied that neither defiance nor danger was enough. Motorbikes and acid 'are both a means to an end, to the place of definitions' but 'the only people who really know where it [the edge] is are the ones who have gone over' (*HA*, p. 323). In other words, the place of definitions is a place you never return from: to be defined is to be dead.

Thompson, or at least, his *Hell's Angels* persona, thus seems motivated by a death-wish, paradoxically in the name of the quest for self-definition and self-realization: it is as if the only way to know the authentic self is to destroy it. One possible source of this drive to eliminate the self is Thompson's felt sense of alienation. By 1967, he had become distanced not only from the American mainstream, but also from the counterculture that he saw was dissolving. Deleuze and Guattari consider what happens when a war machine breaks up. Time is given a new rhythm: an endless succession of catatonic episodes or fainting spells, and flashes or rushes. Catatonia is: 'This affect is too strong for me,' and a flash is: 'The power of this affect sweeps me away,' so that the Self (*Moi*) is now nothing more than a character whose actions and emotions are desubjectified, perhaps even to the point of death. [...] Could it be that it is at the moment the war machine ceases to exist, conquered by the State, that it displays to the utmost its irreducibility, that it scatters into thinking, loving, dying, or creating machines that have at their disposal vital or revolutionary powers capable of challenging the conquering State? (Deleuze and Guattari, 1988, p. 356)

Thus the defeated war machine fragments into myriad smaller units, among them alienated but paradoxically empowered individuals whose experience is geared to the rhythm of the "flash" and the "rush".

There is a close parallel with Thompson in 1967, permanently separated from the Angels and the Haight but nevertheless embracing the dangerous motorcycle riding and hallucinogenic drug use he had inherited from both tribes. Although it would be completely wrong to claim that the counterculture, with its strongly pacifistic hippie and anti-Vietnam War elements, was *literally* a war machine, it was sometimes able to offer a non-hierarchical, geographically and intellectually mobile alternative to the American State, and to offer a version, however temporary and however naively embraced, of the frontier possibilities of freedom and self-definition. The result of the counterculture's eventual failure and dissolution was precisely to produce people like Thompson: or rather, to recall Deleuze and Guattari's term, characters, like the persona he created for himself at the conclusion of *Hell's Angels*, and which he developed into the disillusioned Raoul Duke in *Fear and Loathing in Las Vegas*; isolated, alienated individuals who have gained a sense of autonomous separation from the State and who are, or were, possessed of 'vital or revolutionary powers' but nevertheless feel desubjectified 'even to the point of death'.

3 Gonzo Fists, Guinea Worms and Freaks: The Political Circus

The catalyst for Thompson's political activism was a traumatic moment of radicalization. From 26 to 29 August 1968, he witnessed the police beating protesters and bystanders savagely on the streets outside the Democratic Party Convention in Chicago. Thompson declared he 'went to the Democratic Convention as a journalist, and returned a raving beast' (*GSH*, p. 179). Although crowds of anti-Vietnam War demonstrators had gathered in front of the lines of National Guardsmen surrounding the Convention hall and hotels, the pampered delegates within remained largely oblivious to the fact that 'the American Dream was clubbing itself to death just a few feet away' (*FLA*, p. 117). Thompson himself had been hit with a nightstick when he tried to show a cop his press pass. His experience of the state's willingness to use force on dissidents was so ugly and unforgettable that Chicago came to represent 'a huge turning point in history, so central to his mythology about what bothered him about America and what was wrong with America' (Terry Sabonis-Chafee, cited in Wenner and Seymour, 2007, p. 295).

The beatings became media events. Thompson joined the protesters 'ten feet in front of a row of gleaming bayonets and with plain-clothes cops all around me and cameras popping every few seconds at almost everybody' (*FLA*, p. 114). The protesters were chanting, 'The Whole World Is Watching' (p. 115). The cops responded by trying to suppress coverage; a number of journalists were clubbed and TV cameras broken. This barbaric form of censorship proved a failure; a 17-minute film, which was run unedited on news networks, showed police officers clubbing demonstrators, journalists and bystanders alike and smashing cameras, unaware that *other* cameras were filming them (Kurlansky, 2005, pp. 282–83). The demonstrators, though overcome and dispersed, had won a media victory, as they had 'got themselves onto evening television, revealing to all America, or so they believed, the naked evil of a police state' (Marwick, 1999, p. 669).[1]

Chicago had shown Thompson that the political arena was now a semiotic one, where votes, and therefore social change, were determined by what people observed: by images. This was not only a positive development in that a well-chosen sign could focus dissent, but also a negative one in that the establishment had far more media leverage than any disparate bunch of radicals could hope to wield. Thompson's awareness of the power of the sign was crystallized in a letter he wrote to the left-wing activist Allard K. Lowenstein only weeks after the violence in Chicago, in which he asserted the overwhelming need among dissidents for 'The Word, a unity-concept of some kind, a set of simple directions telling how to make yourself heard in November' (*FLA*, p. 126). Thompson hoped vainly for real political change: 'November' refers to the 1968 presidential election, won by Richard Nixon. The Word was never uttered. There was no unified national protest movement of the sort envisaged by Thompson. Instead, he did the next best thing by creating a local version under the half-serious banner of Freak Power. This tag line contained 'obvious irony' (*FLA*, p. 331) as it embodied the internal contradiction of 'a group of deviates and monsters [...] acting together to accomplish something' (p. 330).

Freak Power, Ideology and the Image: Politics as Simulation Hold-Up

When Thompson formally entered politics in 1970 by standing as the Freak Power candidate for sheriff of Aspen, he followed the principles outlined in his letter to Lowenstein by using an image-saturated campaign that worked on two levels simultaneously: locally, to put out the manifesto he wanted to advocate; and universally, to expose the imagistic basis of *all* political campaigns. Thompson's logo of a black, two-thumbed Gonzo fist clutching a peyote button was his typically twisted appropriation of the clenched fist symbol of the Black Power movement. The Black Power slogan represented 'an assertion of sovereignty over the

---

1 The mayhem was witnessed by Jean Genet, Allen Ginsberg, Terry Southern, Norman Mailer and William Burroughs, all of whom were present (Ginsberg as a protester, the others as reporters). Burroughs saw the hippie-dominated protesters as descendants of the Beat generation: 'These young people challenging the political establishment and battling the Chicago police were in a sense the spiritual offspring of *On the Road*, *Howl* and *Naked Lunch*' (Morgan, 1991, p. 446).

civil rights movement and, as such, a profound statement that blacks no longer needed, or wanted, white help' (DeGroot, 2008, p. 182).[2]

Thompson's Freak Power campaign and Gonzo fist image were similarly intended to revitalize a marginalized and oppressed minority group. However, unlike the original Black Power movement and symbol, they were designed to provoke laughter – whether of joy, amusement or contempt – as much as to subvert and were framed with a high degree of irony. Thompson was, in part, exploiting the fashionable gloss of non-conformity offered by Black Power's connotations: 'the source of Hip is the Negro, for he has been living on the margin between totalitarianism and democracy for two centuries' (Mailer, 1998, p. 213). Freak Power was conspicuously designed as a media event. The Gonzo fist was supported by a number of striking posters and radio and TV spots that carried Thompson's message to the disillusioned local ex-hippie constituency whom he called "freaks". These were radical dissenters who had dropped out of politics after the late 1960s, when 'the old Berkeley-born notion of beating the system by fighting it gave way to a sort of numb conviction that it made more sense in the long run to flee' (*GSH*, p. 166).

In seeking to engage this constituency through mediated irony, Thompson was in fact far closer to the Yippies or the Situationists than to the Black Power movement. The Yippies, or Youth International Party, a hippie protest group led by Abbie Hoffman and Jerry Rubin in the late 1960s, had been responsible for such spectacular acts as running a pig for president and exposing greed at the New York Stock Exchange by throwing dollar bills onto the floor. They believed, essentially, in creating political publicity stunts and thus tricking the establishment media into distributing their heady cocktail of sex, drugs and sedition: 'In Hoffman's view, it was entirely possible to smoke, dance, and fuck for the revolution' (DeGroot, 2008, p. 263). Their contemporaries, the Situationist International, founded in France by Guy Debord in 1957, were influenced by Dada and surrealism, but unlike these modernist art movements, the Situationists sought to criticize and ultimately to overthrow the bourgeois society of the spectacle, meaning 'a social relation between people that is mediated by images' (Debord, 2009, p. 24). Situationism was a

---

[2] The Black Power slogan was originated on a protest march in 1966 by the activist Stokely Carmichael; the pacifist black leader Martin Luther King hated it (DeGroot, 2008, 207, pp. 267–68). Although the struggle for racial equality continues into the present, the Black Power movement was short-lived. The clenched-fist salute had its moment of widest world exposure at the 1968 Mexico Olympic Games, when Tommie Smith and John Carlos, two medal-winning American runners, raised the fist on the podium as a gesture of protest (Kurlansky, 2005, p. 348).

defiant, revolutionary response to the late capitalist world view that had substituted illusion for real life and had co-opted the proletariat into consumerism to the extent that 'alienated consumption has become just as much a duty for the masses as alienated production' (Debord, 2009, p. 38). Revolution against the spectacle could be achieved by the construction of situations, which meant reconstructing everyday life through the prism of the imagination. Situationism is perhaps best encapsulated 'by the French phrase *en situation*, which has something of the force of "in a real-life situation"' (Marwick, 1999, p. 32).

Like Debord, Thompson aimed to live his politics, indeed his whole life, *en situation*; and yet like the Yippies, he wanted to promote his anti-establishment authenticity by the paradoxical means of the mass media. Freak Power was designed to subvert the American political scene by exposing how unreal it had become, to drive home the point that the American people had become so accustomed to images they had forgotten the mediated, artificial basis of their social and political lives: 'The gonzo mode's main enemy is the media overload and its numbing effect' (Green, 1975, p. 210). Thompson's signature method of inciting an event *in order to comment on it* from the centre of the action, exemplified by the Freak Power campaign, might thus be read as an ambiguously dialectical expression of living *en situation* and yet at the same time existing through the images that mediate that situation for mass consumption; "images" in this sense includes film and visual art but means especially the reporter's words.[3]

In this respect, Thompson might be called postmodernist. Jean Baudrillard has written of how the contemporary social order is based on simulation; the images promoted by the political machine and propagated by the media do not bear any resemblance to an underlying reality but feed off other images. In this world of hyperreality, the image does not copy the real or even conceal it, but 'has no relation to any reality whatsoever: it is its own pure simulacrum' (Baudrillard, 1994, p. 6). According to Baudrillard, the very foundations of postmodern politics and the state, including the law, are hyperreal. Therefore, he claims, to *simulate* a crime such as a hold-up is more subversive than to carry out the crime itself, as the simulatory basis of the transgressive act will expose the identical basis of the police and judicial machine brought to bear

---

3 For details of how this dialectic of participation and mediation affected Thompson's work, see my discussions of 'Fear and Loathing at the Super Bowl' and 'The Great Shark Hunt' (Chapter 1), *Hell's Angels* (Chapter 2) and *The Curse of Lono* (Chapter 5). Situationism can also be connected to Hakim Bey's theory of the temporary autonomous zone (see Chapters 2 and 4) and to Thompson's practice of edgework (Chapter 4).

against it. The actions, gestures and rituals of the legal machine are components in an imagistic theatre:

> Parody renders submission and transgression equivalent, and that is the most serious crime, because it *cancels out the difference upon which the law is based*. The established order can do nothing against it, because the law is a simulacrum of the second order [masking a basic reality], whereas simulation is of the third order [masking the absence of a basic reality], beyond true and false, beyond equivalences, beyond rational distinctions upon which the whole of the social and power depend. Thus, *lacking the real*, it is there that we must aim at order. (Baudrillard, 1994, p. 21: emphasis in original)

Thompson's Freak Power campaign was the equivalent of Baudrillard's simulation hold-up.[4] The campaign was an exemplary postmodernist action, fought on the terrain of visual, verbal and auditory signs. Like Abbie Hoffman, the Yippie leader who helped organize the 1968 protests at Chicago, Thompson wanted to expose how the establishment disseminated its ideology: 'We want to fuck up their image on TV. It's all in terms of disrupting the image, the image of a democratic society being run very peacefully' (Hoffman, cited in Kurlansky, 2005, p. 284).

Thompson lost, albeit narrowly. The Freak Power campaign carried the city of Aspen but failed in the outlying districts, largely because the Republican and Democratic parties chose to put on a united front against it. This was the end of Thompson's political activity as a candidate; he later considered running for the Senate in Colorado, but backed away from the idea. In hindsight, Thompson's defeat was not surprising, as his campaign was based on a number of deliberately outrageous manifesto pledges, among them: the Sheriff would only take mescaline when not an active duty; all roads would be ripped up and replaced with grass; Aspen would be renamed Fat City to prevent 'greedheads, land-rapers and other human jackals' from capitalizing on the town's name and image (*GSH*, p. 184); dishonest drug dealers would be given the bastinado while held in a newly erected platform and set of stocks; hunting and fishing would be forbidden to non-residents; the police would never

---

4 As a young man, Thompson had orchestrated several simulated crimes. He arranged for the mock kidnapping of a friend from a cinema queue by a team dressed as gangsters; and he simulated sadomasochistic assaults by using a belt to hit the walls of another friend's New York flat while screaming in fake ecstasy to alarm the neighbours (Whitmer, 1993, p. 48, p. 99).

be armed; another new policy would be 'savagely to harass all those engaged in any form of land-rape' (p. 186). This farrago of pharmaceutical, ecological and anti-capitalist horrors was designed precisely to win the support of disillusioned freaks and to frighten the holiday-home owners and real-estate developers who saw the beautiful environment of Aspen mainly as a source of profit.

'Ripped to the Tits Day and Night': Politics as Junk

Participation in politics, even in the unconventional and ironic guise of a Freak Power candidate, meant involvement with a thrilling but also corrupting and addictive process. Thompson was well aware of this, and frequently brought politics and drugs together in his imagery. He said that the violence of Chicago in 1968 had been 'far worse than the worst bad acid trip I'd even heard rumours about. It permanently altered my brain chemistry' (*GSH*, p. 179).

By comparing his experience to an LSD session, Thompson subverted the system on the level of the trope. In conventional thinking, activism and acid had completely opposed connotations. Politics was associated with reason, action, social change, participation in democracy: LSD connoted unreason, inaction, introspection, dropping out of politics and society. 'Taking LSD was a selfish act which allowed escape from reality. Politics, in contrast, is a group activity demanding engagement with reality, however discordant that reality might be. Drugs and politics, in other words, do not mix' (DeGroot, 2008, p. 214). Many of the hippies and fellow travellers disagreed with this, as they saw tripping as a revolutionary act; the Yippies, for instance, whose leader Jerry Rubin argued that drugs signified 'the total end of the Protestant ethic: screw work, we want to know ourselves' (Davenport-Hines, 2002, p. 266). And yet Thompson undermined *both* positions when he yoked hallucinogenics and politics together in order to claim that exposure to the hard, violent face of power had driven him crazy by changing the chemical make-up of his brain; exactly the thing the establishment claimed illicit drugs such as acid would do.[5]

---

5 LSD was categorized by CIA-funded scientists as a "psychomimetic", a drug that, in their belief, created symptoms nearly identical to those of a psychotic episode: with a bizarre lack of logic, this was seen as evidence that LSD would make a useful interrogation tool (Shapiro, 2003, p. 143). When Britain banned LSD in 1966, a Home Office minister argued that the drug could "induce madness" (Davenport-Hines, 2002, p. 267). Official scare stories were not confined to LSD; in 1967, the US Bureau of Narcotics asserted that cannabis, 'while having very little medical use, is capable of profoundly disturbing the brain cells and inducing acts of violence, even murder' (DeGroot, 2008, p. 213).

Thompson's LSD metaphor seemed at first sight a throwaway, and yet it revealed a fundamental strategy of his political writing. By conflating politics with drugs, he made two points: first, to subvert the outsider status imposed on users by showing how similar to them politicians in fact were; and second, to expose the addictive, mood-altering and hallucinogenic qualities of that most dangerous substance, the American political system. 'Experimenting with drugs can provide feelings of power, self-confidence, illusions of limitlessness, feeling alive and in the moment. So, too, with political experimentation' (Whitmer, 1993, p. 189). This was doubly so during a presidential election campaign, where 'obsessive-compulsive political junkies are ripped to the tits day and night for thirteen straight months on their own adrenaline' (*BS*, p. 6).

Thompson admitted 'that Sheriff's campaign in Aspen was a high that I've never gotten from any kind of a drug. It's mainly an *adrenalin high*' (*CT*, p. 469: emphasis in original). Like the journey of a user seeking to score drugs in defiance of the law, the quest behind the Freak Power campaign was for fun, danger and autonomy. Thompson saw anti-establishment activism as another form of edgework, like fast motorcycle riding or taking hallucinogenics (see Chapter 4).

This exposed Freak Power's weakness as well as its strength. It could lampoon the government and its capitalist backers, but it was ultimately self-limiting; a form of resistance predicated upon the dominance of the system. The edge is a place of danger, as in the edge of a cliff, or the moment of swallowing a pill; but is also a margin, as in the edge of the acceptable, or the fringe. Thompson was aware of this, and therefore of how little real political change Freak Power could create. Only in rare places such as Aspen did success seem possible: writing before his narrow defeat there, he had argued that Freak Power had the potential to 'snap the spine of the local/money/politics establishment', but if it did not succeed, 'then it is hard to imagine it working in any other place with fewer natural advantages' such as the large population of heads (drug users, hippies, anti-establishment fellow travellers) present in the town (*GSH*, p. 184).

In fact, the primary goal of Freak Power lay in the struggle rather than the victory. The participation of the re-energized mass of freaks counted far more than the result: 'our idea was that maybe the means could *be* the end ... The Concept *is* the solution' (*FLA*, 364: emphasis in original). Freak Power not only waved a defiant Gonzo fist in the face of the Man, it also – just like mainstream politics – gave the activist an adrenaline rush not available elsewhere. Its difference from the mainstream was that unlike Thompson, who was consciously engaged in edgework, conventional politicians were in denial, not recognizing the drug-like, compulsive nature of their calling. They displayed exactly the sort of behaviour associated with junkies: 'when they get in a frenzy, they will sacrifice anything and anybody to feed their cruel and stupid habit, and there *is* no cure for it. That is addictive thinking' (*BS*, 7: emphasis in original).[6]

Thompson also used gambling as a metaphor for politics; specifically, gambling on sports. As early as 1849, Thoreau derided the anaemic cynicism of the American democratic process: 'All voting is a sort of gaming, like chequers or backgammon, with a slight moral tinge to it, a playing with right and wrong, with moral questions; and betting naturally accompanies it' (Thoreau, 1992, p. 230). Thompson invoked Thoreau's image to show how not much had changed, but unlike Thoreau he explored gambling not from the outside, as a vice to be denounced, but from the inside, as a kick. As Thompson knew well, gamblers can make or lose fortunes very rapidly when they bet on each individual play of a football game. Such intense hazard creates a thrill remarkably analogous to involvement in a political campaign: 'You'd be surprised how fast the adrenalin comes up, if you stand to lose $1,000 every time the ball goes up in the air. That's why the Aspen Freak Power campaign developed all that fantastic voltage' (*CT*, p. 471).

The drug, sport and betting metaphors in Thompson's political writing blurred conventional conceptual lines in a subversive way, because they revealed that even at the very top, the legally legitimized democratic process had become riven by compulsive desires that were not fundamentally different from the cravings of the junkie or the gambler. The results of this compulsion were hideous. Thompson compared untreated political addiction to a deadly African parasite, the Guinea worm, which buries itself inside the body until finally 'it bursts straight through the skin, a horrible red worm with a head like a tiny cobra, snapping around in the air as it struggles to breathe' (*BS*, p. 7).

The Guinea worm image not only worked to suggest the effect of politics on the participants, including Thompson, but also symbolized how politicians and their cronies were damaging the body politic, gnawing at the Republic from the inside. Thompson knew that the ugliest effects would only reveal themselves when the infestation was at a terminal stage. The 'nightmare of failure that gripped America between 1965 and 1970' (*GSH*, p. 166), prompted by Vietnam and John F. Kennedy's murder, and which led to Nixon's 1972 victory, Watergate and the humiliating exit from Saigon, was merely the thrashing head of the worm, the visible

---

6 Thompson's views here coincided with those of his ideological enemy, Timothy Leary, who told the BBC in 1967: 'You know, politics today is a disease – it's a real addiction' (Roszak, 1971, p. 168).

evidence of the long-festering corruption that had led to the slow death of the American Dream and the closure of the frontier in the sense of space where personal autonomy was possible (see Chapter 4).

Through his images of bestiality and disease, Thompson created a grotesque form of satire, which punctured conventional perceptions by associating politics – something normally reported in economic terms, debated as an intellectual issue or contested through emotive rhetoric – with the body's suppurations, its effluent orifices:

> debasement is the fundamental artistic principle of grotesque realism; all that is sacred and exalted is rethought on the level of the material bodily stratum or else combined and mixed with its images. We spoke of the grotesque swing, which brings together heaven and earth. But the accent is placed not on the upward movement but on the descent. (Bakhtin, 1984, pp. 370–71)

Here Mikhail Bakhtin writes of Rabelais's use of the grotesque. Thompson was thus borrowing from a very old tradition when he located politics in the festering body, and knowingly reduced 'the political world of supposedly complex passions and subtle strategies to his own private allegory of appetite' (Hellmann, 1981, p. 92).

A more immediate influence was William S. Burroughs. Thompson had admired his grotesque 1959 satire *Naked Lunch*, which had strikingly conflated politics, sex and drug addiction. In the 'Hospital' section, for instance, one character is a 'Recharge Connection' who supplies the President of the USA with drugs (Burroughs, 2005, p. 58). They exchange heroin by means of intimate bodily contacts, which appear 'to the casual observer like homosexual practices, but the actual excitement is not primarily sexual, and the climax is the separation when the recharge is completed. The erect penises are brought into contact' (p. 57).

The image of the President of the USA imbibing heroin through his homosexual partner's hard-on was part of Burroughs's wildly fantastical satire, intended to deflate authority through ridicule. Similarly, the medieval and Renaissance festivals discussed by Bakhtin often mocked potentially terrifying figures in effigy in order to parade 'the symbols of fear defeated by laughter. [...] carnivalesque dummies representing in a more or less harmless form the old, receding world' (Bakhtin, 1984, p. 394).

Thompson's satire was less life-affirming than this, because it aimed to show his own and his audience's complicity in the corruption that was debasing them. The TV debates during the 1960 presidential election campaign had encouraged the young Thompson to believe that the old world of the somnolent post-war consensus that had elected Eisenhower could be beaten (see Chapter 4 and below); but after 1968, he knew that political progress would only be possible if Americans came to acknowledge how and why they had chosen to enter the heart of darkness by electing Ike's diabolic heir, Nixon. Thompson knew that the people had been persuaded to accept Republican ideology by skilled image-makers who generated the 'carefully conceived campaign oratory' that propelled Nixon to power (*GSH*, p. 198).

Although Nixon's technicians were deliberately and expertly creating the voters they wanted, this moulding need not always stem from a conscious conspiracy. It is an automatic by-product of the system itself, based on the communication of a message whose aim is to convince; in short, it is based on rhetoric. In his essay 'Ideology and Ideological State Apparatuses' (dated 1970, and thus contemporary with Thompson's early political analyses), Louis Althusser argues that 'ideology hails or interpellates individuals as subjects' (Althusser, 1981, p. 119), meaning when an outside agency addresses an individual and that person responds, the individual is a subject because he or she is being *defined* by that process, regardless of whether the response is negative or positive; to fight, flee, follow or embrace the hailer. In fact, this process of construction and definition has gone on since before the individual is born: 'an individual is always-already a subject' (p. 119). Althusser is aware that his concept of the subject is framed by ambiguity, as it is based on a duality. It means '(1) a free subjectivity, a centre of initiatives, author of and responsible for its actions; (2) a subjected being, who submits to higher authority' (p. 123). Both these senses inform Althusser's notion of the subject in ideology, the individual who is interpellated by messages and whose identity, or subjectivity, is formed through this process.

Thompson's manipulation of the media during the Freak Power campaigns suggested that he understood the importance of interpellation. However, unlike Althusser, he framed the subject as capable of a high degree of agency. Thompson understood politics as 'the art of controlling your environment' (*AGW*, p. 156, p. 242; *KF*, p. 17). Mastery of politics enabled control of one's freedom and rights, and thus one's identity: 'I've used reporting as a weapon to affect political situations that bear down on *my* environment' (*BS*, p. 17: emphasis in original). Thompson was at odds with the American political system, which concentrated power in the hands of an influential few, meaning the leaders of each main party and their financial backers. Despite his support for George McGovern, Jimmy Carter and other Democrats, Thompson knew that the two-party system was a vehicle for controlling the environments of others, and shaping them as subjects according to its own needs rather than anything as quaint as the Founding Fathers' goals of the freedom or self-realization of the individual. He would demonstrate the rotten nature of the system most vividly in his first and most successful political book.

The Ibogaine Effect: *Fear and Loathing on the Campaign Trail '72*

Thompson's best political writing is nonlinear and riven with tensions. Through its often fragmentary, abrasive syntax and episodic structure, it reflects a freedom-seeking individualist's resistance to the power structures that would interpellate him for their own ends. Thompson's 'fable-making is a necessary antidote to the prepackaged language, forms, and concepts with which the corporate media produce illusory images and abstractions' (Hellmann, 1981, p. 99). The most famous example of such aggressively deconstructive fabulation in Thompson's oeuvre is *Fear and Loathing on the Campaign Trail '72*, a series of reports for *Rolling Stone* on the Democratic primaries of that year, and the eventual presidential contest between Richard Nixon and George McGovern, which Thompson later compiled into a book. The reports, in effect, form a campaign diary, as Thompson was filing copy at regular intervals, relating events as they happened and making predictions of the immediate future, rather than writing a retrospective summary.[7]

Throughout *Campaign Trail*, Thompson plays fast and loose with the distinction between fact and fiction; he abandons journalistic objectivity in favour of a blatantly subjective Gonzo concoction of opinion, hearsay, rumour and outright lies. All of these ingredients create a hilarious satire – a powerful antidote to the respectable discourse of the mainstream political press.

Thompson's project was utterly necessary. His colleague at *Rolling Stone*, Timothy Crouse, pointed out that even the conventional journalists covering the McGovern campaign, who were loyal to objectivism and therefore rejected Thompson's approach, had begun to recognize that 'the rules of objectivity were no longer doing the job. The trouble was the staggering inequality between the coverage of the two campaigns' (Crouse, 1974, p. 337). The Nixon PR machine ignored or cut off all meaningful inquiries from the press, whereas the naively accommodating

---

[7] Thompson's monthly reports were published in *Rolling Stone* as soon as possible after writing, except for his concluding article, which first appeared some months after the campaign had finished (*RS*, 5 July 1973, pp. 48–62). This article became the bookends of *Campaign Trail*: the opening 'Author's Note' and the concluding 'November' and 'December' chapters.

McGovern people allowed coverage at a far deeper level: the result was that only McGovern was having his policies seriously questioned in print or on radio or television. Thus a Gonzo account of the campaign became indispensable. Thompson noted that although his language was too direct for many people's tastes, it provided a vital counter to the meek reporting in most of the media: 'Some people will say that words like *scum* and *rotten* are wrong for Objective Journalism [... but] It was the built-in blind spots of the Objective rules and dogma that allowed Nixon to slither into the White House' (*BS*, p. 243: emphasis in original).

Thompson's distaste for objective journalism arose from his individualism. To be objective – or more precisely, to attempt to *write* objectively about politics, despite one's feelings – meant subsuming one's own identity beneath something larger, most often the agenda of one's employer. This was rationalized by journalists as even-handed professionalism or as loyalty to the facts. As one *New York Times* campaign reporter put it, without a trace of irony, 'The *Times* is after all a record of history [...]. I wouldn't want to vilify Richard Nixon if he doesn't deserve vilification – even though *I* may feel he deserves it' (Crouse, 1974, p. 64: emphasis in original).

Thompson could never have suppressed his personal judgement like that. To do so would have denied both his Gonzo method and his philosophy of self-realization. Instead, he let his feelings lead him into wildly implausible digressions. One outrageous example was when he claimed that Senator Edmund Muskie, the initial front runner for the Democratic nomination, was addicted to a mysterious hallucinogenic shrub, ibogaine.

Ibogaine is not a figment of Thompson's imagination: the *iboga* plant is 'the sacred essence of the religion of the Bwiti tribe of Gabon and Cameroon' (Pinchbeck, 2003, p. 30). In the developed world, ibogaine – the active ingredient extracted from *iboga* – has been used in a therapeutic context to treat drug addiction (see Saunders et al., 2000, p. 137), although the treatment is illegal in the USA (Pinchbeck, 2003, p. 31). The ibogaine molecule was patented by Howard Lotsof in 1985, after he had cured his own heroin addiction with it in 1962 (Pinchbeck, 2003, p. 30). One Western user, who took the *iboga* plant during a tribal initiation ceremony, claimed that the experience is like a temporary death: 'Your body cools down, you no longer seem to even breathe and it would look to an outsider as if you were comatose' (Saunders et al., 2000, p. 75).

Thompson makes the deadpan claim that 'not much has been written about The Ibogaine Effect as a serious factor in the Presidential Campaign' (*CT*, p. 144). He reports that he has heard a Brazilian doctor has been flown in to give Muskie the drug, and that therefore there is now a clear explanation for the senator's bizarre behaviour. Thompson presents himself as a concerned and curious journalist in order to smuggle an outrageous falsehood past the reader in the guise of an ugly rumour: 'it had long been whispered that Muskie was into something very heavy, but it was hard to take the talk seriously' (p. 144). Thompson was in fact making the rumour up, but he was so convincing that some readers believed him: 'That wasn't a lie. [... The article] started the rumour, but there was a rumour' (*AGW*, p. 206).

By preceding the ibogaine claim with a lengthy account of the effects of the drug, supposedly taken from 'a study by PharmChem Laboratories, Palo Alto, California' (*CT*, p. 144), Thompson reinforces his self-presentation as an objective, impartial seeker after fact. The study is framed in a pseudo-anthropological style that alleges that African tribesmen use ibogaine when hunting in order to remain motionless for days while retaining mental alertness, and that when they take high doses of the drug, the resultant seizures are carefully monitored by tribal elders for supposed prophetic content. In a development of the Rabelaisian, carnivalesque mode of satire centred on the grotesque, Thompson mocks Muskie, and the political system of which he is a part, by positioning him as the slave of a chemical, and the unwitting centre of a hunting ritual or *juju*; a form of fetishistic magic, in which certain favoured individuals (the candidates) perform at their physical limits and undergo outrageous, mind-warping trials in order to predict the future (the next 4 years in their hoped-for administration) and to hunt their prey (power, success).

Thompson's allegations of fetishism and drug ritual at the heart of the political process of a great democracy formed an extended metaphor. The American presidential race *was* irrational, addictive and mind-altering, but not because the candidates were actually on exotic drugs. If they used any psychoactive substances, they were no doubt as banal as alcohol, caffeine or prescription amphetamines; or in Hubert Humphrey's case, the bizarre cocktail of 'twenty-five One-A-Day Vitamins with a shot of bourbon when he needed some fast energy' (Crouse, 1974, p. 20). During his coverage of the election, Thompson had come to comprehend the more worrying, because more widespread, *systemic* problem; that the political process itself had all the uncontrolled intensity and seemingly overwhelming force of an acid rush.

Political culture's hallucinatory quality was heightened by its emphasis on surface over substance. Like an LSD trip, the 1972 campaign was guided not by fact but by preconception and perception; or in Timothy Leary's terms, by set and setting (see Chapter 2). To shape the voters' *image* of each candidate was the key. Each politician's PR team tried to mould him into the sort of person each block of voters would perceive most favourably: '"Perceive" is the new key word. [...] When you say perceive you imply the difference between what the candidate *is* and the way the public or the voters *see* him' (*CT*, p. 402: emphasis in original). The main exception Thompson saw to the rule of the dominance of the image was the anti-war candidate, George McGovern, for whom he felt a qualified admiration: he had to 'sympathize in some guilt-stricken way with whatever demented obsession' made McGovern think he could lead such a herd of "venal pigs" as the Democratic Party (*CT*, p. 119).[8]

Apart from McGovern, Thompson believed the candidates for the Democratic nomination to be incompetents or hollow schemers. The worst was Hubert Humphrey, whom Thompson demolished as a man utterly without convictions, prepared to say one thing to one constituency and then contradict himself completely when addressing a rival group hours later: 'There is no way to grasp what a shallow, contemptible, and hopelessly dishonest old hack Hubert Humphrey really is until you've followed him around for a while on the campaign trail' (*CT*, p. 199). Thompson was not the only journalist to see this. Timothy Crouse cited his own opinion, endorsed by other reporters, that Humphrey, like Muskie, was 'a whore [...]. He'll sell out to anybody who will give him the Job' (Crouse, 1974, p. 65).

Humphrey was merely an extreme case of an endemic disease. The candidates were subjects of an ideological apparatus that had already moulded them. They were all addicted to the political process. The compulsive rush of politics was why Thompson claimed the spineless Humphrey was addicted to Wallot, a brand of speed (*CT*, p. 144) or Muskie to ibogaine, and why Thompson ludicrously suggested that NBC newsman John Chancellor was taking and distributing LSD 'supplied to him in great quantities, no doubt, by Communist agents' (p. 337). Drug fiends like Doctor Gonzo and Raoul Duke in *Fear and Loathing in Las Vegas* at least *know* what they are taking. But the politicians have, as the ibogaine metaphor suggests, lost their grip. They do not even know that they are addicted. The system distorts their vision just as would any hallucinogenic.

---

8 During the next presidential election, in 1976, Thompson placed a similar faith in Jimmy Carter. Although Thompson would come to believe that Carter was incompetent, once in office (*AGW*, p. 131) he was sufficiently moved by the Georgia governor to approve of him as a candidate. He never went so far as to *endorse* Carter for the presidency; instead, *Rolling Stone* did so on his behalf, to his great annoyance, when the editor Jann Wenner placed the strap-line 'An Endorsement, with Fear & Loathing' on the cover of the issue of 3 June 1976 that contained Thompson's article 'Jimmy Carter and the Great Leap of Faith'.

Thompson's conception of this grotesque addiction is superbly encapsulated by Ralph Steadman's Gonzo illustrations to *Fear and Loathing on the Campaign Trail '72*, which are very much in the style of *Fear and Loathing in Las Vegas*; they expose the unreal vision of the politicians through allusions to popular culture and literature. Nixon, for instance, is depicted as a rampaging Godzilla, thrashing his scaly tail about, lifting his toothy jaws aloft and holding in his claw a half-crushed paper saying 'Peace in Our Time With Honour' an amalgamation of Nixon's 'Peace with Honour' formula for quitting Vietnam and Neville Chamberlain's notoriously naïve declaration of 'Peace in Our Time' following his Munich summit with Hitler (*CT*, p. 52). In an earlier picture, Nixon sits with the Armed Forces top brass at a Mad Hatter's Tea Party, with Nixon as the Hatter, in a reworking of John Tenniel's well-known illustration to Lewis Carroll's *Alice in Wonderland* (p. 40: see Carroll, 1998, p. 61). The point is not only to mock Nixon but also to position him inside a filmic or cartoon-like world of surrealism and illusion that stands as a metaphor for the semiotic game of American politics and the looking-glass world of the nation's policy-making elite.[9]

Watergate: Nixon, Ford and the Politics of Hyperreality

The closure of the 1972 campaign did not end Thompson's, or the politicians', damaging addictions. Thompson was aware that his work on the McGovern candidacy for *Rolling Stone* may have stirred things up on the surface, but had not changed the political system a whit. Nixon's electoral triumph was objectionable, but Watergate was worse. Thompson saw in Nixon not only an evil, corrupt, paranoid egotist, but also a destroyer of the last remnants of the American Dream: a mutant, cancerous cell that was eating the once-healthy body of the Republic from inside. To Thompson, the difference between the two candidates had been clear: 'McGovern made some stupid mistakes, but in context they seem almost frivolous compared to the things Richard Nixon does every day of his life, on purpose, as a matter of policy and a perfect expression of everything he stands for' (*CT*, p. 389). Thus, Thompson pulled no punches with Nixon; he declared himself proud to have been 'the first journalist in Christendom to go on record comparing Nixon to Adolph Hitler' (p. 477). Watergate, though, seemed

---

9 Both these Steadman illustrations accompany the 'January' chapter of the book *Fear and Loathing on the Campaign Trail '72*, but did not appear with the original *Rolling Stone* article. The original illustration by David Richardson was in a similar vein: it showed Nixon as a grotesquely distorted Statue of Liberty, smoke and flames appearing from the hair above his crown, presumably a reference to Nixon- and Kissinger-sponsored bombings in South-East Asia (*RS*, 3 February 1972, p. 6).

the final insult: the system had reached such a nadir that it would allow Nixon to walk away scot-free from heinous crimes with such blatant openness that the contempt of the ex-president and his cronies for the people in whose name they supposedly worked was quite evident.

Jean Baudrillard has described Watergate as an incident that was framed as exceptional but was, in fact, typical. Watergate was merely a tiny visible node of the vast, subterranean, thoroughly amoral socio-economic structure of capitalism. But by making Watergate appear as a shocking departure from the norm, the journalists who exposed it cut it off from this structure and thus unwittingly helped to perpetuate the greater problem even as they revealed the smaller transgression:

Watergate is not a scandal, this is what must be said at all costs, because it is what everyone is busy concealing, this dissimulation masking a strengthening of morality, of a moral panic as one approaches the primitive (*mise en*) *scène* of capital: its instantaneous cruelty, its incomprehensible ferocity, its fundamental immorality – that is what is scandalous, unacceptable to the system of moral and economic equivalence that is the axiom of leftist thought, from the theories of the Enlightenment up to Communism. (Baudrillard, 1994, p. 15: emphasis in original)

Therefore, the restoration of moral order, which was seemingly permitted by the uncovering of the Watergate burglary and cover-up, and the subsequent legal process, did not function simply to expiate a crime; it also unwittingly concealed the workings of capitalism, which were *and had always been* outside morality.

The political left has tried to impose ethics upon the pursuit of profit ever since Karl Marx's denunciation of the bourgeoisie's 'naked, shameless, direct, brutal exploitation' of the proletariat (Marx and Engels, 1992, p. 5). Thompson can, in this limited sense, be associated with the left; his loyalty to the Constitution and what he saw as the founding values of the nation (see Chapter 1), and his early interest in Jean-Paul Sartre's brand of Marxism (see Chapter 5), place him among those who would wish capitalism to be informed by morality. Nevertheless, he was aware of his impotence in this respect. In characteristically humanistic fashion, reminiscent also of the carnivalesque bodily orientation of his satirical imagery, Thompson located his innocence as a biological phenomenon, an internal organ, 'my innocence gland' (*AGW*, p. 178), which had repeatedly been battered by the toxic onslaught of politics.

The relationship between Thompson's disillusionment during Watergate and his drug use was evident in 'Fear and Loathing in Limbo: The Scum

Also Rises' (*RS*, 10 October 1974, pp. 28–36, pp. 49–52), anthologized in *The Great Shark Hunt*. The article begins with an epigraph from *Heart of Darkness*, where Conrad's narrator Marlow admits: 'my speech or my silence, indeed any action of mine, would be a mere futility. [...] The essentials of this affair lay deep under the surface, beyond my reach, and beyond my power of meddling' (Conrad, 1990, p. 190: cited in *GSH*, p. 318). Thompson shares Marlow's sense of powerlessness in the face of evil.[10]

Like Marlow, however, Thompson is not simply an observer of his sinister, deranged subject (Nixon/Kurtz) but appears uncannily dependent on him for energy and focus: 'My interest in national politics withered drastically within hours after Nixon resigned' (*GSH*, p. 324). Time and again Thompson claims that the actions of Ford and Nixon have reduced him to rage, scuppering his deadlines, interfering with his writing to the point where he collapses in 'hysterical exhaustion and screeching helplessly for speed' (p. 323); but even at these points of collapse, Thompson is aware that it is the politicians' heinous skulduggery that has determined the content and structure of what he is putting on the page. Thompson's dependency on the president and his sidekick even extends to his consciousness of self, by informing his awareness that he now exists on a hazy, drug-ridden borderline between life and death. When told by a friend that Ford has pardoned Nixon, he claims he goes through a near-death experience, just like 'that long, long moment of indescribably intense sadness that comes just before drowning at sea, those last few seconds on the cusp when the body is still struggling but the mind has given up' (p. 323).

Thompson's sense of self-annihilation and existential despair is paralleled by the structure of 'Fear and Loathing in Limbo: The Scum Also Rises', which, in Gonzo fashion, splits into dissociated fragments after the opening statement of disgust with Ford and Nixon. Several sections follow in which Thompson claims to be reproducing his notebooks from the time immediately before Nixon's resignation on 9 August 1974. The suggestions of difficulties in water continue. On the morning of the resignation, Thompson has fallen asleep in his wet swimming trunks (p. 327); he adds, 'My eyes were swollen shut with chlorine poisoning' (p. 328). Thompson has, in fact, been swimming in the hotel pool but he never mentions this, let alone describes it, until much later (p. 336), so his symptoms become detached from any clear cause, and his battered,

---

10 Thompson also shares Conrad's satirical irony and wit. When he said he considered Conrad 'one of history's greatest humorists', Thompson had his tongue only partly in his cheek (*AGW*, p. 89). 'He had long thought the novel [*Heart of Darkness*] hysterical' (Brinkley, 2005, p. 42).

poisoned body becomes a metaphor for his exhausted state of being. He then begins to narrate Nixon's resignation from his own point of view, leading with the suggestion that when served a subpoena for the Oval Office tapes, the president 'began losing his grip on reality' (p. 330). Again the co-dependency of Nixon and Thompson is suggested. It is when events intensify around the president's resignation and pardon that Thompson likewise, in his Gonzo persona, begins to feel his hold on reality weaken.

The article thus reaches beyond its immediate topic: it offers a sketch of the fragmentation and destruction of the free individual by means of ideology. Thompson believed in an authentic self that could be realized through the American Dream, even though what the Dream meant was never entirely clear (see Chapter 4); but just as on a personal level Thompson's co-dependent relationship with Nixon threatened to erode his autonomy, so on a cultural level the political system with its bombardment of interpellation threatened to remodel the American individual as a subject in the sense of a tool of its own social logic.

And yet, at the same time, the article's fragmentation suggests a strategy of resistance to this process. Through its Gonzo style and structure, with its ellipses, rambling sub-headings and semi-fictional digressions about Thompson's early experience of robbing gas stations, the article sketches out for the reader a means of opposing the system. Disrupt truth, refuse linear narrative, eschew objectivity and intercut memory with conjecture and lies and you have at least a working basis for rejecting the master narrative handed to you by the state. Thompson's Gonzo writing has much the same political impact as William S. Burroughs's cut-ups. These were collages of fragments Burroughs had cut and pasted from newspapers, magazines and other sources, which aimed at once to be 'a parody of newswriting, with its claim to objectivity and "just the facts, ma'am"' (Morgan, 1991, p. 425) and 'a way to avoid manipulating the reader' in order to recreate instead 'the nervous, distraught, uncertain quality of contemporary life' (Morgan, 1991, p. 451).

After expressing his outrage at Nixon's flagrant disregard for the Constitution, Thompson cuts to an imaginary conversation between the discredited president and Ron Ziegler, his press secretary. Ziegler, inspired by the Boss's shining example even at this dark hour, is compared to another group of fools despised by Thompson: he represents 'the political flip side of every burned-out acid freak who voted for Goldwater and then switched to Tim Leary until [...] Jesus or Maharaj Ji lured him off' (*GSH*, p. 333). Thompson here refers to his own attack on Leary and the acid culture in *Fear and Loathing in Las Vegas*, which had first appeared in *Rolling Stone* only 3 years before (see Chapter 2). In his slavish devotion to Nixon, Ziegler is the obverse of the drop-out devotees of acid shamans or religious gurus; the opposite face of the same fundamental structure. This structure is one of dominance and submission, of dissolution of the self 'in the wake of another perfect master' (p. 333). In Thompson's view, this was exactly the opposite of the sort of individualistic self-fashioning that LSD could have made possible, had the drug culture not been taken over by the slavish desire to worship authority and borrowed from the very political, religious and military institutions it professed to despise.

Thompson's account of Ziegler's fawning is not meant to be believed. The press secretary's camp emotions are a satirical joke: but the joke goes beyond making the target look ridiculous, which is the primary goal of satire. It exposes the complicity of the counterculture in the hierarchical power relations of mystification favoured by Nixon, and develops Thompson's long-running metaphor of politics as a drug. Nixon's resignation left a desperate sense of withdrawal for all 'the Watergate junkies who never even knew they were hooked until the cold turkey swooped into their closets' (p. 340).

Yet again, Thompson constructs politicians as slaves to a hideous compulsion, citing the 'mutant energy' of the 'unexplainable addictions' of the political and entrepreneurial classes (p. 341). This bears comparison with Burroughs's *Naked Lunch*, where addiction is framed in terms of the unspeakable, as well as of economics and the law: 'Followers of obsolete unthinkable trades, doodling in Etruscan, addicts of drugs not yet synthesized [...] servers of fragmentary warrants taken down in hebephrenic shorthand charging unspeakable mutilations of the spirit' (Burroughs, 2005, p. 45).

Thompson juxtaposes this section with an account of Nixon's oddly compulsive need to tape every syllable he uttered in the White House, ascribing it to Nixon's typically vain desire to record his actions for posterity and thus earn his place in history (*GSH*, pp. 358–59). This connects Nixon's addictive behaviour to his capitulation before the dominance of the image; what mattered to him, as much as his own place in posterity, was turning everything into a copy, to have it all reproduced: 'the State is concerned primarily with Simulation rather than substance' (Bey, 2003, p. 99).

Like his arch-enemy, Thompson understood the power of recording and reproduction, especially of the visual image. He placed great importance on Steadman's illustrations to his Gonzo work; his Freak Power campaign depended to a great extent on posters; and he knew to what extent politicians could be exposed by photography and television. While indicting Nixon's Gang of Four – the President, Spiro Agnew, Henry

Kissinger and J. Edgar Hoover – he commented, 'A group photo of these perverts would say all we need to know about the Age of Nixon' (*BS*, p. 245). Thompson believed that Nixon had been fatally exposed by television in his pre-election debates with John F. Kennedy: 'When Nixon finally had to face the TV cameras for real in the 1960 presidential campaign debates, he got whipped like a redheaded mule' (*BS*, p. 243); 'the mushrooming TV audience saw him as a truthless used-car salesman' (pp. 243–44).[11]

Thompson had been hugely influenced by the television images of the Nixon-Kennedy debates; he cited them as the root cause of his decision to manage the mayoral campaign of Joe Edwards, the first Freak Power candidate: 'That was when I first understood that the world of Ike and Nixon was vulnerable' (*FLA*, p. 260). And yet, he expressed disappointment over the pathetically complicit press and TV coverage: the television companies had staged 'a political batting-practice instead of a World Series' (*PH*, p. 235). Thus, although the image had considerable power, it was liable to be weakened if not properly exploited by those journalists and executives responsible for it. It was not surprising, then, that Thompson turned to television – both as a topic and a viewing medium – in the last of his books devoted exclusively to political journalism, *Better Than Sex: Confessions of a Political Junkie*, first published in 1994.

Clinton and the Mediated Image: *Better than Sex*

Thompson followed Bill Clinton's 1992 presidential campaign from Woody Creek, using the TV set. Although this was largely for pragmatic reasons, such as the obstructive fame that had kept him from covering the 1976 Ford-Carter race on the ground, *Better than Sex* allowed Thompson to focus on television itself more than he ever had before. He notes how the 1990–1991 Gulf War was timed by President George Bush (senior) with a view to maximizing his popularity through blanket coverage of air strikes before the election and thus 'whipping the voters into a patriotic frenzy. […] it was true, but he was forced to deny it repeatedly on national TV' (*BS*, p. 110); 'The first strike was originally set for noon on Monday (dot-zero Washington) to make the network evening news deadlines' (p. 111).

Thompson urges a robust response to this deadly propaganda tool: 'There is a huge difference between merely "watching" TV and learning

---

11 Thompson held much the same view of the effect of television on George W. Bush: 'Did you see Bush on TV, trying to debate? Jesus, he talked like a donkey with no brains at all' (*FH*, p. 58).

to respond aggressively to it. The difference, for most people, is the difference between the living and dying of their own brains' (p. 52). Thompson's rhetoric is reminiscent of the 'campaign junkie' passages of *Campaign Trail*, yet here the drug is not politics but television itself. Like acid, mescaline or any other hallucinogenic that can intensify sensation to nearly unbearable levels, television can be utilized, rather than running away in fear, but must be handled carefully and with knowledge. It is the responsibility of the user to manage the medium with appropriate control. In Thompson's world, the nightmare of television lies in the dignity it can lend the base, and the cloak of sincerity with which it can cover lies. Thompson draws attention to how high-quality TV equipment can give the sensation that Clinton's huge, idol-like head is speaking as if inside you (p. 52): television can lend a speciously disembodied, even divine quality to the image of such a shallow politician, allowing his interpellations to be internalized all too easily.

Thompson implies that whereas television and the American political class have both grown more powerful and sophisticated, their audience has not: unlike Nixon, Clinton has learned to hide his lies on television so cleverly that the American public swallows them. Thus, Clinton must be met face to face and be exposed for what he is. *Better Than Sex* records a meeting between Clinton and several *Rolling Stone* journalists, including Thompson, on 31 July 1992. Thompson presents Clinton with a saxophone reed, because, in a masterstroke of populist opportunism, the candidate had played the saxophone on *The Arsenio Hall Show* during the campaign. In a superbly Rabelaisian oral motif, Thompson has Clinton stare at the reed, throw his head back and howl: 'Then he grasped the wicker basket of French fries with both hands and buried his face in it, making soft snorting sounds as he rooted in the basket, trying vainly to finish it off' (*BS*, p. 104).

Thompson's faked account is a reworking of the *Campaign Trail* fantasy about Muskie and ibogaine. Clinton's porcine lust for the food represents metaphorically the power of his egocentric urge to gratify his instincts without inhibition. Needless to say, the French fries incident did not actually happen. Thompson's interview with Clinton 'was relaxed, yet formal. [...] There were no shenanigans' (Whitmer, 1993, p. 296). Moreover, Clinton gave a robustly anti-drug answer to a question from Thompson about the Fourth Amendment: 'We were all unprepared for the intensity of his response, and Hunter was especially taken aback. [...] Hunter essentially withdrew [from the interview]' (Jann Wenner, cited in Wenner and Seymour, 2007, p. 308).

Thompson believed that Clinton was a superficial but crafty politician who knew how to project an appealing image. To expose his duplicity,

Better Than Sex foregrounds the importance of presentation over content. In accordance with this, it is a highly visual text, but not in the manner of Thompson's earlier work, which had benefited so much from Ralph Steadman's Gonzo illustrations. Thompson had difficulty compiling the book, and enlisted the aid of the historian Douglas Brinkley, who would later edit Thompson's letters. Brinkley realized that '*Better Than Sex*, at that point, was like a deck of cards in disarray' (Wenner and Seymour, 2007, p. 310). Even the published version looks somewhat disorganized. William McKeen saw the book's lack of a clear structure as a weakness: 'much of it was made up of faxes and photocopies. Though amusing, it was also the least substantial work he produced, reading like an unedited diary' (McKeen, 2008, p. 321).

This underestimates *Better Than Sex*. The text gains from its fragmentary structure, regardless of whether it stemmed from Thompson's brilliant awareness of the zeitgeist or merely from his laziness or incapacity. Born of Thompson's characteristic *bricolage*, *Better Than Sex* forms a pastiche that signifies its own complicity in the cut-and-paste process of the mediated fabrication of contemporary reality. The book is cut up into different fonts; frequently, there are facsimiles of letters typed, or faxes scrawled, on Thompson's personalized *Rolling Stone* paper. The text is intercut with blatantly faked photographs, such as the one of Thompson at Woody Creek in the snow, standing shoulder to shoulder with a cardboard cut-out of a grinning Clinton in a dark suit: the cut-out that poses beside Thompson is merely the largest of a line of identical figures that diminish as they disappear into the distance (p. 70). There are also fictitious newspaper reports, in the manner of the intercalated snippets in *Fear and Loathing in Las Vegas*, such as an account of the death of the independent candidate Ross Perot, under the by-line Raoul Duke, in which Perot is 'killed by a crazy, bushy-haired hit man from the Crips gang' (p. 84). The implication throughout is that politicians are as specious and ephemeral as their images: in the real political world, as well as in Thompson's book, two-dimensional cardboard Clintons are manufactured like dolls on a production line and hapless Perots are metaphorically killed and/or resurrected by the press at every turn.

In this context, nothing that Thompson writes can be taken at face value: we are in the Gonzo realm of having to decide what, if anything, on the page is true. Clinton and his crew 'are politicians, nothing more. The truth is not in them' (p. 127). Likewise, one of Thompson's correspondents tells him that the Republican Convention did not happen, but 'was a videotape produced by the GOP and given to all networks for playback', allegedly to save money (p. 119).

Better Than Sex is thus the conspiracy theorist's ideal political primer, as it presents all truth as being manufactured by the media. The text includes an ironic sop to history, when at seemingly random intervals a highlighted strip across the page introduces a timeline with the dates of key events in bold type. This purportedly stabilizing device in fact fails to maintain any semblance of order amid the riot of facsimiles, handwritten scrawls, photos, drawings and letterheads. Some of the more bizarre timelined events, such as 'New planetary object detected beyond Pluto' (p. 130), seem irrelevant unless they are taken as symbols of the deepening strangeness of the campaign: Thompson hints that we are entering uncharted space here, discovering new political bodies orbiting the fringes of our knowledge, like the bizarre Ross Perot.

Hakim Bey has written of the success of some temporary autonomous zones that managed to last 'whole lifetimes because they went unnoticed, like hillbilly enclaves – because they never intersected with the Spectacle, never appeared outside that real life which is invisible to the agents of Simulation' (Bey, 2003, p. 99). Thompson never allowed himself such convenient invisibility. Although he intended Owl Farm to be an autonomous enclave, he deliberately *courted* the spectacles and simulacra produced by the capitalist state by remaining permanently immersed in commercial media, especially television. Thus, he was able to respond to state interpellation in the best way he knew: through his informed satirical books such as *Better than Sex*, and through his columns anthologized in collections such as *Hey Rube*.

'We are At War now': 9/11 and *Hey Rube*

When Thompson's Freak Power campaign is compared with his later columns on 9/11, a remarkable consistency emerges. In each case, Thompson displays his understanding of the simulatory basis of the political system and his penchant for irony and shock tactics. His immediate reaction to the atrocities of 11 September 2001 was very prescient. He saw the attack as the start of a war against an unspecified enemy: 'It will be Religious War, a sort of Christian Jihad, fuelled by religious hatred and led by merciless fanatics on both sides. [...] Osama Bin Laden will be a primitive "figurehead"' (*HR*, p. 90). Thompson then personifies himself ironically as a combination of Davy Crockett and a trigger-happy helicopter gunner out of *Apocalypse Now*, as he sits in his mountain fortress: 'I shoot into the darkness at anything that moves. Sooner or later I will hit something Evil, and feel no Guilt. It might be Osama Bin Laden. Who knows?' (p. 93)

Thompson turns himself into a symbol of America: blindly blasting ammo into the void, knowing the foreign Other is out there, but having no effective means of distinguishing terrorists from innocent bystanders. In Gothic mode, Thompson personifies Bin Laden as Nosferatu, a catalyst for mass hysteria: 'Osama Bin Laden is like a vampire that casts no shadow, yet his shadow is over us all. People call me on the phone and jabber like fruit bats in heat' (p. 96). The bat image suggests that hysterical Americans have taken on something of the quality of the undead terrorist predator they all fear.

Thompson takes this one stage further by bringing the Other home: in the world of the War on Terror, anyone can conspire to destroy America – even Americans. The job of the right-thinking citizen, Thompson argues, is now to watch his neighbour for signs of deviancy: 'With luck, you might catch him in the act of fondling a foreign flag or prancing around his parlour wearing nothing but a turban and a black jockstrap' (p. 105). Foreignness here becomes a ludicrous pose – a farrago of comic signs that no real terrorist, bent on escaping surveillance, would ever display.

Fortunately, the good Dr Thompson is on hand to offer a word of caution to the over-zealous patriot on the lookout for subversives. He advises that even a foreign flag, turban or jockstrap should not justify terminating a suspicious neighbour immediately: 'There is a big difference between croaking a harmless pervert and callously murdering a close relative of the Saudi Ambassador' (p. 106).[12] The passage mocks the perceived ignorance of the USA, which since 9/11 seemed to Thompson to be thrashing about, unable to distinguish between its allies and its enemies. In this hysterical, xenophobic environment, all foreigners are strange and prone to do things that in an upright American citizen would be labelled as perversions.

Thompson suggests that to the vast majority of Americans not directly involved, 9/11, like Watergate, was played out as spectacle. It formed a semiotic, ideological episode of image-formation and interpellation. The coverage of the event had a role in disciplining the population. Americans were warned that the state had a new, hidden enemy, Al Qaida; but they were simultaneously reassured that the government would remorselessly hunt the terrorists and dispense justice. This message was a reaction to the massive insecurity felt by Americans in the wake of the attack. However, the system in which they lived *promoted* insecurity, through the forced instabilities created by globalization, and the imagistic basis of contemporary society:

---

12 Thompson in fact had Prince Bandar, former Saudi ambassador to the USA, as a neighbour for some of his time in Aspen (*AGW*, pp. 164–65; see also *BS*, p. 132).

The system [...] causes a general principle of uncertainty to prevail, which terrorism simply translates into total insecurity. Terrorism is unreal and unrealistic? But our virtual reality, our systems of information and communication, have themselves too, and for a long time, been beyond the reality principle. As for terror, we know it is already present everywhere, in institutional violence, both mental and physical, in homeopathic doses. Terrorism merely crystallizes all the ingredients in suspension. It puts the finishing touches to the orgy of power, liberation, flows and calculation which the Twin Towers embodied, while being the violent deconstruction of that extreme form of efficiency and hegemony. (Baudrillard, 2003, pp. 58–9)

Baudrillard here refers to his theory of the four stages of the image, which begin in mimesis and culminate in hyperreality; the system has moved 'beyond the reality principle' and is, like the terrorism that attacks it, based on a self-referential and self-perpetuating complex of images. Like terrorism, the New World Order is mediated, and breathes the oxygen of publicity.

Thus the mysterious enemy that Thompson accurately predicted America would be fighting for the foreseeable future was nebulous and elusive precisely because it was a semiotic constellation, subject to change at any moment and fundamentally unstable. Hence Thompson's satirical account of the neighbour with the turban and jockstrap, fondling a foreign flag and being shot by an over-zealous right-thinking American mindful of the Patriot Act. What motivates the vigilante is not knowledge but connotation: in the hyperreal culture of constant high alert, certain *signs* qualify one as a terrorist, regardless of one's actual beliefs or actions.

Conclusion: Authenticity and the Semiotics of Violence

Thompson's work implies that when the ground of the human subject is the sign, but one seeks to resist this state of affairs through authentic action, then a self-consciously dissident subject is more likely than ever before, at least in modern American culture, where the real, territorial frontier no longer exists, to end up practising edgework, exploring borderlands of chemicals, sub-cultural living, dissident politics, guns and motorized speed (see Chapters 2 and 4). Thompson's dangerous and excessive behaviour therefore was not only idiosyncratic, with its roots in personal psychological issues, but also, and much more importantly, *culturally* significant: 'the proper use of freedom is to abuse it, and make excessive use of it. And this includes taking responsibility for one's own death and that of others' (Baudrillard, 2003, p. 67).

Despite his propensity for danger, Thompson never used violence as a political tool. Although he was interested in weapons and civil disobedience, it would be inappropriate to equate Thompson with terrorists. Apart from anything else, one thing that points him away from such armed resisters of globalization and towards mainstream American thought is his humanism, meaning the value he placed on human life, or 'existence and freedom' (Baudrillard, 2003, p. 68). Instead of fighting the system with bullets, Thompson used the political arena as a space to campaign for individual liberty: not through a revolutionary impulse to overturn the existing order, but through a radical impulse to return that order to its authentic, forgotten roots in the Constitution and Declaration of Independence.

Baudrillard has argued that what is at stake in the War on Terror is 'the eschatological passion for the Real' (Baudrillard, 2003, p. 75), a concept he borrows from Slavoj Zizek:

> The ultimate and defining moment of the twentieth century was the direct experience of the Real as opposed to everyday social reality – the Real in its extreme violence as the price to be paid for peeling off the deceptive layers of reality. (Zizek, 2002, pp. 5–6)

Thompson's quest for authenticity, then, was a definitively twentieth-century moment. In this sense, 9/11 might be seen as the last gasp of the previous century rather than the ugly birth of the current one. What Thompson sought in his engagement with politics was freedom for an autonomous subject seeking to embrace the Real and resist interpellation, even at the cost of exposing the grotesque reality beneath the simulations propagated by the state: he revealed this reality through attacking the state not by military means, as terrorists do, but in print.

With that said, Thompson was always *prepared* to fight, to face 'the Real in its extreme violence'. On the night of the Freak Power election in 1970, he dug in at Owl Farm with guns and several companions, fearing attack and ready to repel it, although the attack in fact never came. He did *write* about violence as a political device, and toyed with the idea of distributing the sort of information that might counter police intimidation at demonstrations, but when he considered making these ideas public, he was already thinking in terms of the same self-deprecatory irony that the phrase Freak Power had embodied. He considered putting out 'a regular weapons feature' under the Raoul Duke by-line in the satirical magazine *Scanlan's Monthly*, including suggestions on how to disable police vehicles (*FLA*, p. 326). He aimed to create, through Duke, 'a virtual clearing-house for information on all forms of violence' (p. 325).

The Duke persona was a very thin disguise; Thompson was not a terrorist in hiding, but an artist attacking the system through satire. Although he was far from averse to physical resistance to what he saw as establishment oppression, he understood from early on that the most effective means of creating the space in which the individual could remain or become authentic was on the semiotic, ideological ground on which the system operated first and most effectively in the lives of ordinary Americans.

Hence his scathing, Rabelaisian images: Muskie as an ibogaine addict, and politics as the Guinea worm. Thompson's political writing aimed not to overturn the existing order but to shift *the image* of the system forever by associating politics not with noble endeavour and fair debate but with everything that debased the mind and body: drug addiction, gambling and deadly parasites. Tying these together is a nexus of compulsion, enslavement and corruption. One is addicted to chemicals or one bets on a sport obsessively, at the expense of wealth, health and personal relationships; one's cells are attacked by rapacious predators or opportunistic infections; or one participates in politics. The body invaded, for Thompson, is both the individual body and the body politic; human beings and the nations they inhabit are corrupted alike by a system that has become rotten. As the next chapter will investigate, Thompson attempted to respond to this corruption in the best way he knew: by chronicling its effects on a critically ill patient, the American Dream.

4 The Elusive American Dream; the Edge, the Lodge and the Frontier; Gonzo Sex and Gender

In 1977, Thompson made it clear that Duke and Gonzo's fruitless search for the American Dream in *Fear and Loathing in Las Vegas* was a metonym for his generation's failed quest: 'There are worse ways to spend your life than chasing the American dream. But once you've found it [...] it is generally just a slab of burned-out concrete in Las Vegas called the old Psychiatrist's Club' (*AGW*, p. 94). Thompson acknowledged that for many Americans, the Dream was 'sort of the guiding ethic for enterprise, democracy, honesty, truth, beauty, things like that' (p. 94). But, as he knew very well, this definition was hopelessly vague. The Dream in effect constituted a national utopian myth, so nebulous as to apply to almost anything.

In fact, Thompson had no clear idea of what the Dream was: 'Was it Horatio Alger, rags to riches [...]? Or was it a dream of freedom? Personal freedom ... or the concept of freedom that the founders brought into the [...] world?' (McKeen, 2008, p. 118). Following his first major publication, *Hell's Angels*, he had been commissioned by Jim Silberman of Random House to write a book on the death of the Dream. He soon bitterly regretted signing the contract, as he had no idea of how he was going to complete the project. He spent years attempting to break the agreement. Writing to Silberman on 30 August 1969, he complained that 'That "American Dream" notion becomes increasingly meaningless [...]. You might as well have told me to write a book about Truth and Wisdom' (*FLA*, p. 205). This was no isolated incident of writer's block. As early as 9 June 1968 he had written to Silberman to claim that 'I'm losing any hope of a focus' (*FLA*, p. 92).

By the mid-to late twentieth century, the Dream had become so blurred and contentious that it was highly troublesome to a thoughtful commentator like Thompson. But only a generation earlier it had been defined with a clarity that must have seemed enviable. In his 1931 book *The Epic of America*, the historian James Truslow Adams had popularized the phrase:

But there has been also the *American dream*, that dream of a land in which life should be better and richer and fuller for every man, with opportunity for each according to his ability or achievement. It is a difficult dream for the European upper classes to interpret adequately, and too many of us ourselves have grown weary and mistrustful of it. It is not a dream of motor cars and high wages merely, but a dream of a social order in which each man and each woman shall be able to attain to the fullest stature of which they are innately capable, and be recognized by others for what they are, regardless of the fortuitous circumstances of birth or position. (Adams, 1945, p. 415: emphasis in original)

Although Adams acknowledged that some Americans had already grown sceptical about the Dream, it was nevertheless relatively easy for him to outline. His definition involved two key elements, with an implied tension between them: the realization by every *individual* human being of his or her full potential, regardless of background; and the creation of a *social* order open enough and yet structured enough to make such self-realization possible.

Later interpretations of the Dream, although bitterly opposed to one another, implicitly acknowledged the duality underlying Adams's definition. Timothy Leary and other idealistic hippies of the 1960s believed that a turned-on individual could 'Drop acid and change yourself, change yourself and then change the world' (Stevens, 1993, p. 20). In the same decade, Lyndon B. Johnson shared the same assumption that social transformation was inextricably linked to individual fulfilment. He stated that his aim was to create a civilization that served 'not only the needs of the body and the demands of commerce but the desire for beauty and the hunger for community' (cited in Kearns, 1976, p. 211).

Although ideologically far apart, Leary and Johnson both recognized that riches were not enough. So did Thompson. He had come to realize the hollowness of the Horatio Alger myth of economic advancement, and was concerned with 'the fallout from the dream's failure' (Sickels, 2000, p. 71).[1] In *Vegas*, Thompson distances himself from Alger through

---

1 Alger was the composer of a number of formulaic nineteenth-century novels in which the earnest protagonist found success through his own efforts, such as *Strive and Succeed; or, the Progress of Walter Conrad* (1872) and *Brave and Bold; or, the Fortunes of Robert Rushton* (1874). Alger's biographer John Tebbel summarized his creed as: 'the United States is a place where anyone, no matter what his origins, no matter how poor and obscure he may be, can rise to fame and fortune' (cited in Sickels, 2000, pp. 61–2).

irony. In the final sentence of the novel, after snorting an amyl nitrite, Raoul Duke cynically calls himself 'a monster reincarnation of Horatio Alger ... a Man on the Move, and just sick enough to be totally confident' (*LV*, p. 204). As Duke's wry self-denunciation suggests, he is the antithesis of Alger, as he is 'deceitful, lazy, and self-indulgent' (Grassian, 2000, p. 103).

Thompson did not mourn the demise of Alger's ideas. To claim that the rags-to-riches myth was his main concern, and that 'lamentations on what he sees as the death of Alger's version of the American Dream can be seen throughout his work' (Sickels, 2000, p. 62) somewhat simplifies his relationship to the Dream, because it ignores the problem of definition that prevented him from producing his contracted book. As an inheritor of the individualist tradition derived from the Founding Fathers, Thompson was committed to a problematic and elusive ideal of self-realization: he knew that the American Dream was – or rather, *ought* to have been – based on a far nobler ideal than the capitalist myth that anyone could get rich through hard work.

In the post-war years of relative peace and prosperity under Eisenhower, the Dream seemed, to some, to have been realized in the USA. Thompson knew this impression was superficial. He understood how limited an outlook it took to see 'motor cars and high wages' as sufficient. His parents' generation had fought the War, but had then meekly traded liberty for security by voting for Eisenhower and retreating 'to the giddy comfort of their TV parlours, to cultivate the subtleties of American history as seen by Hollywood' (*HA*, p. 310). Nevertheless, even at the centre of this television-numbed society, there was a sense that material prosperity was not enough, and that the administration was not offering any clear direction. One joke of the period claimed that to make an Eisenhower doll work properly, one simply wound it up and it did nothing for 8 years. Hannah Arendt called Ike senile in private, while the journalist Joe Alsop called the administration 'a dead whale upon a beach' (Rorabaugh, 2002, p. 3).

Thompson was well aware of this. He called his society 'so far adrift and puzzled with itself that its president [Eisenhower] feels called upon to appoint a Committee of National Goals' (*HA*, p. 306), and noted that because of this directionlessness, alienaton was popular. Indeed, a number of disparate, more or less alienated minorities pursued unconventional aims during the 1950s and 1960s, creating their own Dream in opposition to the shallowness of that of the majority. Thompson wrote of the rebellious urges of dissenters who had internalized 'the sense of new realities, of urgency, anger and sometimes desperation in a society where even the highest authorities seem to be grasping at straws' (*HA*, p. 307).

Some of the most prominent of these dissidents were writers. The Beat Generation's leading figures, like William S. Burroughs, Allen Ginsberg and Jack Keruoac, came of literary age in the 1950s. In their works they poured scorn on the dominant ideologies of capitalism and consumerism. Ginsberg's 'America' ironically complains of poverty amid the plenty of the 1950s: 'When can I go into the supermarket and buy what I need with my good looks?' (Ginsberg, 1959, p. 39, 1. 15). In 'A Supermarket in California', Walt Whitman appears to Ginsberg in a vision, asking bathetic questions: 'Who killed the pork chops? What price bananas?' (Ginsberg, 1959, p. 29, 1. 5). The Rio Grande Valley section of Burroughs's *Junky* (1953) offers a get-rich-quick travesty of the American Dream, in which hapless town dwellers try to become entrepreneurial farmers, pursuing the illusion of a fast buck: 'All the worst features of America have drained down to the Valley and concentrated there. [...] The very rich are getting richer and all the others are going broke' (Burroughs, 1977, p. 108). Kerouac's *On the Road* (1957) includes a parody of the Horatio Alger myth, in which Dean Moriarty's father and a friend try to sell flyswatters to make a living during the Depression: 'after two whole weeks [...] hustling in the heat to sell these awful makeshift flyswatters they started to argue about the division of the proceeds and had a big fight on the side of the road' (Kerouac, 1991, p. 207).

On the Road, Kerouac's long, originally paragraphless scroll that fictionalized his and his friends' travel across the States, became one of the templates for *Fear and Loathing in Las Vegas* (see Chapter 1). But between the two novels came the 1960s, where the Beatniks morphed into hippies who then became freaks. Thompson knew an ideal had died by the end of the decade, but it had never been clear exactly how and why it had perished, and even what it was. Instead, he perceived the disappearance of a huge opportunity; he saw that his generation had not even had time to articulate its vision of a future before that future was snatched away. In *Vegas*, Raoul Duke cites the blissful self-righteousness felt by the hippies and fellow travellers like himself in the mid-1960s: 'There was a fantastic universal sense that whatever we were doing was *right*, that we were winning' (*LV*, p. 68: emphasis in original). The hippies' sense of the coming victory is 'fantastic': Duke uses this adjective in the colloquial sense, meaning it felt good, but the term also connotes fantasy. Likewise, the phrase 'whatever we were doing' carries positive connotations of self-belief, implying the hippies' every activity was sanctioned by a sense of mission, but it also suggests the imprecision that arose from the counterculture's lack of a coherent programme of action.

The destruction of the young generation's half-formed vision of its future was exemplified by the assassination of John F. Kennedy, an incident that traumatized Thompson, but – much to his anger – did not appear to shock some others, whom he called "giggling scum" (*PH*, p. 419): 'It is the triumph of lunacy, of rottenness, the dirtiest hour in our time. [...] It is the death of reason. From here on out, the run is downhill for us all – and I mean all' (p. 418). Kennedy's symbolic value to Thompson was enormous: 'The shits were surely killing us, and now they have killed the only hope on the American horizon' (p. 418). He feared a victory for the right-wing Republican senator Barry Goldwater in 1964 and a return either to Communism or to Fascism (p. 419). Writing to his Marxist friend Paul Semonin, Thompson declared his disgust with these totalitarian doctrines and his loyalty to his old-fashioned vision of his country, which was based on loyalty to the Constitution and the ideas of the Founding Fathers: 'I fully intend to go down with it before I give in to either of the other shitty camps' (p. 419).

Writing on 22 November 1963, the day of Kennedy's assassination, Thompson used the phrase 'fear and loathing' for the first time, as a description of his gut reaction to the murder (p. 420). He perhaps borrowed it unconsciously from Søren Kierkegaard's nineteenth-century existentialist interpretation of the story of Abraham and Isaac, *Fear and Trembling*.[2] Thompson later denied the connection with Kierkegaard: the phrase 'came straight out of what I felt. [...] I just remember thinking about Kennedy, that this is so bad I need new words for it' (*AGW*, p. 234). Douglas Brinkley states that Thompson's source for the phrase 'fear and loathing' was Thomas Wolfe's novel *The Web and the Rock*, published posthumously in 1939 (Wenner and Seymour, 2007, p. 128). *The Web and the Rock*'s protagonist, George Webber, is appalled by the squalor of his own background: 'Drowning! Drowning! Not to be endured! The abominable memory shrivels, shrinks and withers up his heart in the cold constriction of its fear and loathing' (Wolfe, 1975, p. 81).[3]

Whatever its literary sources may have been, Thompson's intense personal pain arose from his sense that cherished public institutions were

---

2 Kierkegaard situates the phrase 'fear and trembling' in a passage that offers an uncannily appropriate description of the older Thompson: 'When the old campaigner approached the end, had fought the good fight, and kept his faith, his heart was still young enough not to have forgotten the fear and trembling that disciplined his youth and which, although the grown man mastered it, no man altogether outgrows' (Kierkegaard, 2005, p. 5).

3 Thomas Wolfe (1900–1938) is not to be confused with Thompson's contemporary Tom Wolfe, the New Journalist and writer of *The Electric Kool-Aid Acid Test*. According to Brinkley, Thompson told him 'it was too much of a hassle [to acknowledge the Thomas Wolfe source], that people would think he meant Tom Wolfe' (Wenner and Seymour, 2007, p. 128).

being shattered: 'fear and loathing' therefore tapped a nerve in his culture. The horror writer Stephen King took Thompson's slogan as a synonym for terror, an emotion that 'arises from a pervasive sense of disestablishment; that things are in the unmaking' (King, 1981, p. 22; cited in Bridgstock, 1989, p. 119). The phrase had political as well as personal connotations. It meant 'a dread of both interior demons and the psychic landscape of the nation around him' that enabled Thompson to articulate 'the mind-set of a generation that had held high ideals and was now crashing hard against the walls of American reality' (Gilmore, 2005, p. 47).

As far as Thompson was concerned, the Kennedy assassination had killed much more than the president himself. It had destroyed an aspect of the American Dream, articulated in a literary masterpiece: 'Neither your children nor mine will ever be able to grasp what Gatsby was after. No more of that' (*PH*, p. 420). *The Great Gatsby*, published in 1925, was F. Scott Fitzgerald's ambiguously ironic comment on the dazzling façade put on by a rich criminal of humble origins named Gatz, who invented himself as Gatsby, along with a fake privileged background and the story of a legitimate basis for his fortune, in order to explain his existence and to try to win back his former lover, Daisy Buchanan. To Thompson, it felt like the product of a literary Golden Age: an imaginary era that had permitted an intensity of artistic aspiration that was no longer possible.

The Great Gatsby also suggested a negative model to Thompson, in the shape of Richard Milhous Nixon, another aspirational faker, a debased contemporary incarnation of Gatz, who wooed the nation with lies. Even in 1968, 6 years before Nixon's resignation over Watergate, Thompson believed he had the future president nailed: 'Nixon is a monument to all the bad genes and broken chromosomes that have queered the reality of the "American Dream." Nixon is the Dorian Gray of our time, the twisted echo of Jay Gatsby' (*FLA*, p. 50).[4]

As well as echoing Thompson's characteristically Rabelaisian metaphors of bodily corruption (see Chapter 3), the references to genes and chromosomes suggest a post-Darwinian discourse of devolution: Thompson believed that Nixon was reversing the development of USA by debasing any remnants of the original national quest for life, liberty and the pursuit of happiness. Nixon was a Gatsby who had gone over to the dark side. Thompson compares the president to Conrad's Mister Kurtz, who dies after becoming deified in horrifying blood

---

4 This came in a letter. Thompson barely deviated from this formula in an article of the same year, 1968: 'a monument to all the rancid genes and broken chromosomes that corrupt the possibilities of the American Dream' (*GSH*, p. 197).

rituals, and is completely corrupted by dwelling in the heart of darkness: 'Mistah Nixon, he dead' (*GSH*, p. 299).

Nixon's was not the only character Thompson derived from *The Great Gatsby*, as he also saw his own persona there. Fitzgerald's novel depends on the narration of Nick Carraway, an observer who is nevertheless involved in events. At the end of the novel, Carraway observes the limits of Gatsby's illusion, and implies the evasiveness of the American Dream:

> his dream must have seemed so close that he could hardly fail to grasp it. He did not know that it was already behind him, somewhere back in that vast obscurity beyond the city, where the dark fields of the republic rolled on under the night. (Fitzgerald, 1991, p. 168)

Carraway notes what he believes are Gatsby's limitations, and by implication records the failure of his generation's quest. However, his observations are never neutral: they cannot be separated from his preconceptions. *The Great Gatsby* is a subjective narrative that nevertheless claims to offer a detached outsider's perspective both on Gatsby's character and 'the dark fields of the republic', the national psyche from which Gatsby's ambiguous fakery emerges.

Like Thompson's other personas, Raoul Duke became Gatsby *and* Carraway, a figure who could make a doomed effort to piece together the tattered remnants of the American Dream by setting out on a quest to discover and enact a vision of personal freedom, and yet at the same time report on his own failure: 'Like Nick Carraway before him, Duke, serving as both prophet and a microcosm of the American people, emerges from his experiences physically unscathed, but forever disillusioned' (Sickels, 2000, p. 73); 'Duke is pursuing the American Dream, in all its Gatsbyesque splendour' (DeKoven, 2004, p. 97); 'Thompson stretches another Fitzgerald technique, that of simultaneously leading the parade and heckling oneself from the curb, to capture the spirit of the age in himself' (Klinkowitz, 1977, p. 34).

Thompson had derived the Duke persona from his strong, though never systematically articulated, Gatsby-like belief in American individualism and the quest for self-realization, which was combined with – and often undermined by – the stance of a Carraway-like observer-participant who could chronicle with sometimes withering irony his own dysfunction and complicity in capitalist exploitation. Duke notes that when you are high on ether, 'you can actually *watch* yourself behaving in this terrible way, but you can't control it' (*LV*, p. 45: emphasis in original). As

Duke and Gonzo, ethered to the gills, stagger towards the Circus-Circus casino, they are mistaken by the staff for drunks. They are not turned away because of this: on the contrary, to the predatory gambling establishment, they represent 'fresh meat' (p. 46).

A generation earlier, T. S. Eliot could refer to ether to create an objective correlative for his feelings of inner hollowness: his alienated persona J. Alfred Prufrock sees the evening sky as 'Like a patient etherised upon a table;' (Eliot, 1974, p. 13, l. 3). In Duke's case, though, the drug is not a simile: Thompson's, rather than Eliot's, was the first truly etherized generation. This incident encapsulates in miniature the counterculture's abandonment of its own ideals, a capitulation that Thompson saw as symptomatic of the death of the American Dream. Duke and Gonzo stumble through the turnstiles stoned because they have no sense of a goal, of anywhere to go to.

To a degree, Thompson shared Duke's lack of direction. In his work, he stated very clearly what he was *against* (cops, corrupt politicians, establishment journalists, acid gurus, naïve idealists, exploitative businessmen) but he was usually much less explicit about what he stood *for*. His ideals were sometimes incarnated in figures problematic with promise, like John F. Kennedy. He told Random House that he wanted to chronicle 'the death of that whole era that began, for me, one night in 1960' when he saw the first Kennedy-Nixon debate on TV (*FLA*, p. 124). Not coincidentally, he had been on a Kerouac-influenced hitchhiking trip across Oregon at the time and watched the debate in a roadside tavern. Although Kennedy had not yet delivered anything significant, he seemed to herald a new, more humane form of government.[5] Until he saw the young senator defeat Nixon before the cameras, Thompson had never realized 'that politics in America had anything to do with human beings' because it had seemed to him merely 'a world of old hacks and legalized thievery' (*FLA*, p. 260). Thompson found himself responding to Kennedy's *image*, because it seemed to embody one of his core beliefs: humanism (see Chapter 1).

---

5 It is uncertain whether Kennedy did actually achieve this. He personified the promise of the early 1960s that offered such a contrast to the torpid Eisenhower years, but he arguably delivered little actual change. He projected charm and mystique, but although 'these techniques along with his mastery of television guaranteed his popularity, which remained unusually high throughout his presidency, they did not enable him to accomplish much as president' (Rorabaugh, 2002, p. xx). Kennedy's relationship with television continued after his death and affected the nation's perception of politics and of itself: 'The ceremonies of laying him to rest made television not only the national mourning place for a weekend but, ever after, the first assembly place of national emotions or national attention to the great events of our times' (White, 1982, pp. 174–5).

Despite the murder of Kennedy, which so intensified Thompson's loathing of the establishment and his fear that his ideals were under threat, he failed to produce the book for Random House about the death of the American Dream. Paradoxically, the frustration of this ambition was to catalyse his subsequent work, which became an attempt to construct America as having failed in a mission that, although urgent, was nevertheless neither definable nor even fully understood. Bruce-Novoa has argued that Thompson developed his Gonzo style in the 1970s as a response

> to the fear and loathing he felt for what was happening to the American Dream. Like so many sixties radicals, Thompson believed in that Dream, in the terms of the individualist, the nonconformist, the frontiersman, the doer as opposed to the watcher. (Bruce-Novoa, 1979, p. 39)

Thompson's inability to articulate the death of the Dream for the Random House project suggests that the concept was somewhat less clear to him than this. Although he undoubtedly valued non-conformity and the frontier spirit, and wrote Gonzo journalism in response to the forces that threatened to kill that spirit, he was also aware that the American Dream was problematic, because plastic; it was too vague and too malleable to stand simply for one set of values, even his own.

Thompson was very well read and extremely articulate in print, but he was not a philosopher or even an intellectual. He was, first and foremost, a journalist, who preferred to seek the Dream and report on the quest rather than to theorize about it. He never sat down to formulate his ideas systematically in the abstract; instead, he composed everything in response to some experience. He was a materialist and an empiricist, seeking the foundations of his writing in the lives of actual human beings and in the evidence of his sometimes chemically deranged senses.

This was one reason why the Dream proved so elusive. Thompson, like Raoul Duke, was 'a crusading cultural detective, hunting for the secret cultural truth that governs American ideology and behaviour', but he knew that the Dream itself, as its name implied, was a fantasy (Grassian, 2000, p. 102). Such a chimera could never be contained in prose. Instead, Thompson produced fragments, or 'Notes' on the Dream and its death: *Fear and Loathing in Las Vegas* was subtitled *A Savage Journey to the Heart of the American Dream*; his third volume of Gonzo papers, *Songs of the Doomed*, was subtitled *More Notes on the Death of the American Dream*. Each fragment was loosely connected to the others, forming a disjointed, not always internally coherent but nevertheless consistently significant account of American life in the last half of the twentieth century.

'The Edge is Still Out There': Thompson and Edgework

In the powerful final passage of *Hell's Angels*, Thompson describes a high-speed motorcycle ride. He attempts to rationalize it in terms of a philosophy of danger:

> The Edge ... There is no honest way to explain it because the only people who really know where it is are the ones who have gone over. [...]
>
> But the edge is still Out there. Or maybe it's In. The association of motorcycles with LSD is no accident of publicity. They are both a means to an end, to the place of definitions. (*HA*, p. 323)

Excessive speed on a motorcycle is a route to risk, up to and including fatal peril. For Thompson, it is also a means of self-realization, through the manipulation of space – one's own small stretch of America – on one's own terms, by traversing it so quickly that the journey becomes potentially lethal. Like an acid trip, high-speed motorcycle riding might be described as mind-revealing: fast driving is one of a number of sports that have 'a certain psychedelic aspect, a power to transform space and time. They are non-competitive, essentially solo activities, which induce in the participant a sense of danger, dizziness and disorientation that he finds attractive' (Brown, 1976, p. 26). The parallel with hallucinogenics is clear. Both offer risks and thrills but can also clarify the self's presence in the instant of experience by vastly amplifying the senses: 'The [Hell's] Angels' trip was the motorcycle and the [Merry] Pranksters' was LSD, but both were an incredible entry into an orgasmic moment, *now*' (Wolfe, 1996, p. 154: emphasis in original).

The sociologist Stephen Lyng defines such voluntary risk taking as "edgework", a term he takes from *Fear and Loathing in Las Vegas* (*LV*, p. 80). Lyng dismisses psychological models of risk that assume that the individual is motivated by anticipated reward. Instead, his work focuses on those who 'place a higher value on the *experience* of risk-taking' than on the results, even to the extent that risk becomes '*necessary* for the well being of some people' (Lyng, 1990, p. 852: emphasis in original):

> The idea of edgework is the product of several diverse influences. The term itself is borrowed from the journalist Hunter S. Thompson, who has used it to describe a variety of anarchic human experiences, the most infamous being his experimentation with drugs. Thompson's journalistic accounts of many different types of edgework give a powerful expression to the essential character of this

experience. Indeed, negotiating the boundary between life and death, consciousness and unconsciousness, and sanity and insanity is a central theme in Thompson's work. (p. 855)

Thompson's edgework is about using psychedelic sport, in all its forms, in order to experience liminal states where one can glimpse an inner boundary, and even briefly travel along it, at the risk of crossing over permanently.

According to Lyng's interpretation of Thompson, the edge is the dividing line between ordinary life (rationality, sanity, order) and a state or place of desirable but dangerous Otherness. Thompson compares drug use to negotiating dangerous bends on a motorcycle: 'I like to just gobble the stuff right out in the street and see what happens, take my chances, just stomp on my own accelerator. [...] you have to be *good* when you take nasty risks, or you'll lose it' (C, 8–9, cited in Lyng, 1990, p. 858: emphasis in original). Thompson took pride in the skill required: only the few who were good enough at riding the chemical motorcycle would step off it in one piece. Thompson shared the 'elitist orientation' of some edgeworkers (Lyng, 1990, p. 860).

Edgework was a form of self-testing for Thompson. It was his way of validating and continually measuring the progress of the quest for self-realization that forms a major part of the American Dream. The other part, creating a social order that allows self-realization to happen, proved more problematic. He found that no such order could exist except on a local, temporary level – for instance among groups of bikers speeding on the interstate, or freaks using drugs in San Francisco or in rural retreats. The American establishment was absolutely inimical to it. Richard Nixon, despite his spectacular ascent from humble origins in 'a rustic Californian clapboard cottage which had no electricity, no running water, no wireless, no telephone, and no inside privy' (Wright, 1996, p. 442), would do anything rather than allow others to realize themselves. On the contrary, he would swindle them and blind them with fakery; he was 'a cheap thug, a congenital liar' (C, p. 24), 'a half-mad used-car salesman' (p. 26).

How, then, in the era of Nixon and Lyndon B. Johnson could the American Dream be realized? With no geographical frontier left, and a political order either apathetic (Eisenhower) or repressive and corrupt (Nixon, Johnson), what chance did the Dream stand? Thompson appeared to be a man in retreat from an environment that would not allow him to realize his ideals. Apart from the Freak Power candidacy, he was not a political activist. What was left was his edgework and the satirical writing that represented it. The result was Thompson's Gonzo style: a fragmented account of broken national aspiration, in which self-realization became a distant chimera, replaced by the urgent need for holding the self together under pressures, which were often chemically induced.

In a section of *Fear and Loathing in Las Vegas* supposedly transcribed from a tape left by Duke, he and Gonzo drive around, fruitlessly trying to locate the American Dream. Abstract ideals and banal realities are hopelessly blurred. During a farcical conversation with a waitress at a taco stand on the outskirts of Las Vegas, the attorney tries to explain their quest: 'We're looking for the American Dream [...]. That's why they gave us this white Cadillac, they figure that we could catch up with it in that' (*LV*, p. 164). The waitress and the cook eventually narrow the Dream down to the Old Psychiatrist's Club. The attorney summarizes their description as, 'Big black building right on Paradise: twenty-four-hour-a-day violence, drugs' (p. 167). The editor's closing note suggests that Duke and the attorney did find the site, but it was only vacant lot, a decrepit shell. There is nothing left of it, and the waitress and cook are not convinced that it was ever called the American Dream anyway. It is an illusion and the quest for it is absurd. In fact, Duke never even writes it up, as '*At this point in the chronology, Dr. Duke appears to have broken down completely*' (p. 161: emphasis in original), thus forcing the editor to rely on imperfect tape recordings, corrupted by an ambiguous 'viscous liquid encrusted behind the heads' (p. 168).

This comic, reflexive sequence articulates Thompson's feelings about the death of the Dream and his frustrated failure to find it. The curse of the unfulfilled contract for Random House lies behind this section, as does Thompson's reworking of the literary tradition of the frustrated quest: his literary precedents here are *On the Road* and *The Great Gatsby*, not to mention *Don Quixote*, *Moby Dick* and *Waiting for Godot*. Duke and Gonzo's mission is pointless. They are seeking an illusion, just like Don Quixote, whose horse Rozinante is replaced here by cars, the Great Red Shark and the White Whale (itself an allusion to Melville). They appear exhausted, beat. They are condemned to exchange useless badinage, like an acid-addled update of Beckett's Vladimir and Estragon. Duke's initial explanation of their quest, as given to Gonzo in Los Angeles, relies on 'the faux-naïve, self-mocking Gatsby motif' (DeKoven, 2004, p. 94), as captured in Duke's parody of insouciant Jazz Age banter: 'I tell you, my man, this is the American Dream in action!' (*LV*, p. 11).

Even so, Duke and Gonzo are not traditional literary figures. Duke's formulation of the Dream emphasizes presentness: 'The American Dream. Horatio Alger gone mad on drugs in Las Vegas. Do it *now*: pure Gonzo journalism' (p. 12: emphasis in original). Duke connects the Dream to past writing, but only in a mocking way, when he alludes to the nineteenth-century champion of self-help, Alger. Like Duke, Thompson felt the need to act *now*. In the early 1970s, he knew that the social and political moment was all-important and that it had to be seized, or the Dream would be irrevocably lost. In 1974, writing his opening memo to the eight participants of a secret conference of Democratic Party luminaries he had convened at Elko, Nevada, Thompson claimed that looking ahead, 'I saw the 1976 elections as either a final affirmation of the Rape of the "American Dream" or perhaps the last chance any of us would have to avert that rape' (*FLA*, p. 582). When Thompson wrote after Watergate, only 2 months later, there was a distinct change in tone: 'The Impeachment Of Richard Nixon, if it happens, will amount to a de facto trial of the whole American Dream' (*FLA*, p. 588). In the Elko address, the American Dream was the victim: it was either raped or threatened with rape. Following Watergate, it was the defendant, on trial.[6]

Thompson does not mean the same thing by 'American Dream' in each case, but the disparity points to more than the semantic flexibility (or vagueness) of the whole concept that had so frustrated him. The difference in the two meanings also suggests a change in his thought about the matter, as if the Dream itself had become culpable, and had had its contradictions and corruption exposed by Nixon. As Thompson put it in 1990, 'Nixon was a monument to everything rotten in the American dream – he was a monument to why it failed' (*SD*, p. 148).

'I Need My Freedom': The Frontier and the Lodge

Thompson's American Dream was mapped onto the old frontier, a long-vanished open space that permitted individual freedom. For Thompson's generation, there was no frontier in the received geographical and historical sense of a border between an expanding USA and unknown territory. The coasts and the continental interior had been settled, the Indian and Mexican wars were over and the Union was stable. As early as 1893, unexplored territory was already an anachronism: beginning his history of the frontier, Frederick Jackson Turner pointed out that the superintendent of the US census of 1890 had declared that 'there can hardly be said to be a frontier line' any more and that discussions of its 'westward movement' or 'extent' were no longer meaningful (Turner, 1963, p. 1). Turner concluded that 'the frontier has gone, and with its going has closed the first period of American history' (p. 58).

The death of the frontier meant that individualism shifted from a practical necessity to an ideology: 'In 1893 the frontier was closed, even if its legends were slow to fade. […] it called for initiative, ingenuity and

---

6 Thompson later included this letter in a *Rolling Stone* piece, 'Fear and Loathing in Washington: The Boys in the Bag' (*GSH*, pp. 300–18).

self-reliance; it was hostile to remote authority because it was remote and because it was authority' (Wright, 1996, pp. 7–8). Despite its disappearance, and because of its individualist, anti-authoritarian ethos, the frontier continued to exist as a concept and an object of desire. Because of 'the closure of the map' in which the 'last bit of Earth unclaimed by any nation-state was eaten up in 1899' (Bey, 2003, p. 100), freedom-seeking Americans pushed the frontier either into conceptual space or real but temporary zones: 'the map is closed, but the autonomous zone is open. Metaphorically it unfolds within the fractal dimensions invisible to the cartography of Control' (Bey, 2003, p. 101).

Thus, in Thompson's writing, instead of being a literal borderland or unsettled zone, the frontier is an idea, connected to two related but mutually contradictory concepts. First, the edge, or space of personal danger: the theatre of edgework. Second, the lodge, or *Walden*-like area of peacefully isolated domestic security and/or independent communal living, an autonomous zone far away from state power, where outside pressures such as deadlines and the grander march of history can be resisted, at least temporarily.

In 1960, Thompson set up home beside the idyllic rocky coastline of Big Sur, California, with the aim of 'writing the Great Puerto Rican Novel' (*PH*, p. 242), the project that was eventually published as *The Rum Diary* in 1998 (see Chapter 5). His experience of Big Sur was blighted by poverty, but he had at least found a place that he enjoyed living in: 'Big Sur is [...] "the tall walking nuts." But a man on the crest of a new wave can hardly afford to retire, so all signs point to my imminent return to the strife and struggle of cold-war reality' (*PH*, p. 257). Thompson saw himself as temporarily secure in Big Sur: as isolated from the conflicts of the wider world, in a sympathetic environment where, despite penury and other practical difficulties, he could finally grind out great literature, supported by his loyal wife Sandy.

But Big Sur was hardly an original discovery by Thompson: it already had a reputation as an artists' colony. A recent resident had been the controversial novelist Henry Miller, who was most famous for having had several of his works banned for obscenity in the USA. By the time Thompson arrived, self-consciously following in Miller's footsteps, the older writer had fled to Europe 'for what may be a permanent vacation' (*PH*, p. 269). Thompson admired Miller's work hugely, particularly *Tropic of Cancer* (1934) and *The World of Sex* (1940).[7] William McKeen quotes a

---

7 *The World of Sex* was a particularly rare text: Miller published it privately in 1959, but it only received commercial publication in 1965. Thompson sent a precious 1959 copy to Norman Mailer in 1961, but did not receive a reply (*PH*, p. 546).

passage from *Tropic of Cancer* that, as he rightly points out, might equally have been a self-portrait by Thompson:

> I am a free man – and I need my freedom. I need to be alone. I need to ponder my shame and my despair in seclusion; I need the sunshine and the paving stones of the streets, without companions, without conversation, face to face with myself, with only the music of my heart for company. (Miller, 1994, p. 66; cited in McKeen, 2008, p. 62)

Thompson knew that Miller had been hounded by fans and would-be lovers during his time at Big Sur, hence his flight. All Miller had wanted was 'peace and solitude' (*PH*, p. 267), the very things sought by Jack Kerouac, who had stayed there seeking 'six weeks just chopping wood, drawing water, writing, sleeping, hiking' (Kerouac, 2006, p. 7). These simple, Thoreau-like pleasures were denied to Thompson in the end, partly due to his anti-social behaviour, including drunkenness and shooting out his own windows, but mostly because of an article he had published in *Rogue* magazine, 'Big Sur: the Garden of Agony' (*PH*, 264–77), which his landlady believed defamed the community, causing her to evict him. After leaving in 1961, he soon registered his disillusionment: 'the myth of Big Sur attracts talent, but the reality of Big Sur erodes talent' (*PH*, p. 466).

Although Thompson had been attracted to Miller's vision of peace and solitude, he in fact needed other people for self-realization, as did Miller. In *The World of Sex*, Miller's narrator 'saw within the frame of the actual the potential being which I am', but realized that this potential could manifest itself only in the context of the 'deep and lasting connection between myself and all the other human beings' (Miller, 2007, p. 22). In accordance with this vision of personal fulfilment through interpersonal relationships, the next incarnation of the lodge for Thompson was a communitarian one. It came in 1964 in San Francisco, where Thompson rented an apartment at 318 Parnassus – only a few blocks away from the emerging hippie community of Haight-Ashbury – which, like Big Sur, he helped turn into an object of nationwide publicity by publishing articles about it (see Chapter 2).

In 1966, Thompson fled San Francisco for Colorado. Apart from the impending collapse of the Haight under a huge influx of would-be hippies, the reasons for Thompson's flight had been 'indirectly political' (*PH*, p. 590); he had been affected particularly by the jailing of Ken Kesey, the breaking of a student strike at Berkeley and the election of the despised Ronald Reagan as governor, 'a grinning whore who will probably someday be President' (*PH*, p. 492).

The final and most successful incarnation of Thompson's lodge was not a bohemian enclave but an isolated homestead, Owl Farm. In *Walden*, Thoreau had used the house as an extended metaphor, an image for the self that ought ideally to be fashioned autonomously:

> There is some of the same fitness in a man's building his own house that there is in a bird's building its own nest. Who knows but if men constructed their dwellings with their own hands, and provided food for themselves and families simply and honestly enough, the poetic faculty would be universally developed, as birds universally sing when they are so engaged? (Thoreau, 1992, p. 31)

Thoreau believed creative fulfilment and self-realization depended on the construction of one's own domestic space in isolation, preferably in a wilderness. Thompson took his cue from this outdoor variant of transcendentalist idealism. Owl Farm was a concept before it became a reality; in California in 1964 he and the pregnant Sandy had inhabited 'a sort of Okie shack' that he called Owl House, where, in a scaled-down imitation of Thoreau, he built his own writing-desk from a disused door (*PH*, p. 439).

In the spring of 1967, he arrived at what was to become the final Owl Farm. The countercultural tone was set by his writing room, 'painted red, white and blue by a dope freak that I hired from the trailer court', and by the Bob Dylan records he blasted 'out of an alcove full of paint cans and dirty brushes' (*PH*, p. 610). He claimed hippies kept turning up at the house to sell him drugs. The influx of freaks into this rural backwater made him write of the resulting local tensions in a mock-Gothic tone: 'wild shrieks in the night, dog packs, flutes screaming in unison, ugly behaviour. [...] The Siege of Woody Creek will go down in history as the Watershed of Dope' (*PH*, p. 618). He had begun to joke of Owl Farm as a "fortress" (p. 618), and he mockingly called it a fortified compound in his book blurbs. Looking back in August 2000, he acknowledged that it had acted as 'a very important psychic anchor for me, a crucial grounding point where I always knew I had love, friends & good neighbours. It was like my personal Lighthouse that I could see from anywhere in the world' (*FLA*, p. xxii).

'They're a Different Race': Thompson, Gender and Sexuality

During the move to Owl Farm, Sandy Thompson was Hunter's helpmate, 'keeping the house quiet when he slept, feeding him a lavish breakfast when he woke, and tending to his every need at the expense of her own'

(McKeen, 2008, p. 115): 'I had no life. [...] My whole world revolved around Hunter' (Wenner and Seymour, p. 220).[8] It was Sandy who had kept Thompson afloat in San Francisco by working at a series of short-term, poorly paid jobs. In the lodge, a domestic space, Thompson demanded a woman at the hearth to provide security, whereas the edge was an all-male zone of danger and excitement. This discriminatory separation was reflected to a great extent in Thompson's fiction: 'the world that Duke projects in *Fear and Loathing in Las Vegas* is strictly male-dominated and misogynistic – the female is purposely excluded' (Grassian, 2000, p. 108); 'misogynistic sexual fear and (self-) loathing violently abjected and projected onto women is part of the fear and loathing [felt by Duke and Gonzo]' (DeKoven, 2004, p. 98).

However, Thompson's writing did sometimes question patriarchal attitudes, despite the 'characteristic sixties sexism' that he shared with other males of his generation (DeKoven, 2004, p. 75). In a 1967 article for *Pageant* magazine, entitled 'Why Boys Will Be Girls', he relished the fruitful connection between the subversive utopianism of the Haight and the hippies' flouting of gender conventions: 'there were men wearing flowers, kilts, and necklaces, and girls dressed in sweat shirts and Levi's, with their hair cropped short like Army recruits' (*WB*, p. 94): 'what is it? Have the Reds already put LSD in the public waterworks? [...] How can a mighty nation like America wage war with an army of transvestites?' (p. 96).

Thompson also questions sexism in his fiction, although this is usually done indirectly, through an implied critique of the protagonists' actions. In *Vegas*, for instance, Gonzo seems to enjoy exploiting women: he gives the naïve young Lucy LSD and, it is implied, abuses her sexually; he believes a woman reporter is in love with him after she merely requests an interview; and most graphically of all, he turns on a waitress at the North Star Coffee Lounge, a downmarket diner. Focusing on the woman 'out of boredom' (*LV*, p. 158), he pulls a knife after she objects to his writing 'Back Door Beauty?' (a barely disguised invitation to anal intercourse) on a napkin and passing it to her (p. 159). 'The sight of the blade, jerked out in the heat of an argument, had apparently triggered bad memories. The glazed look in her eyes said her throat had been cut' (p. 160). Duke does not directly criticize Gonzo's behaviour, but he hardly endorses it. He tacitly permits the scene to happen, letting Gonzo do as he wants, but he finds himself 'stupid with shock, not knowing whether to run or start laughing' (p. 159). The reader is left to draw his

---

8 Hunter's dependency on Sandy ended when she endured a protracted miscarriage, 'an agony that stretched over several months of enforced bed rest' (McKeen, 2008, p. 115).

– or her – own conclusions about Gonzo's perpetuation of the cycle of violence and abuse.

In a 1976 interview, Thompson made a self-mockingly essentialist claim about gender: 'I don't understand women. That's one of the reasons I don't write about them. […] They're a different race. They fascinate me, but I'd be worried about writing about them until I learn to speak their language' (*AGW*, p. 62). Despite Thompson's tongue-in-cheek tone, a reductive view of women as Other comes across here. Nevertheless, although Thompson acknowledged the patriarchal subdivision of women into categories such as mommas, bimbos and hookers, he attempted to distance himself from this crude classification. He implied that *real* women were none of these, but that he did not understand them, and rarely met them: 'You don't seem to run across them as much as mommas' (p. 62).

Thompson was exaggerating for effect. He had encountered plenty of real women whom he respected. Those most closely associated with him knew that he did not classify them as bimbos: they believed that whatever his personal faults, his work deserved complex analysis. For Sandy, his first wife, Thompson's talent had attracted her even as his behaviour came to repel her: 'I was living for Hunter and his work – for this great person, this great writer, who was so disciplined […] who loved me and who was also terrifying me' (Wenner and Seymour, 2007, p. 220). His second wife, Anita, found that he was fascinated by female fiction-makers like Anaïs Nin and Ayn Rand, and he read their work 'to better understand how smart women thought' (Thompson, 2007, p. 29).

Even if he loved specific women but still saw females in general as essentially Other, Thompson was well aware of sexual politics. He knew that sexuality was a social issue, rather than simply a natural drive. As Anita put it, 'Hunter knew the difference between love and sex, and the combination of the two became a driving factor in his craving for knowledge about the world around him' (Thompson, 2007, p. 29). The legislation and industrialization of sex could be a barometer of power. In the mid-1980s, as a research project, he took a job as night manager of the O'Farrell Theatre in San Francisco, an adult revue bar.[9] As ever, he saw

---

9 The O'Farrell Theatre was run by the brothers Jim and Artie Mitchell. After showing hardcore pornographic films in the 1960s, the Mitchells graduated to making their own, such as *Behind the Green Door*, which featured group sex, interracial sex and a shot of a man ejaculating, and thus 'offered audiences the sense of participating in a world of "far-out" sexual fantasies' (Allyn, 2000, p. 235). By the 1980s, the theatre had become a live sex club where 'lap dancers writhed with customers. The dancers did just about anything, masturbating for an audience, masturbating clients, or fellating them. The O'Farrell was a sexual theme park' (McKeen, 2008, p. 283).

the political implications of the environment he happened to be in, and drew connections between local events and national politics: 'It was a nice place to work in those money-mad years of the Reagan Revolution. [...] Huge expense money was the oil that kept that national economy going, and sex was everywhere' (*KF*, p. 22). To Thompson, the O'Farrell Theatre and the pornography industry were merely the most obvious evidence of the exploitative sexual dynamics of patriarchy, in which outwardly respectable men *and* women colluded: 'All political power comes from the barrel of either guns, pussy, or opium pipes and people seem to like it that way' (p. 26).

The same was true of the Hell's Angels. Thompson understood that the sexism of the bikers mimicked the power imbalances of wider society. He writes of how the Angels divide their girlfriends into old ladies and mamas, with the former belonging to one Angel exclusively, and the latter being sexually available to the whole chapter (*HA*, pp. 198–99). Thompson likens these women, especially mamas, to other groups of people who are exploited and remain voiceless. In a reference to the human traffic of the days of slavery, he recounts an incident in which a mama, her body auctioned for beer money, attracts only a joke bid: 'It would be interesting to hear, sometime, just exactly what it feels like to go up on the auction block, willing to serve any purpose, and get knocked down for twelve cents' (p. 199).

Typically, despite his sympathy for the woman, Thompson approaches this dire event not as a feminist but as a humanist. He universalizes the mama's situation, suggesting that *all* voiceless people like her should be heard from. The discourses of reportage and literature worsen the problem, rather than expose it: those "men" whose deeds enter 'the public prints' are less worthy of report than the "people" (women, slaves, the poor) who are left out of them simply because they are considered worthless by the capitalist social order (p. 199).

Thompson further exposes the commodification of women in *Fear and Loathing in Las Vegas*. Gonzo has suborned the naïve teenage runaway Lucy and fed her LSD. Duke then suggests what they might do with her in the context of the District Attorneys' Convention they are attending. He claims that the cops will 'go fifty bucks a head to beat her into submission and then gang-fuck her' (*LV*, p. 114). Duke is being sarcastic, but the stoned Gonzo misses this entirely. Duke's point is that Lucy is Gonzo's problem; he must now do something about her, before both men suffer the consequences when she recovers from the drugs and realizes what has happened (p. 116). Duke himself has 'never even coveted the goddamn girl, much less put my hands on her flesh' (p. 177).

Although one critic has characterized Duke's urging Gonzo to get rid of Lucy as the product of misogynistic fear, and of his need to eliminate 'any possible weak spot where his individuality might crumble' (Grassian, 2000, p. 108), the narrative makes clear that here, as in many instances in Thompson, the Gonzo protagonists are not so much eccentric woman-hating deviants as satirical exaggerations of the majority of men. Duke's imaginary cops who would pay $50 each to rape Lucy are a metonym of the patriarchal, sexually predatory social order of a town like Las Vegas, where an ingenuous, stoned girl may soon find herself a victim or a commodity to be traded. By treating Lucy as they have, Duke and, in particular, Gonzo are complicit in this gender traffic. As Duke stands and argues with the attorney, he wearily concludes that anyone watching them would assume they were disputing 'who had "rights to the girl." It was a standard scene for a Vegas parking lot' (p. 118).

The tone of this passage is deliberately dark, and is in tune with *Hell's Angels*, where Thompson treats rape as a widespread imaginary possibility rather than an occasional physical reality. Though sexual assault is brutally real to its victims, even more worrying is the power dynamic of American society that allows it become part of patriarchal mythology and fantasy, and thus to be tacitly accepted. Rape is 'a horror and a titillation and a mystery all at once' (*HA*, p. 222). Thompson concludes that the Angels' occasional gang rapes, however heinous, stem from attitudes that are not exceptional. They represent a brutal exaggeration of mainstream patriarchal values: 'in this downhill half of our twentieth century they [the Angels] are not so different from the rest of us as they sometimes seem. They are only more obvious' (p. 230).

At the heart of Thompson's account of rape lies his humanist protest against the awful things society can do to the individual. A social order of capitalist competition is designed to produce winners, but this means there must also be losers. Among these are not only the victims of rape, and all sexually abused women, but also those men, like many of Thompson's protagonists, who are duped by the ideology of domination of which rape is the most visible manifestation.

On the evidence of his work, Thompson was far from a feminist. One account of *Vegas* suggests that his implied disapproval of the protagonists' sexist attitudes is a mere cover for his misogyny: his fiction offers a 'loathsome fear and loathing of women (in which Thompson, like Burroughs, one of his major influences, clearly participates at the same time that he distances himself from it)' (DeKoven, 2004, p. 106). If true, this may have arisen from Thompson's tendency to engage in often painful self-examination. Rather than ignoring his own misogyny, he dissects it in his texts, at the expense of his persona. The same has been said of

Oscar Zeta Acosta, the prototype of Dr Gonzo, who 'is a unique figure among male Chicano novelists, in that his bitter, honest reflections [on his masculinity] do nothing to enhance his machismo' (Stavans, 1995, p. 54).

In fact, rather than expressing hatred of women, Thompson's writing suggests another form of sexism, in that it often virtually ignores them or uses them as incidental bystanders to male-dominated scenes. The mamas and old ladies are less important to Thompson's work than are the Hell's Angels; Lucy and the waitress matter far less to *Fear and Loathing in Las Vegas* than Duke and Gonzo; the political scene described in *Fear and Loathing on the Campaign Trail '72* is largely a battle between masculine antagonists, reported by a nearly all-male press pack.[10]

Given the Gonzo principle of placing the journalist at the centre of the story, a masculine focus in Thompson's work would seem inevitable. Nevertheless, the Gonzo protagonist sometimes has his macho self-importance punctured by transgendered individuals, gays and others who impinge on his world. Some of Thompson's protagonists are violently anti-queer, but his writing remorselessly charts the damaging effects that their prejudice has on them. In *The Curse of Lono*, Thompson and his friend Captain Steve are stopped at a traffic light by what appears to be a group of prostitutes. When one of them leans in and tries to grab Steve, Thompson repels her by jabbing her hand with his lit cigarette. It turns out the prostitute is actually a transvestite mechanic who used to work for Steve: 'I made a real effort with Bob, but he got too weird for the clients' (*CL*, p. 84).

Steve then explains why he fired Bob: after Bob had gone to work one day with the ass cut out of his Levi's, a group of offended Japanese tourists tried to kill him, and threw him into the sea. Bob was stabbed several times with fish hooks, but survived. Steve managed to bribe the tourists to avoid losing his captain's licence, but found himself charged with sexual assault, presumably because he allowed himself to be blamed for the crime, and thus took the rap in place of the homophobic tourists whose silence he needed to preserve his job (p. 85). Thompson's conclusion is deadpan: 'I said nothing. The story made me uncomfortable. […] Captain Steve seemed okay, but the stories he told were eerie. They ran counter to most notions of modern-day sport fishing' (p. 85).

---

10 Timothy Crouse points out how rare and yet how effective the women reporters on the campaign trail were in 1972. One example was Cassie Mackin of NBS, who fortunately 'had neither the opportunity nor the desire to travel with the all-male [press] pack; therefore, she was not infected with the pack's chronic defensiveness and defeatism' and could report Nixon's lies and evasions without compromise (Crouse, 1974, p. 282).

This is a typical Thompson tactic. An outrageous series of events is presented to the reader, but the numbed protagonist refuses to react outwardly – just like Duke in the North Star Coffee Lounge in *Vegas*. Unlike Duke, Thompson participates in the violence by using his cigarette on Bob, but his last statement suggests his creeping sense of discomfort and guilt. Thompson's persona is here discovering that he is part of the reactionary aggression all around him: he is not objectively distant from the heart of darkness, but inhabits it.

In fact, Thompson himself had committed violent homophobic acts in Big Sur in the early 1960s. In a letter, he claimed that these contributed to his dismissal from the community: 'I am about to be evicted for splitting a queer's head with that billy club' (*PH*, p. 280). When he discovered that the nearby swimming pool, of which he was caretaker, was a gathering place for gay men, Thompson would drive them away with his gun (McKeen, 2008, p. 63; Perry, 2009, pp. 62–3).

In his fiction, though, Thompson shows how homophobia is a trap for the abuser as well as the victim. In *The Rum Diary*, a gay man attempts to pick up the protagonist Kemp in a Puerto Rico hotel bar. Kemp has already outed himself as something of a degenerate: 'a new face in the snakepit, a pervert yet to be classified' (*RD*, p. 27); and yet, when he is offered an opportunity *to be* perverse, he panics by threatening violence: he accepts the man's proposal of a walk on the beach, but says he must first 'borrow a meat-whip from the kitchen'; the man looks nervous and Kemp asks, 'Don't you want to be flogged?' (p. 110). After the man leaves, Kemp realizes, 'I was shaking. Jesus, I thought, maybe I'm getting the DTs' (p. 110).

Kemp is more disturbed by the incident than he would like to admit. He is experiencing the conditioned reaction of the male heterosexual subject to the realization that he could become an object of gay desire, or be perceived as gay by outsiders, or may even *be* gay without ever having known it. Such panic forms part of a homophobic structure of control, in which:

> no man must be able to ascertain that he is not (that his bonds are not) homosexual. [...] So-called 'homosexual panic' is the most private, psychologised form in which many twentieth-century western men experience their vulnerability to the social pressure of homophobic blackmail. (Sedgwick, 1985, pp. 88–9)

Here, unlike in *The Curse of Lono*, there is no actual homophobic violence, only the threat of it, but both texts investigate the complex impact of homophobia on the perpetrator as well as the intended victim.

'A Male Nightmare': Thompson and Homosocial Desire

The ludicrousness of much homophobia and homosexual panic is exposed by the Hell's Angels' male-on-male kissing in public, especially before photographers, which is designed mainly to embarrass spectators and the media: 'This is a guaranteed square-jolter, and the Angels are gleefully aware of the reaction it gets. [...] The sight of a photographer invariably whips the Angels into a kissing frenzy' (*HA*, p. 234). The Angels' kissing is also the most visible evidence of their homosocial desire, meaning strong same-sex friendship or emotional bonding that is not sexual but has the *potential* to become so, even if it is aggressively homophobic on the surface. The term homosocial 'is applied to such activities as "male bonding," which may, in our society, be characterized by intense homophobia, fear and hatred of homosexuality' (Sedgwick, 1985, p. 1). There is 'a continuum between homosocial and homosexual – a continuum whose visibility, for men, in our society, is radically disrupted' (Sedgwick, 1985, pp. 1–2). Thus, homosocial relations between men form part of a structure of desire that links them to homosexuality; but in Western culture, this link, far from being readily accepted, has caused considerable discomfort, even down to homosexual panic and outright homophobic violence. The kissing Angels are exploiting this discomfort in their audience, without having put a name to it.

In Thompson, the edge is not only a place for self-discovery by the individual subject, but is also a homosocial zone of intense male rivalry and desire. This is one reason for the role of the sidekick in his writing. Duke and Gonzo need each other, just like Thompson and Steadman in *The Curse of Lono* or 'The Kentucky Derby'. Such bonding allows Thompson's work to explore gender performativity, meaning the construction of masculinity through actions such as speech and dress codes:

> acts, gestures and desire produce the effect of an internal core or substance [of gender], but produce this *on the surface* of the body, through the play of signifying absences that suggest, but never reveal, the organizing principle of identity as a cause. Such acts, gestures, enactments, generally construed, are *performative* in the sense that the essence or identity that they otherwise purport to express are *fabrications* manufactured and sustained through corporeal signs and other discursive means. (Butler, 1990, p. 136: emphasis in original)

The Hell's Angels' gang rituals, for instance, might be read as a *creation* rather than a mere demonstration of one form of American masculinity, achieved through a play of signifying surfaces; the badged denim of the uniforms, the metal of the bikes and Nazi helmets, the provocative gestures involved in showing "class" to the local squares (see Chapter 2). The Angels make themselves men through acting out their quest for a liberated frontier in an overdeveloped, technological, over-regulated society.

Apart from the motorcycle itself, the most potent catalyst of the Angel's maleness is his colours, or club badge sewn into the back of his denim jacket. Thompson demonstrates how the Angels initiate a new member. Although the club president Sonny Barger would later claim this passage was pure fantasy (Barger, 2001, p. 127), Thompson's striking images present in symbolic form the homosocial patterning of the gang: 'dung and urine will be collected during the meeting, then poured on the newcomer's head in a solemn baptismal. Or he will take off his clothes and stand naked while the bucket of slop is poured over them' (*HA*, p. 54). If this passage is Thompson's fabrication, even though introduced in pre-Gonzo fashion without obvious subjective bias, then it is all the more remarkable for its figurative insight into the Angels' homosocial subculture. They are dropouts and losers whose primitive right-wing values include a strong though crude sense of American patriotism (see Chapter 2); their homosocial bonding is cemented by xenophobia and commodity fetishism.

The Angels' motorcycles are Harley-Davidsons, an iconic American brand. Japanese bikes are anathema within the club. Thus, through buying and using a US-made consumer durable, the Angels express their commitment to a frontier myth, a variant of the American Dream: 'The motorcycle is an example *par excellence* of the consumption process whereby the universal human longing for a better life becomes identified with the use of commodities' (Alt, 1982, p. 134). In Thompson's account, another American commodity, the denim of the colours, forms the medium by which the initiate receives the club's traditions through the members' collected excrement, symbolically soaking up the values of the chapter. The Angels' shared affection for the Harley furthers this process; the 'crankcase drippings' from the bike are another form of intimate fluid allowed to seep into the new member's clothes (*HA*, p. 54).

Duke and Gonzo, hurtling through Las Vegas, are bonded in a similar way. They act out their masculinity through drug use and fast driving. Their shared fetish objects are chemicals, cars and weapons: they drive together, get stoned together, sometimes go naked in front of each other in the hotel suite, and pull knives and Mace cans on each other. Gonzo, in the bath, asks Duke to assist his planned suicide. Duke asks for confirmation of his intent, and the exasperated Gonzo replies, 'Fuck yes [...]. I was beginning to think I was going to have to go out and get one of the goddamn *maids* to do it' (*LV*, 60: emphasis in original). Later, the hapless chambermaid Alice walks into their room to clean it and finds both men naked, with the tripping Gonzo vomiting into his shoes, believing he has reached the lavatory bowl. The two men seize Alice and in a comic double-act, manage to convince her they are undercover cops and everything is under control, before they shoo her out of the door (pp. 181–5).

In each instance, Duke and Gonzo's nudity and drug-intensified homosocial conflict and intimacy are linked to the banishment of a female. Again, as with the Angels, the frontier of risk, where the edge can be traversed, appears to be a patriarchal space, where women are not welcome, 'a male nightmare that must be worked out among other males' (Grassian, 2000, p. 108):

> if emotions were the main avenue through which men distinguished themselves from women before, during and after edgework, they may have felt that their appropriate gender performance – their very masculinity – would be threatened if they were to display emotions associated with a feminized edgework performance [such as anxiety or fear]. This interpretation resonates with [...] 'hegemonic masculinity', which is sustained because it dominates over other gendered forms [... including] any kind of femininity. (Lois, 2001, p. 403)

One particular vector of gendered hegemony is through 'the division of labor, the social definition of tasks as either "men's work" or "women's work", and the definition of some kinds of work as more masculine than others' (Carrigan et al., 2002, p. 114). Edgework is a form of labour that can be gendered like any other. Hegemonic masculinity is enforced through male edgeworkers' display of emotional control, or their venting of stereotypically masculine responses to edgework, such as homosocial bonding, aggression, excitement and elation.

Thompson's protagonists do, in fact, exhibit feminized responses to edgework some of the time: Gonzo is in 'catatonic despair' after his failed suicide attempt (*LV*, p. 62) and is tearful after a traumatic elevator journey when tripping on acid (p. 24); Duke is terrified when he attempts to register at the Mint Hotel, and the female desk clerk turns into a poisonous moray eel (pp. 23–4: see Chapter 2). However, these emotions occur within the context of an androcentric adventure, in which women appear only as incidental hazards or exchangeable objects of desire. This is the central form of sexism in Thompson's work: outright misogyny, though present in his writing, is rarer than the consistent exclusion of females from the frontier and the edge, and therefore from Thompson's project of self-realization.

Conclusion: A View from a Hotel Room

Thompson's attempts to realize the mutually exclusive dreams of the edge and the lodge help to explain his paradoxical interests: in rural conservation and explosives, in ecology and dangerous driving, in anti-war protest and firearms. His version of the American Dream required space in which to adventure, but security in which to write; his space needed to be open and free, but also closed off from interference. His needs, in short, were contradictory, not just on a personal domestic level but in a literary and ideological sense.

The space of the hotel room, where much of the chaos of *Vegas* takes place, as well much of the political reflection in *Campaign Trail*, embodies these contradictions. It is a common but ambiguous location in Thompson's writing. There are many instances of success and frustration in such rooms, when deadlines are met or more usually missed, or scenes of drugged debauchery take place: often, the debauchery and the deadlines are combined in a deadly synergy. It is a place where failure shadows success, where the Gonzo protagonist finds himself embroiled in the pleasures of work and the pressures of leisure; in grinding out mechanical paragraphs stoned, looking down on ordinary citizens below, feeling exhausted but absurdly privileged.

The first paragraph of Thompson's 1969 piece 'First Visit With Mescalito' encapsulates the ambiguous role of the hotel. Thompson is on the 11th floor of the Continental in Los Angeles, on the balcony overlooking the road, when he sees four freaks below. One of them waves, they exchange V-signs (Winston Churchill's victory sign, co-opted by Richard Nixon, and appropriated by the hippies to mean "peace") and one of them asks what he is doing up there. Thompson replies, 'I'm writing about all you freaks down there on the street' (*SD*, p. 119). The incident with the four street freaks sounds fictional, because it forms such a conveniently clear image of Thompson's sense of distance from the street yet empathy with it. He muses on the isolation of the privileged political classes by imagining Hubert Humphrey looking down on the violence in Chicago in 1968, from the comfort of his hotel suite. If Humphrey had had a balcony, he might have behaved differently, as 'Looking out a window is not quite the same. A balcony puts you out in the dark, which is more neutral – like walking out on a diving board' (p. 119).

Thompson implies that the balcony is another incarnation of the edge. It is a liminal line over which lies death; a dangerous "diving board" just outside the hotel room. Thompson is aware of the privilege that keeps him literally on the level of Humphrey and other members of the establishment, but also of the bitter experience of being down below that has made him know at first-hand the violence that a political class detached from the people is capable of: his recollection of the police brutality in Grant Park was still vivid, as it took place in August 1968, only 6 months before 'Mescalito'. Later in 'Mescalito', Thompson will turn away from politics and look inwards, to the self-fashioning medium of hallucinogenic drugs, as he tries to write. The rest of the piece describes his first encounter with mescaline (pp. 122–28).

In all his experience, and especially in his writing, Thompson was perpetually searching for his own version of the American Dream. If the edge was the subjective limit he strained towards so often, and the lodge was the locus of domestic security that he needed in order to write and rest, the frontier was the space of adventure and self-discovery that would catalyse the fully realized humanity he sought for himself and others. The hotel room, especially seen in the context of drugs and writing, as in 'Mescalito' and much of *Vegas*, was a mixed, ambiguous space between all three: a temporary home, with some of the services of the lodge but none of its domestic comforts or security; a hired theatre for creativity, edgework and dangerous chemical hedonism; a space symbolically distanced, often by its height and always by its price, from the street outside and the freaks who lived there. The most resonant image of this space in Thompson's work is that of Raoul Duke, trapped in a Las Vegas hotel suite he cannot afford, reminiscing about the great acid wave of the mid-1960s in California. Duke's imagery suggests he is symbolically looking out from a height, like the tower of his hotel, over a deserted shore, seeing where the wave rolled back (*LV*, p. 68).

Indeed, the wave had broken: as Thompson increasingly came to realize, the fantasy of the American Dream had been replaced by the reality of the US Empire. During the last quarter of the twentieth century, after the setback of Vietnam, America consolidated its status as a world power by subtler means than war: advertising; propaganda; overseas aid; the spread of corporate investment and influence; in short, through globalization. The next chapter examines how, in his writing, Thompson formulated his own image of the imperial American nation, and of his place within it, as the USA extended its power over the planet and tightened its grip on dissident elements within its borders.

5 'Bash the Buggers Silly; Bomb the Insane': Thompson and the American Empire

The postcolonialist thinker Benedict Anderson locates the construction of the nation in two written forms, the novel and the newspaper, that express a new conception of time suited to national consciousness:

> [the nation depends upon] an idea of 'homogeneous, empty time', in which simultaneity is, as it were, transverse, cross-time, marked not by prefiguring and fulfilment, but by temporal coincidence, and measured by clock and calendar.
> Why this transformation should be so important for the birth of the imagined community of the nation can best be seen if we consider the basic structure of two forms of imagining which first flowered in Europe in the eighteenth century: the novel and the newspaper. For these forms provided the technical means for 're-presenting' the *kind* of imagined community that is the nation. (Anderson, 1983, p. 30: emphasis in original)

Anderson goes on to analyse several realist novels to show how in narrating the simultaneous actions of subjects who never encounter one another but are nevertheless connected within a space, the genre allows the nation to be born. Likewise with journalism, Anderson examines the newspaper as a narrative vehicle and remarks that he is 'struck by its profound fictiveness': the arbitrariness of the links between juxtaposed news items shows that 'the linkage between them is imagined' (p. 37). Through the temporal coincidence of events within them, and by their connection to an increasingly self-aware market sharing a language and a space, the novel and the newspaper are ideal breeding grounds for national identity: we share this land, we are here together and therefore, we are a nation. Anderson argues that fiction and journalism share a comfortable role of ideological reinforcement, where 'fiction seeps quietly and continuously into reality, creating that remarkable confidence of community in anonymity which is the hallmark of modern nations' (p. 40).

Thompson aimed to mix the genres in a totally different way. Through his Gonzo style, he aimed to smash the cosy nation-building consensus between fiction and journalism by creating conspicuously subjective, implausible narratives whose often outrageous style and content questioned the comfortable assumptions of 'objective' reporting and realist novels.

Race was one faultline along which this challenge could be pursued. Issues of ethnicity and nationhood informed Thompson's writing throughout his career and his unconventional approach to them formed part of his resistance to received wisdom. As his appropriation of the Black Power clenched fist for Freak Power suggests (see Chapter 3), Thompson viewed race and national identity as issues that, like a number of others, required ethical choice and yet could be played with ironically and made into vehicles for satire.

Thompson was not blind to racial discrimination, but he saw it as one more means of economic exploitation. In this respect, he was clearly aligned with the Marxist side of the dialectic between Marxist and sociological approaches to colonialism in which 'the former approach privileges class, and the latter race in understanding colonial societies' (Loomba, 2005, p. 108). Early in his career, he evolved a theory that *any* downtrodden person, regardless of race, could be classified as a 'Nigger': despite the offensiveness of the word, he intended it not as an insult, but as a recognition of marginalization (*PH*, p. 411). In the 1970s, he persisted with this blurring of black and white. He felt that if the American establishment were given free rein, 'There'll be a nigger hanging on every telephone pole ... along with a lot of Blacks, too' (*FLA*, p. 342). He claimed that he identified with the black activist Charles Evers, as he felt like 'a Nigger Mayor in Mississippi' (*FLA*, p. 305).

Thompson was aware of the unpleasant connotations of his language, but was remarkably honest about where his casual use of racial epithets came from. He admitted to 'a strain' of racism, but pointed out that in every black-white confrontation he had seen, 'I've had to admit the negroes were Right' (*PH*, p. 449).[1] However, this concession had limits, defined humanistically. When he heard Malcolm X's call for arming the Black Power movement and blowing heads off, 'there the dialogue ends

---

1 Thompson's friend Bob Geiger pointed out that Thompson used racist language casually but his political beliefs were 'the opposite'; in the mid-1960s he even hatched a never-fulfilled scheme to run guns to the South to allow civil rights activists to fight back against the Ku Klux Klan (Wenner and Seymour, 2007, p. 72).

[...] Malcolm X is a black Goldwater, and apparently just as dense' (p. 449). He believed that forming a Black Nationalist party would energize too many people who are 'just waiting for an excuse to act like the racists they are' (p. 449).

The racists Thompson referred to were black as well as white. Thompson was here marginalizing the racial specificity of Malcolm X and of Barry Goldwater, who was of Jewish descent, because, in his view, they were *both* violent idiots, and Goldwater's slogan 'extremism in the defence of liberty is no vice' (FLA, p. 70), with its coded incitement to self-righteous reactionary violence, was as wrong-headed as Malcolm X's exhortations. Instead, experience reinforced Thompson's humanism by teaching him that people were basically alike, regardless of race: 'You can try to convince me that Africans are different [from South Americans], but I will take a lot more convincing now than I would have a year ago' (PH, p. 358).

Thompson's work nearly always features a human centre, the protagonist, which cannot hold under the pressure of alienation, or fear and loathing, heightened by alcohol and/or drugs. Thompson's individualist focus on the alienation of the protagonist led his work to appear to marginalize race by framing the colonial encounter as a backdrop to the subjective experience of a white male (see, for instance, the sections on *The Rum Diary* and *The Curse of Lono* below). This approach led to critical remarks from his friend, the Chicano activist and lawyer Oscar Zeta Acosta, who was the model for Dr Gonzo in *Fear and Loathing in Las Vegas*: 'You think you know about the issue of race in this country, which has led you to conclude that it is not really an issue at all' (FLA, p. 281). However, rather than ignoring race, Thompson was treating it as one important factor among others in the formation of subjectivity: or in his terms, of what makes someone human.

Thompson's position can be aligned with recent postcolonialist thinking such as that of Couze Venn, who wishes to distance postcolonialism from the identity politics of race, class, gender and sexuality:

> in the background of the problem of identity one finds quite basic questions about the 'who' – of action, of agency, of lived experience, the one who answers the call to responsibility – and about belonging and ontological security, questions that are as old as the emergence of human self-consciousness. (Venn, 2006, p. 78)

Venn distances himself from the Cartesian dualisms of body/mind, self/other, black/white, in order to align his work with thinkers like Foucault, Althusser and Butler, who promote dynamic models of the mind, body and other in which subjectivity is constantly being created and reformed with reference to ideology, power and performativity.[2]

Nevertheless, underlying Venn's model is a humanism revealed when he champions that 'simple humanity without which one loses sight of what is really important: the dignity and fragility of human life, and so loses heart' (p. 118). Thompson shared this sympathy. He did not dedicate his life to civil rights activism, apart from his semi-satirical Freak Power campaign, but he did dedicate it to exposing the death of the American Dream in print, and chronicling the dehumanizing corruption, including racism, that had ruined American society and destroyed its ideals; this debasement was, for him, chiefly personified by the Republican Party and more particularly by Richard Nixon.

Thompson's focus on subjective hate figures was hardly surprising, given that, for him, objectivity was not only impossible in journalism, but also impossible, and undesirable, in life. As Venn argues when critiquing the traditional Marxist conception of ideology, it 'presupposes a domain of objective reality and rational unitary subjects who can objectively weigh up the arguments' and thus escape the false consciousness that ideology creates (p. 91). But if ideology in fact works to *constitute* subjectivity, as Althusser argues (see Chapter 3), then objective scrutiny of the self and its world is impossible.

Thompson acknowledged this, and lived it out in his work: he could not see outside himself and did not try. Instead, he created his own subjectivity continuously by means of his writing. Encounters with racism and racial Otherness were catalysts for his identity-building narratives. For Thompson, these were also nation-demolishing narratives, as his visions of a fragmented, self-conflicted, imperialist USA and of a Gonzo observer-participant, possessed by fear and loathing, shaped themselves simultaneously.

Thompson, Marxism, Sartre and Fanon: *The Wretched of the Earth*

Writing to his friend Paul Semonin in January 1964, Thompson expressed a number of typically contradictory views. He was sympathetic to Semonin's

---

2 Michel Foucault's work proposes a dynamic relationship between the subject and power, in which the individual's self-definition and the state's self-concept depend on their mutual interaction: 'Power relations are rooted in the whole network of the social' (Foucault, 2002, p. 345). Subjective agency is essential to power relations, which are far from being simple systems of state domination: 'there is no relationship of power without the means of escape or possible flight. Every power relationship implies, at least in potential, a strategy of struggle' (p. 346). For further discussion of Foucault, see Chapters 1 and 6. For Althusser on ideology, see Chapter 3; for Butler on gender performativity, see Chapter 4.

Marxism, but was at bottom an individualist. Thus, although he believed material inequality was evil, he saw government as an equally serious problem, rather than as a solution to poverty: 'You accuse me repeatedly of being "anti-Marxist." I am not [...]. My position is and always has been that I distrust power and authority' (*PH*, p. 429). This tension played itself out in his approach to the problems of the developing world, which in his view arose from the imperialism that imposed a debased copy of democracy on colonized nations while economically exploiting them.

A month after the letter to Semonin, Thompson wrote to Dwight Martin of *The Reporter* to pitch for a review of Frantz Fanon's anti-colonialist book *The Wretched of the Earth*. Thompson was particularly interested in Jean-Paul Sartre's introduction to the text. Not knowing that Fanon had died, but assuming correctly that he 'is a West Indian, and presumably black' (*PH*, p. 438), Thompson went on to précis Sartre's interpretation of Fanon's thesis: 'there is no sense in talking to ex-colonial peoples in terms of Western Values (specifically, the doctrine of Humanism) that have never really taken hold' (p. 438).

Thompson's engagement with Fanon and Sartre raises two important contradictions. First, as Thompson knew, Fanon and Sartre's doctrinaire Marxism asserted that Western humanism was not the universal philosophy of the human condition it claimed to be, but an expression of colonialist values and ultimately a tool of Western capitalism. And yet, despite his sympathy with their ideas, Thompson was fundamentally a humanist himself. Often, his assertion of his own values privileges those who are, or who can act like, human beings – a phrase he always uses positively (see Chapter 1).

The second contradiction is that although Thompson agreed with Fanon about the speciousness of journalistic objectivity, he had different reasons for his views. Where Thompson saw objectivity as conformity to the values of a self-interested establishment, and thus a means of tricking journalists and their readers, Fanon saw the problem from the perspective of the native who is written about. He distrusted the colonizer's tactic of reporting in an allegedly objective way about the native, which in fact *objectified* him:

> In the war in Algeria, for example, the most liberal-minded French reporters make constant use of ambiguous epithets to portray our struggle. When we reproach them for it, they reply in all sincerity they are being objective. For the colonized subject, objectivity is always directed against him. (Fanon, 2004, p. 37)

Fanon's solution to this problem was to expose the truth of the situation through a *genuinely* objective, Marxist political discourse that saw through the fakery promoted by ideology. Thompson's solution was completely the opposite: to question orthodox 'truth' by asserting the value of the subjective in a seemingly chaotic manner whose ultimate expression was Gonzo journalism: 'Facts are lies when they're added up [...] you have to add up the facts in your own fuzzy way, and to hell with the hired swine who use adding machines' (*PH*, p. 529).

Thompson's central problem, then, when confronting colonialism and issues of race, was to report events without resorting to the pseudo-objective tone of conventional, tacitly pro-imperialist journalism but without at the same time compromising his bedrock humanism. He needed to rise above the level of the co-opted 'swine', which meant loyalty to his own 'fuzzy' approach at the expense of any totalizing political doctrine. His humanism is often masked by a comic, cynical pose. With curmudgeonly irritation, he suggests in a letter that he might take up his gun and blast away at a 'herd of beatniks' grazing below his house, then concludes 'I have come to the point where I think I could kill humans as easily as deer or wild pigs, which probably makes me good timber for Africa' (*PH*, p. 358). As a way of acknowledging his own jadedness, Thompson poses as a colonizer, able to rationalize violence through dehumanizing the victim.

As his ironic embrace of the gun suggests, Thompson shared with Fanon an understanding of the central role played by violence in shaping all societies, particularly colonial ones. According to Fanon, violence 'governed the ordering of the colonial world' by systematically destroying the native social fabric and culture (Fanon, 2004, p. 5). However, he believed that the exact same violence would be 'vindicated and appropriated' by the colonized during the revolution (p. 6). Reporting from Peru for the *National Observer* in 1962, Thompson wrote that the country had no democratic tradition, and anyone trying to introduce one 'is going to meet violent opposition' (*GSH*, p. 373): 'It is only in times of crisis that it [the power bloc that rules Peru] puts on the jackboots and goes into the street with truncheons. In times of peace it wears mufti' (p. 374).

Writing of the military takeover in Peru, after free elections inconveniently put a left-leaning party in government, Thompson cites a general who berates the deposed socialist president for 'lack of objectivity' in not having annulled the elections himself (p. 376). Here, the discourses of objectivity and of domination connect. Thompson sees objectivity as a term in the language of oppression: a rhetorical weapon possessed by those with power, and lacked by the marginalized, who are supposedly driven to irrational actions by their failure to see the situation objectively. Fanon argued that when clearing his country of the colonizer, the native will appropriate European violence, but will rid himself of specious

European liberalism and humanism: 'Challenging the colonial world is not a rational confrontation of viewpoints. It is not a discourse on the universal, but the impassioned claim by the colonized that their world is fundamentally different' (Fanon, 2004, p. 6). Thompson too challenged the colonial world in a way that overthrew the universalist, objective style expected of the Western reporter; but unlike Fanon, he spent his working life resisting the idea that colonized and colonizer were different; instead, he believed in their common humanity.

'Anti-Gringo Winds': Colombia, 1963

Thompson's early *National Observer* reports from South America often echo Fanon's views, but problematize them by taking the subjective viewpoint of the journalist from the colonizing power, Thompson himself in persona, whose sensibilities are warped by the experience of the colonized country. Fanon insists on the primacy of a duality of space, demographics and of race in the colonial context: such a sustained dichotomy is required for colonial society to function. 'The colonial world is a compartmentalized world' (Fanon, 2004, p. 3):

> The 'native' sector is not complementary to the European sector. The two confront each other, but not in the service of a higher unity. Governed by a purely Aristotelian logic, they follow the dictates of mutual exclusion. (p. 4)

The Aristotelian law of the excluded middle, which insists that something cannot be one thing and its opposite at the same time, leads Fanon to the idea that the two sectors are 'inhabited by different species' (p. 5): the spatial division of sectors is a material expression of the dualistic construction of race that is the basis of colonial society, that allows the dehumanization of the native and his/her exclusion from the imperialist ideology that claims to be improving the country for the sake of the native, who mysteriously cannot do it himself/herself.

The passage from Fanon about the city divided into sectors, as cited above, is used by the postcolonialist critic Edward Said as a prime example of the sort of politicized writing that makes 'untenable the opposition between texts and the world, or between texts and speech' (Said, 1991, p. 49). This is exactly the same opposition that Thompson's project aims to break down. His reporting, especially his Gonzo journalism, cannot be said to inhabit a privileged literary space cut off from the world it engages with, because it is an impassioned account of the protagonist's participation in actual events such as the Kentucky Derby or the Mint 400: and yet, at the same time, it foregrounds its own artificiality by breaking linear narrative and refusing to pose as transparent reportage or to use the five Ws structure (see Chapter 1).

The strong engagement of Thompson's writing with the colonial world can be seen in the short article 'Why Anti-Gringo Winds Often Blow South of the Border', first published in the *National Observer* in 1963. It is one of Thompson's most politically committed pieces: it is a report, and thus refuses the aesthetic privilege of literature; but it also does not allow itself the specious distance of objectivity. It comments directly on the spatial and racial separation addressed by Fanon. In the lead paragraph of Thompson's piece, a jaded British expatriate stands on a high hotel balcony in Cali, Colombia and drives golf balls over the 'white adobe blockhouses of the urban peasantry' without the faintest idea or interest in where they will land (*GSH*, p. 369). On the table behind him sits a long gin and tonic, which he occasionally refills.

As Thompson puts it, this could not have happened in London, but in Colombia it is quite commonplace because 'where the distance between rich and poor is so very great, and where Anglo-Saxons are automatically among the élite, the concept of *noblesse oblige* is subject to odd interpretations' (p. 369). The natives, continues Thompson in ironic vein, consider this practice 'bad form indeed', and resent it, perhaps because 'they lack sporting blood, or maybe a sense of humour' (p. 369). The result is a brilliant, impassioned satire on the colonial duality of space: the randomly whacked golf balls signify not only the one-way violence that maintains spatial division – because shooting downwards into the *barrio* is acceptable, unlike shooting upwards into the hotel – but also the ignorance that makes such violence completely unremarkable.[3]

Thompson goes on to explain how even well-meaning white expatriates in South America are made cynical by their surroundings, especially by the corruption they see around them:

> Objectivity is one of the first casualties of 'culture shock' – a term for the malady that appears when a North American, with his heritage of Puritan pragmatism, suddenly finds himself in a world with different traditions and a different outlook on life. (*GSH*, p. 373).

---

3 William McKeen finds this to be one of Thompson's strongest passages of political comment and compares the narrator's outrage to that of Thompson's favourite singer, Bob Dylan, in his lament for the victim of a callous, racially motivated murder, 'The Lonesome Death of Hattie Carroll' (McKeen, 1991, pp. 21–22).

The article offers two simultaneous descriptions of racial Otherness: the natives are strange creatures, passionate and violent, but do not respond directly to the provocation of the fired golf balls; and the golfer's fellow expatriates, because they are in an alien environment where objectivity vanishes, do not even think to criticize his behaviour. For Thompson, *both* groups are foreign, estranged and dehumanized: 'the colonist always remains a foreigner. [...] The ruling species is first and foremost the outsider from elsewhere' (Fanon, 2004, p. 5).

The cause of culture shock appears to be a cultural and environmental difference that is insurmountable, at least for the North American. Instead of leading to understanding, culture shock creates a focus on survival at the expense of communication. Thompson imagines a typical expatriate who arrives in South America full of ideals. Worn down by the petty corruption, theft and squabbling endemic to his environment, the white incomer eventually decides that the locals are 'a bunch of rotten ingrates, stupid and corrupt to the last man' (*GSH*, p. 371). His newfound convictions are compounded by the expatriate community, who are often 'more snobbish than the Latins themselves' (p. 371). Moreover, they end up not disseminating the American values of liberty and democracy, but by becoming hybrids; they imitate reactionary models of identity and behaviour in order to adapt to their surroundings, as they mimic the 'wealthy, anti-democratic' native elite of the Latin country, and even sometimes beat them at their own game (p. 371).

The expatriate's objectivity and compassion are exposed as shallow when they vanish in an environment of colonial exploitation. However, by demonstrating the corrupting effect of context, Thompson is not simply vindicating Fanon's thesis that humanism is a fig leaf for imperialism. Instead, his article assumes, and sympathizes with, a basic liberal fairness in the expatriate that is remorselessly ground down by the venal colonial system. Thompson describes how odd it is to return from South America and then read a book 'by some expense-account politician' whose visit has only brought him up against senior figures, and involved discussions of policy (*GSH*, p. 373). Reading such a book, the bemused ex-colonist will find the issues 'suddenly become quite clear – as they never were when you were right there in the midst of them' (p. 373). Thompson views the privileged, blinkered lifestyle of the visiting diplomat with irony but nevertheless implies, in a nod to traditional Marxism, that a degree of objectivity *is* possible, at least as regards material conditions; infrastructural issues of economics are much the same everywhere, even if they are usually occluded by the drudgery and corruption of day-to-day life in the colonized country.

The Loud American: Puerto Rico, 1960

Thompson explored colonial exploitation, corruption and culture shock in his second attempt at a novel, *The Rum Diary*, begun in the early 1960s but not published until 1998. Like most of his other writing set abroad, it is centred on the alienation of the white protagonist. In this, it followed Hemingway's lead: like *Prince Jellyfish*, Thompson's first, as yet unpublished novel, *The Rum Diary* was 'in truth, largely Hemingway-derivative, albeit with an original, double-edged twist of sobering invective and inebriated humour' (Brinkley, 2005, p. 36). In the mould of the autobiographical adventurers who populate Hemingway's travel novels, Kemp, a reporter in Puerto Rico, is loosely based on Thompson, who spent time there as a young journalist.

Near the beginning of the novel, hearing some American tourists in a bar in San Juan, Kemp pauses to listen to them. His judgement is condescending but revealing. He decides that they originate from 'some flat little town where they spent fifty weeks of every year' and they make him feel 'like a man with no country at all' (*RD*, p. 28). Kemp constructs himself as stateless: as cut off both from these mediocre provincial Americans and from the native Puerto Ricans among whom he lives. The colonial context is felt as a scene of oppression, but only on a personal, existential level: it is a theatrical space that highlights Kemp's sense of dissociation. Thompson later characterized this alienating scenery as 'The San Juan drink/drug/madness underground, as a backdrop to the American Dream destroying one of its main worshipers' (*FLA*, p. 399). Accordingly, Kemp is an American expatriate who is busy losing his illusions of self-determination, freedom and success and who therefore does not identify with his mother country.

The novel ends with a sense of restlessness and oppression: 'Sounds of a San Juan night, [...] people getting ready and people giving up, the sound of hope and the sound of hanging on, and behind them all, the quiet, deadly ticking of a thousand hungry clocks' (*RD*, p. 204). The alienation that Kemp felt at the beginning of the story is redoubled, reinforcing his sense of dissociation from place and from nation. Kemp's Spanish is very limited and his involvement in Puerto Rican culture restricted to bars, parties and the carnival. He wants to move on, to realize his ambitions, but has no idea where or how he is going to do this. His feelings contrast with the sense of hope and possibility he feels near dawn: 'There is something fresh and crisp about the first hours of a Caribbean day, a happy anticipation that something is about to happen' (p. 190). Thus Kemp is not just encountering foreign people, but a foreign chronotope, where space and time play out in different ways.[4]

He is also *creating* this chronotope by projecting his hopes, fears and ambitions onto the landscape and people: the Puerto Ricans and their loosely ordered society are seen by Kemp as a catalyst for drunkenness, violence and sexual transgression on the part of the American colonizers, including himself. After the San Juan carnival, he encounters about two hundred inebriated people, mostly Puerto Ricans, looting a liquor store. A number of whites participate enthusiastically. In the middle of the crowd, a giant Swede wearing a blue jockstrap is blowing blasts on a trumpet: meanwhile, a fat American woman raises two magnums of champagne and smashes them together, 'laughing wildly as the glass and the booze rained down on her bare shoulders' (p. 147). Kemp and his friends join in the looting and then run away. In a side street, they pass a jeep marked with a misspelled 'Poleece', where a uniformed man is 'half asleep, idly scratching his crotch' (p. 147). The Puerto Rico of *The Rum Diary* is a party colony; a place of permissiveness, disorder and colonial exploitation, where Europeans and Americans come to have a good time away from the legal and social restraints of home.

The dark climax of the colonists' party comes when Chenault, the white girlfriend of Kemp's colleague, gets drunk and ends up dancing with a black man, in front of a whooping crowd (pp. 155–7). The man strips her as she dances, and she is too inebriated to care: as her breasts are exposed, they become 'Full, pink-nippled balls of flesh, suddenly cut loose from the cotton modesty of a New York bra' (p. 156). There is a frisson of inter-racial sexuality here that was still potent at the time Thompson wrote; indeed, he decided to add a mixed-race sex scene in a late draft, in a bid to 'enliven' the narrative and 'shock readers' (McKeen, 2008, p. 91). However, in the final version, the sex, probably rape, takes place off stage, after Kemp sees the black man dragging the naked Chenault away.

Chenault's drunken exhibitionism and consequent abduction, and Kemp's impotent observation of the event, form Thompson's metonym for the weaknesses and excesses of his country in the wider world; for the collapse of America's naively assured sense of its own sophistication and self-control under the pressure of confrontation with another culture. A

---

4 The term 'chronotope' means space-time configuration, and is applied to literature by Mikhail Bakhtin: 'We will give the name *chronotope* (literally, "time space") to the intrinsic connectedness of temporal and spatial relationships that are artistically expressed in literature' (Bakhtin, 1981, p. 84: emphasis in original). This enables Bakhtin to write, for instance, of the chronotopes of the road (p. 243), castle (p. 245) and provincial town (p. 247).

literary precedent is Graham Greene's *The Quiet American*, first published in 1955, a novel Thompson had admired as it 'gave the Vietnam experience a whole new meaning' (*C*, p. 152) and which he quoted as an epigraph in 'Dance of the Doomed', his report on the fall of Saigon for *Rolling Stone* (*DD*, p. 56: see below). Alden Pyle, Greene's main American character, comes to symbolize the devious yet clumsy foreign policy of his nation. He is an outwardly ingenuous young man who has taken most of his views on Indochina from historians and textbooks, but who is nevertheless perpetrating terrorist acts at second hand in an effort to destabilize the French colonial government and promote American interests in the region (Greene, 2005). Another influence is Ernest Hemingway's *Fiesta: The Sun Also Rises*, first published in 1927, a story of love and despair among American expatriates in France and Spain. Jake Barnes, Hemingway's narrator, has a subtle metaphorical connection to his mother country. He is an influential but ultimately powerless American, who is in love with the sensuous English noblewoman Brett Ashley, but is impotent due to a war wound. He facilitates Brett's affairs with American and Spanish lovers (Hemingway, 2004a).

The Rum Diary does not quite achieve the symbolic scope or political complexity of Greene's and Hemingway's novels. However, Kemp's fatigued sense of despair comes to articulate the limitations of America's vision of itself as an imperial power when it is faced with the reality of foreign peoples: 'In a twisted way, it will do for San Juan what *The Sun Also Rises* did for Paris' (*PH*, p. 278).

'Strange Rumblings in Aztlán': Los Angeles, 1971

During Thompson's correspondence with Oscar Zeta Acosta, the two men frequently argued about issues of space and race. Acosta sent Thompson plays and short stories, asking for an honest critique, but was upset when Thompson told him what he thought. The embattled Chicano, struggling against the oppression felt by his ethnic minority community, was particularly riled by Thompson's suggestion that he quit Los Angeles and find a refuge somewhere rural, as Thompson himself had done by leaving San Francisco for Aspen: 'What in God's name makes you think that that [sic] government would leave us alone?' (*FLA*, p. 254). Thompson replied by asserting the benefit he had found from Owl Farm, 'a place where I can live like a human being when I get tired of all the screaming bullshit that comes with trying to change a nation of vicious assholes' (*FLA*, p. 273).

This exchange suggests that Thompson saw Acosta's problems partly in spatial terms and saw Acosta as in one respect like himself: as a man in need of the lodge (see Chapter 4), an autonomous zone free from urban tensions, where he could recuperate from the exhausting effort of trying to make a difference to the state. Again, Thompson's humanism underlies his discourse. Acosta is not an exotic racial Other; he is just like Thompson, wanting to 'live like a human being' but swamped in fear and loathing of an intolerable nation that violently oppresses its own dissidents, whether Chicanos or freaks.

Acosta was an important source for the article 'Strange Rumblings in Aztlán ', published in *Rolling Stone* in 1971, in which Thompson engaged with the identity politics of the East LA Hispanic community when he set out to investigate the police murder of Ruben Salazar, a Chicano investigative journalist. After his death, Salazar's name became a rallying point, not just for activists but also for the entire Chicano community.[5] Thompson's essay is set in Aztlán, a territory constructed by Chicano activists to represent Texas, New Mexico, Arizona and Southern California – once about half the Mexican nation, signed over to the United States over a hundred years ago after 'the invasion that gringo history books refer to as the "Mexican-American War" (Davy Crockett, Remember the Alamo, etc.)' (*GSH*, p. 137). Aztlán is an imaginary space, 'more a concept than a real definition' (*GSH*, p. 137). Recognizing the significance of the palimpsest formed by Aztlán and California, Thompson uses the article to weave a narrative out of the tension arising from a conflict over space and identity. The Chicanos want to be just that, rather than Mexican-Americans. The choice of terms signifies the difference between politicization and co-option into the system, as between black and negro.

However, for Thompson, there were limits to how far he could concentrate on the problems of one ethnic group. His tendencies, as ever, were first to universalize the issue in characteristically humanist fashion, and secondly to fictionalize his narrative and make it subjective. Thompson links the killing of Salazar to the establishment's oppression of *all* non-conformers, when he cites it as a regional example of 'the standard Mitchell-Agnew theme: Don't fuck around, boy' (*GSH*, p. 153). In a typically subjective and possibly fictional aside, he mentions how he used Mace spray on one of Acosta's activist friends, Frank, 6 months earlier during a shared mescaline trip. Frank had told Thompson that if he ever showed up in East LA, he would carve the word 'Mace' all over his body. But now, somewhat worryingly, Thompson finds

---

[5] Salazar was a professional reporter with experience of Vietnam, who worked for the *Los Angeles Times* (*GSH*, p. 141). He became news director for KMEX-TV, the local Mexican-American station, and began to broadcast increasingly anti-establishment coverage, including allegations of police brutality. The death of Salazar is fictionalized in Acosta's autobiographical novel *The Revolt of the Cockroach People* (Acosta, 1989b).

Frank standing in front of him, chopping meat with a butcher's knife. Another Chicano asks what that 'goddamn *gabacho* pig writer' is doing there, as he knows enough to put them all in prison (p. 154).

Acosta's attitude to Thompson sometimes matched this. In a letter, he exhorted Thompson to 'quit playing the role that I'm some fucking native, a noble savage you discovered in the woods' (*FLA*, p. 447). Thompson's ambiguous response was to fictionalize Acosta in *Fear and Loathing in Las Vegas*, written at the same time as the article, and to mutate him into a Samoan rather than a Chicano, a larger-than-life figure who could stand for a marginalized, oppressed freak whose racial Otherness was just one more reason for the mainstream to reject him.[6]

Othello on Acid: Las Vegas, 1971

Fear and Loathing in Las Vegas was loosely based on the two trips Thompson made to Las Vegas with Acosta in early 1971. They were looking for a break from the extreme tension of Los Angeles: a temporary refuge where they could discuss the Salazar situation openly. Both men sought to articulate the failure of the 1960s project of radical social change:

> Both Thompson and Acosta chronicle the defeat of the sixties dream and attribute its demise to the same source. Each sees that his respective community prefers to remain locked within its traditional myopia, in its racist intolerance, in its isolated introversion. True, both men witnessed and participated in the efforts to change the society as well as in the key occurrences of official repression [...]. And both pour their disappointment out in Gonzo literature. (Bruce-Novoa, 1979, pp. 47–8)

Bruce-Novoa characterizes Thompson's Gonzo writing as the response of a defeated man. This is too pessimistic. In *Fear and Loathing in Las Vegas*, Thompson achieves a critique of his society's racism, orientalism and corruption that suggests militancy as much as disappointment. Its ethnic

---

6 Acosta replied to Thompson's treatment when he put Thompson into *The Revolt of the Cockroach People* as Stonewall, a white journalist with powerful connections who claims he can help Buffalo Z. Brown, Acosta's alter ego, but in fact offers little concrete support (Acosta, 1989b, p. 20). Thompson also appears in *The Autobiography of a Brown Buffalo* as Karl King. Acosta mockingly plays on Thompson/King's construction of him as a generic racial Other: 'I wanted to give her the Samoan bit again as I had done all those years of my search for a reconciliation with my ancestry. But it would not come. I could not joke about it as I had with the *americanos*' (Acosta, 1989a, p. 190).

comedies and ironies are part of its aggressive satire. *Vegas* seems to be a chaotic recreation of lived spontaneity, but was in fact written by Thompson some time after his visits to Las Vegas, in a relatively sober state, during breaks from composing the 'Strange Rumblings' article (see Chapter 2). With its superficially slapdash fragmentation, the novel artfully constructs a broken, divided reality, one of whose faultlines is race.

Ostensibly because of Thompson's fear of incriminating him, Acosta appeared in *Fear and Loathing in Las Vegas* in the guise of Raoul Duke's Samoan lawyer, who is never named except as Dr Gonzo, a patently ludicrous alias, or by his role, as 'my attorney' (*LV*, p. 4). Gonzo is not quite 'the person of color alter ego of classic American fiction' that one reader has claimed he is (DeKoven, 2004, p. 89). He is too protean and postmodern a figure for this. His ethnicity appears to be a minor detail, and to be highly variable.[7] In the opening paragraphs of the novel, Dr Gonzo is seen wearing Spanish sunglasses (*LV*, p. 3); however, by the time of the hotel scene, an hour or so later, the glasses have mysteriously become Brazilian (p. 24). When they check into the Mint 400 race later on, the sunglasses are Danish (p. 33). The attorney's ethnic mutability, suggested by his perpetually migrant sunglasses, is heightened by his bizarre attempt 'to facilitate the tanning process' by pouring beer onto his chest; in effect, to darken his complexion, to brown up (p. 3).

This is ironic given Acosta's status at the time as a leading advocate of the militant Chicano Brown Power movement and his own anger, revealed in correspondence with Thompson, at his failure to fit in with the privileged Anglo culture around Aspen, an exclusion which in his view was motivated by racial prejudice. He had 'mixed with the comfortable anglo' but 'Could Not Make It'; hence his return to Los Angeles and to Chicano politics (*FLA*, p. 253). This came in a letter the year before the trips to Las Vegas that gave rise to the novel. Acosta's experience of Anglo xenophobia is recapitulated when Duke and Gonzo pick up a hapless young hitchhiker. Duke explains to him: 'This man at the wheel is my *attorney*! [...] in spite of his race, this man is extremely valuable to me' (*LV*, pp. 6–8: emphasis in original). Gonzo's foreignness is dismissed as unimportant, but is mentioned nevertheless, as a hurdle that has to be cleared before Duke can explain their alleged mission. Likewise, when

---

7 Indeed, in the famous Ralph Steadman illustration of Duke and Gonzo in their car, with a stylized mesa in the background, that usually precedes Part One of the novel and often goes on the cover, Raoul Duke appears distinctly black and Gonzo white.

Duke acquires the money for the trip, in the form of an advance cash payment, he chides Gonzo: 'You Samoans are all the same [...]. You have no faith in the essential decency of the white man's culture' (p. 11). Total strangers give Duke dollar bills, and this is 'the American Dream in action!' (p. 11).

This is intended as a satirical comment on the arbitrariness and venality of gringo culture. Far from incarnating the Horatio Alger version of the American Dream, in which anyone can become successful through talent and hard work, the white man's USA is a greed-driven lottery. Gonzo's Samoan-ness is a pretext for Thompson to imply this, through Duke; the attorney's race works as a device to throw Anglo culture into relief.[8] Peter O. Whitmer has called Gonzo's anonymous foreignness 'a brilliant piece of symbolism', because even an unknown racial Other can aspire to power in America (Whitmer, 1993, p. 179). However, Gonzo is as disempowered as Duke. By making Gonzo an outsider, Duke can throw all sorts of supposedly informative explanations of US culture at him, which they both know are satirical asides.

The novel addresses racial tensions, but in the background; on the whole it prefers to concentrate on divisions of class and subculture, particularly between the drug culture and the mainstream. As Gonzo says, the American Dream is bullshit and should be forgotten; what they need to concentrate on is 'the Great Samoan Dream' (p. 20). He promptly chews up a blotter of acid. The Samoan dream is nothing to do with the real Samoa, which is co-opted as a sign of alterity to stand for the hedonistic ambitions of the depoliticized drug culture that by 1971 had abandoned its radical ideals and merely wanted to get as twisted as possible. The Samoan's comment is immediately followed on the radio by John Lennon's simplistic agitprop song 'Power to the People', which Duke comments wryly is 10 years too late (p. 21).

Despite appearances, the apolitical chemical excesses of Duke and Gonzo form part of a strategy of resistance by Thompson. His novel inverts the classic manoeuvre of power in capitalist society by which a social issue is privatized so that it is 'reconfigured as a problem arising from the psychological or mental health of particular individuals'

---

8 Like American tourists abroad, Duke and Gonzo wear Acapulco shirts and visit a Polynesian bar (p. 12). Again, as with Gonzo's Samoan appellation, foreignness becomes a metaphor. When reflecting on the hapless Okie hitchhiker's comment that he had never rode in a convertible before, the guilty Duke says he feels like King Farouk (p. 17): that is, one of the anti-democratic native elite, a member of the privileged few in a vastly unequal society.

(Venn, 2004, p. 97). Privatization would cause problems for Thompson later on, when his personas such as Raoul Duke became more visible and important than his own lived identity. Thompson's work was increasingly treated as a crude autobiographical narrative, a titillating display of the hang-ups and addictions of its central character, taken to be Thompson himself. This compromised the political force of his writing: the privatization of culture by corporations and the media 'has perverting effects in not only narrowing the range of the models of emplotment that are available or have authority in the process of reconfiguration – for instance, in relation to the cult of the celebrity – but in eliminating counter-hegemonic narratives' (Venn, 2004, p. 112). *Vegas* creates its own counter-hegemonic narrative by reversing the process of privatization, using the 'private kinkiness' (*LV*, p. 182) of the drug-saturated, dysfunctional Duke and Gonzo as a mirror to expose the legitimized hedonism and materialism of the society around them, and its propensity to violence and racism, fused above all in the Vietnam War.

Of all the characters he could have identified with, Duke chooses that of a displaced black soldier: 'I felt like Othello. [...] we'd already laid the groundwork for a classic tragedy. The hero was doomed; he had already sown the seed of his own downfall' (p. 122). The novel's action, like that of *Othello*, is conducted against a constant ground bass of conflict. Vietnam and Laos are on the television in the protagonists' hotel rooms, and the attorney, when drunk, pretends to be a traumatized Vietnam veteran to annoy some rednecks at a stoplight (pp. 151–2).

Vegas implies that a society that can create the Vietnam War is more criminal and less sane than a subculture that uses hallucinogenic drugs. In fact, war creates delusions as powerful as those generated by acid: meeting some militant race-goers out in the desert, the hung-over Duke and Gonzo see on the side of their jeeps paintings of 'Screaming Eagles carrying American Flags in their claws, a slant-eyed snake being chopped to bits by a buzz-saw made of stars & stripes', reminiscent of the morale-boosting designs added by soldiers to their aircraft and vehicles (p. 39). One jeep also sports a machine-gun mount. The militants ask the protagonists 'What *outfit* you fellas with?', and Duke and Gonzo have to assure them they are 'friendlies – hired geeks' and 'just good patriotic Americans like yourselves' (p. 39: emphasis in original). These crazies are cruising around the desert, living out their own hallucination of Vietnam, on an imaginary search and destroy mission whose target is unspecified but is implied to be anything unpatriotic or un-American; in short, anything foreign. Duke claims that a nearby journalist was responsible for *The Selling of the Pentagon*, a television documentary critical of the military, and the crazies immediately rush after him (p. 40).⁹

In the newspapers that Duke reads, the war is linked to the trade in heroin, to torture and to racist murder: one officer is reported to have shot his interpreter, claiming '"She was just a slope, anyway," meaning she was an Asiatic' (p. 73). Duke is relieved to feel that against this backdrop even he is 'a relatively respectable citizen', but is disturbed to find out that Muhammed Ali has been sentenced to 5 years for *refusing* to kill 'slopes' (p. 74).

In *Fear and Loathing in Las Vegas*, Vietnam, Laos and South-East Asia are the dwelling places of the slant-eyed and the slopes: Thompson's novel shows how this racist vocabulary denies the cultural identity of others 'by reducing the adversary to his biological physiognomy' (Anderson, 1983, p. 135). These undifferentiated, de-cultured spectres are used as catalysts to deliver the novel's account of the craziness that has taken over America, a nation that in Thompson's view once had a worthy identity but had come to compromise it fatally through fantasies of colonial domination. The Other is used as a sign to reveal the self, but the novel appears fully conscious of this process, unlike the orientalist tradition of Western scholarship and literature, which promotes 'the specially legitimated antipathy towards and downgrading' of the object of study that is so dominant in the orientalist's consciousness that it 'obscures the actualities before his eyes' (Said, 1995, p. 289).

'These Menacing Times': Laos and Vietnam, 1975

Thompson did not just chronicle the effects of the war in America: he travelled to Vietnam in 1975 to witness the fall of Saigon, the capital city of what was, in effect, a US colony. Thompson's arch enemy Richard Nixon had 'failed to recognize the organic nature of the insurgency or its substantial revolutionary component. Additionally, as a product of the previous ten years of U.S. policy, Nixon clung to the external aggression thesis explaining the war' (Carter, 2008, p. 244). American foreign policy during the late phase of the war was still

---

9 *The Selling of the Pentagon* was a 1971 CBS film about the military-industrial complex's PR effort. It aimed as much to expose the complicity of TV as to reveal the machinations of the military: '*The Selling of the Pentagon* was a milestone in the development of the television documentary, not so much for what it contained, but because it represented a clear statement that the networks could not be made to bend to government control in the technological era' (Jowett, 2010, n.p.).

predicated on the assumption that the Soviet Union and China were destabilizing a sovereign non-Communist state, South Vietnam. The fact that the South was an artificial client regime, created by the partitioning of Vietnam in 1954, was conveniently elided. Thompson makes clear his contempt for the South's puppet government in his account of the former premier Nguyen Cao Ky, a protégé of Lyndon B. Johnson, who had made sure 'that American correspondents who interviewed him understood that his personal hero was the late Adolf Hitler' (*DD*, p. 50).[10]

The US establishment either failed to see, or chose not to do anything about, the odious nature of the regime it was supporting and consistently refused to recognize the conflict as the uprising of one nation, Vietnam, seeking to unite itself. Instead, Johnson had escalated the war despite evidence that this was fruitless: 'Johnson had a legitimate choice on which way to proceed in Vietnam, a choice laid out *at the time* by both the opponents and proponents of negotiations' (Logevall, 2008, p. 89: emphasis in original). Thompson witheringly denounces America's colonial client state, and recognizes its debilitating effect on him, and by implication, the US as a whole: 'In its last hours, it [Saigon] became a desperate, overcrowded nightmare full of thieves, losers, pimps, con men, war junkies and many, many victims. Including me – although I am just beginning to understand this' (*DD*, p. 50).

Thompson's account of the fall of Saigon is prefaced by deliberately incongruous, absurd scenes. He describes how he heard the song 'Bye Bye Miss American Pie' with its refrain *'This'll be the day that I die* [...] booming out over the muzak in the air-conditioned top-floor bar of the [Hotel] Continental' while he watched incoming artillery shells explode in a rice paddy a mere five miles away (*DD*, p. 52: emphasis in original). He also visits Laos, writing of how:

> every time I think of Laos, my mind slips strangely out of focus and I see a chorus line of transvestites dancing in a sort of hypnotic trance at an all-night fertility festival while the government crumbles and grinning little men wearing huge wooden dildoes pass out leaflets saying the first act of the new Communist regime will be to legalize the use and cultivation of opium. (*DD*, p. 50)

---

10 References are taken from the *Rolling Stone* article 'Dance of the Doomed' (*DD*). A slightly different version appeared in *Songs of the Doomed* (*SD*, pp.161–79).

This skit is very reminiscent of William Burroughs, whose *Naked Lunch* Thompson had absorbed early in his adult life as part of 'the required reading of his generation' (McKeen, 2008, p. 41).[11] *Naked Lunch* is full of perverse erotic spectacle, often in the context of the same US satellite states covered by Thompson's early reports. Describing a Chimu fiesta, Burroughs's narrator takes on the pose of a bemused American outsider: 'Gentle reader, the ugliness of that spectacle buggers description. Who can be a cringing pissing coward, yet vicious as a purple-assed mandrill, alternating these deplorable conditions like vaudeville skits?' (Burroughs, 2005, p. 34).

Thompson's dildo dance passage can also be interpreted as an ironic recapitulation of Jean-Paul Sartre's account, in his preface to Fanon's *The Wretched of the Earth*, of ritual dancing as a vain response to colonialism on the part of the dehumanized subject peoples. For the natives, the dance 'relaxes their painfully contracted muscles' and articulates 'the No they dare not voice, the murders they dare not commit' (Sartre, 2004, p. liii). The dancing is originally enacted as a revival of old rituals for a new purpose not always understood. It is ideal fuel for the orientalist fantasy travestied in Thompson's Laotian vaudeville; the transvestites' and dildo-wearers' antics are evidence of what Thompson, parodying racist psychology, calls 'the understandably scrambled Indochinese mind [...] in these menacing times' (*DD*, p. 47). It is, presumably, this 'Dance of the Doomed' that gives Thompson's piece its title, but the dance could equally refer to the clumsy and increasingly desperate steps of US foreign policy.

The transvestite skit does not prepare the reader for a jarring juxtaposition. Comic perversity turns into serious politics: in the next two paragraphs, Thompson writes of how Saigon was surrounded by fifteen to twenty Communist divisions, and details the collapse of South Vietnamese banking and communications prior to a North Vietnamese/Viet Cong victory accomplished 'more or less on American terms, by means of brute force and sheer military skill' (*DD*, p. 50). Here the native is beating the colonizer at his own game, responding to violence by imitating it with surpassing ruthlessness. This is exactly the response Fanon urged on the dispossessed of the colonies. Religious revivals and dances are mocked and abandoned by the native when 'the colonized subject,

---

11 Thompson hugely admired Burroughs as an archetype of the free individual: 'he was the first white man to be busted for marijuana in my time. William was the Man. [...] He was my hero a long time before I ever heard of him' (*LY*, p. 40). He later met Burroughs, and fired guns with him; Burroughs, then 80 years old, still 'shot like he wrote – with extreme precision and no fear' (*TS*, p. 54).

machine gun at the ready, finally confronts the only force which challenges his very being: colonialism' (Fanon, 2004, p. 20). Thompson propels his reader from the high camp of an imaginary Laos to the military camps of the real Vietnam, from a nation still in a colonial mentality of articulating resistance as theatre to one that has progressed to driving the colonizer out.

'A Fool Lies Here Who Tried to Hustle the East': Hawaii, 1980–81

Five years later, Thompson shifted his focus from the hard, military colonialism of Vietnam to the soft power evident in another US outpost, Hawaii. On the morning of 7 December 1980, exactly 39 years after Pearl Harbor, he stood on the site of the atrocity, watching the Honolulu Marathon and wondering what 'kind of sick instinct' (*CL*, p. 69) had created the grotesque display he saw before him: 'There's no sane reason at all for these runners' (p. 73). Haunting Thompson's bafflement is the spectre of US cultural hegemony. Recreational running, a fad of the American bourgeoisie, now so favoured by 'Every rich liberal in the Western world' that it is treated as 'a goddamn religion' (p. 38), has become globally exported, leading to a worrying depoliticization of all concerned. Thompson observes mockingly that those who burned their draft cards in the 1960s are now masochistic fitness fetishists, 'torturing themselves in the streets' and creating a 'half-wit spectacle' (p. 78).

William McKeen has described *The Curse of Lono*, Thompson's novel that emerged from the trip, as 'perhaps his most underrated work' (McKeen, 1991, p. 88). Indeed, it is an important part of Thompson's oeuvre and shows significant development from his 1970s writing, although it has been critically neglected.[12] It is a critique of late twentieth-century US neo-colonialism and therefore anticipates the current globalization

---

12 *The Curse of Lono* sold 'about 200,000 copies' (Perry, 2009, p. 217), but had fallen out of print until revived by Taschen in 2004, the year before Thompson's suicide. It has been marginalized or dismissed in most accounts of Thompson's life and work: '[The part about the marathon] was Hunter in his top form. [...] The rest of the book was mostly a series of false starts and half-baked ideas' (Rob Fleder, cited in Carroll, 1993, p. 212); 'Since *The Curse of Lono*, his books had become pastiches of previously published material' (McKeen, 2008, p. 320); 'a best-seller for a short while, but far from his best work' (Harold Conrad, cited in *C*, p. 66); 'There are some wonderful things in that book, but it was also the beginning of the end' (Alan Rinzler, cited in Wenner and Seymour, 2007, p. 233); 'I never read it. It just seemed like an indulgence' (Jann Wenner, cited in Wenner and Seymour, 2007, p. 235).

debate.¹³ At the same time, it wrestles with the connected problem of its author's acknowledged status as a celebrity, or branded American product (see Chapter 1).

Thanks to the success of his earlier work, Thompson had become trapped in his Gonzo persona, but he still depended on it for financial reasons. *The Curse of Lono* reflects his consequent commercialization of the Gonzo formula. Although Thompson's persona in the novel, who shared the author's name (*CL*, p. 19), was essentially the same drug-slugging reporter as before, he was far more slickly packaged: it was as if Thompson had finally drifted away from the outrageous, of-the-moment journalism of his key works and towards the staid, reflective banality of the coffee table book. On first reading *The Curse of Lono* seems merely to repeat the Gonzo formula. In basic plot terms, it has exactly the same premise as *Fear and Loathing in Las Vegas*: the Thompson character and his sidekick, in this case Ralph Steadman, travel to an exotic location, ostensibly to cover a sporting event, but in the process engage in a stoned, picaresque ramble through city and landscape, enraging the locals.

As ever with Thompson, the plot begins in the author's experience but almost immediately spirals into cartoon-like surrealism. In 1980, Thompson was commissioned by Paul Perry, executive editor of *Running* magazine, to write an article on the Honolulu Marathon. Thompson accepted the commission and flew to Hawaii with his fiancée. Steadman also came. The marathon is over soon after the story begins. Thompson and Steadman then take refuge in rented houses on the Kona coast of Hawaii, a supposedly sheltered area which turns out to be battered by constant waves and storms. After a fishing trip, Thompson returns with a huge marlin he has caught, in an echo of Hemingway.¹⁴ When Thompson

---

13 'Globalization, of course, is not one thing, and the multiple processes that we recognize as globalization are not unified or univocal' (Hardt and Negri, 2001, p. xv). The term has been defined as 'the removal of barriers to free trade and the closer integration of national economies' (Stiglitz, 2002, p. ix), but is also acknowledged to be 'political, technological and cultural, as well as economic' (Giddens, 1999, p. 10). It is difficult to pin down: 'multiple conversations coexist (although few real dialogues), which do not readily afford a coherent or definitive characterization' (Held and McGrew, 2003, p. 2). Globalization attracts controversy rather than agreement, but there is a limited consensus: 'globalization is being shaped by technological changes, involves the reconfiguration of states [and ...] involves more intensive interaction across wider space and in shorter time than before, in other words the experience of a shrinking world' (Nederveen Pieterse, 2004, p. 8).

14 The most obvious allusion is to *The Old Man and the Sea* (Hemingway, 2004b), but Thompson also echoes Hemingway's non-fiction on fishing, such as 'The Great Blue River' (Hemingway, 1967, pp. 403–16).

finally comes into harbour, he has the revelation that he is the Hawaiians' god, their deified, long-departed ruler, Lono: he shouts this out to the crowd.[15]

Thompson is thus repeating, in somewhat altered form, the story of Captain James Cook, the explorer who discovered Hawaii in 1779: Cook, who had unwittingly arrived at the season prophesied for the return of Lono, was worshipped and then murdered in a dispute over a missing boat. Thompson, having broken local taboos with his blasphemous announcement of his own godhead, and, just as importantly, having damaged the local real-estate business with his outrageous behaviour, has to go into hiding at the City of Refuge, a traditional sanctuary, after the local realtors send thugs to kill him. At the sanctuary Mitch Kamahili, a park ranger, conceals him and supplies him with beer. The text ends with Steadman's double-page illustration of a departing Boeing 747, with Thompson's head sticking out of the top and the airline logo on the tail replaced by 'Aloha Lono' (*CL*, pp. 206–7).

As this suggests, *The Curse of Lono* mocks its Gonzo protagonist as both a tourist and a buffoon: it comments on the subjectivism of Gonzo ironically, pushing celebrity to its ludicrous limit by making the protagonist a god. At the same time, the novel demonstrates how authorship can emerge from the historical forces that shape subjectivity, such as globalization:

> globalisation is not a 'natural event'. It is not an ahistorical happening that takes place within a cultural and political vacuum. It is part of an ongoing set of processes, mapped into the very idea of history that lies at the heart of Western narratives of self-identity. (Cox, 2007, p. 98)

Thompson was well aware that by the 1980s, Gonzo had become a marketable commodity. Steadman reported that 'Hunter had developed an unhealthy hunger for anything that generated money' (Steadman, 2006, p. 184). A new Gonzo project was the ideal source of cash. Accordingly, the project had to appear as distinctively branded as possible. Steadman placed great importance on the literal signature of both author and illustrator: 'Much of the layout incidentally will require my distinctive

---

15 There is an echo here of Steadman's Leonardo da Vinci project, which he was working on at the same time as he and Thompson composed *The Curse of Lono*. After much frustration, Steadman had his creative breakthrough about two-thirds of the way through the project: 'Why didn't I try to *be* Leonardo? *I, Leonardo* became the title' (Steadman, 2006, p. 202: emphasis in original).

handwriting – and yours. Chapter headings, titling, etc. It is a necessary part of the characteristic style of the subject' (Steadman, 2006, p. 230).

'A High Mix of Memoirs & Madness That is Also a Milestone': the Gonzo Brand and Thompson's Audience

Thompson branded *The Curse of Lono* in a letter to his publishers. With characteristic hyperbole leavened with irony, he outlined the significance of his as yet unwritten text to its prospective audience:

> If we can create a high mix of Memoirs & Madness that is also a Milestone with even a hint of continuity into this weird new world of the '80's, I think we can lash out a classic that will sell at least a million copies, if it's properly managed. We are looking at a whole generation of refugees out there who desperately need a book (or a film or a statement in some form) to give them a sense of personal continuity in a world they never expected to have to cope with. […] Yes. We will skulk off the plane in Honolulu with the hopes & dreams of a whole generation in our hands. (cited in Steadman, 2006, pp. 193–4)

Thompson thus set out to reach the disillusioned 1960s generation, the decline of whose ideals was articulated in *Fear and Loathing in Las Vegas* (see Chapter 2). Thompson hoped *The Curse of Lono* would chart the shallows his generation had to navigate in the 1980s, the time of the Reagan presidency: 'a very nasty decade, a brutal Darwinian crunch that will not be a happy time for free-lancers' (*CL*, p. 78). Thompson was thus positioning his product, working out the development of the Gonzo franchise by planning his own performance of the author function, or 'the determination of [… the author's] individual perspective, the analysis of his social position, and the revelation of his basic design' (Foucault, 2000, p. 215: see Chapter 1).

The text is doubly branded: by Steadman's artwork and by the positioning of its subject, Thompson, as the Gonzo icon of the hard-working reporter in the middle of exotic and dangerous Otherness. Thompson's text reinforces this iconography. At the end, Thompson finds himself holed up in a hut in the City of Refuge: 'I am in here with a battery-powered typewriter, two blankets from the King Kam, my miner's headlamp, a kitbag full of speed and other vitals, and my fine Samoan war club' (*CL*, p. 197).

In reality, Steadman states, neither he nor Thompson ever entered the hut because of their superstitious fear of the interior. Instead, Steadman 'nipped over the spiked, wooden fence and Hunter, now accomplice to this act, took a Polaroid picture of me standing with the gods – our fathers' (Steadman, 2006, p. 223). This furtive, rather amateurish tourism contrasts comically with the macho portrait of the Gonzo reporter drawn in the book, and vividly demonstrates the naivety of confusing Thompson with his persona.

In the final City of Refuge scenes, as from the outset, *The Curse of Lono* is based on fictitious characters. It establishes itself as the product of *two* personas, Thompson's and Steadman's, and sets out its structure accordingly: the first subject will have the experience and the second will mediate it visually, with the illustrations generally juxtaposed with the corresponding prose. The viewpoints of Thompson's sources are introduced, which complicate the matter further: these include Mark Twain's *Letters from Hawaii* and Richard Hough's *The Last Voyage of Captain James Cook*. The result is a highly effective evolution of, and commentary on, Thompson's celebrity and the Gonzo brand. The text foregrounds the parallel of Thompson and James Cook as interlopers and false gods, and hints at the fundamental ambiguity of the novel: its critique of US neo-colonialism through a celebrity protagonist who participates in tourism.

'The First Thing I Saw on the Outskirts Was a Texaco Station': Globalization and Colonialism

Thompson writes that when he came in on a fishing boat, having caught the large marlin, he was screaming '*I am Lono!*' at the superstitious crowd, who were upset by the spectacle (p. 194: emphasis in original). Here, albeit in an ironic tone, Thompson inverts colonialist xenography by becoming the stranger himself. He is the foreigner, the reincarnation of Cook, the alien visitor who nevertheless has a religious claim on the Hawaiians. Upon finally realizing that he is Lono, Thompson 'immediately shed all religious and rational constraints, and embraced a New Truth' (p. 196).

This is a recapitulation of Thompson's Gonzo technique of making a beast of himself, as seen in 'The Kentucky Derby is Decadent and Depraved' and *Fear and Loathing in Las Vegas*. However, by the time of *The Curse of Lono*, Thompson and his Gonzo persona were famous: accordingly, Thompson's character had by now metamorphosed into an object of fear and worship, the deified centre of the ritual. It is as if the depraved journalist of 'The Kentucky Derby', in his new incarnation as Lono, had become fused with a more self-conscious update of Conrad's Mister Kurtz.

And yet, this is far from the Africa of *Heart of Darkness*. In Hawaii, Thompson is more ambiguously situated than Marlow: he is both abroad *and* in the USA. Rather than simply venturing into a mysterious world of Otherness, he is, at the same time, a mere tourist with ideas above his station. Lindsey Michael Banco has called *Fear and Loathing in Las Vegas* a novel of 'anti-tourism' and has shown how Raoul Duke is in fact similar to the conservative, money-grubbing, drinking and whoring tourists he affects to despise (Banco, 2010, p. 101). *The Curse of Lono* recapitulates the earlier text, but it is not so much anti-tourist as an exposure of a major vector of globalization – the mediated corporate homogeneity that spreads a veneer of American-ness over Hawaii and then allows the mainland to claim it.

Although Thompson wanders across 'a desert of hostile black rocks, mile after mile of raw moonscape and ominous low-lying clouds' he finds that 'the first thing I saw on the outskirts was a Texaco station, then a McDonald's hamburger stand' (p. 82). Thompson's lunar image and his point about the isolation of the land suggest that he is not in the USA he knows, despite the familiar corporate logos. He is crossing an old, solidified lava flow, implying that this ugly landscape is part of a temporarily habitable, alien planet of flux, where the tectonic plates of overlaid American values will be subject to unpredictable tremors.

In keeping with this, quotations from Hough's *Last Voyage of Captain Cook* and other sources are interwoven with the main narrative so as to block the flow of the story and create juxtapositions that expose the sometimes sinister, sometimes bathetic echoes of Cook that occur in Thompson's exploration of the islands. At the climax of the novel, Thompson-Lono comes to personify the overweening brutality of American neo-colonialism. The reader is prepared for the incident by an excerpt from Hough which describes the murder of Cook by a crowd of natives in the surf just off the shore. Cook is first stunned with a club, then stabbed with a *pahoa* (knife), then mutilated: 'The natives fell on the corpse like wolves upon a fallen moose' (p. 176). Cook's body is cut up and the parts distributed amongst the chieftains, with the greatest part going to the king (p. 177).

Soon afterwards, Thompson arrives on the pier, screaming and brandishing his war club and declaring himself to be Lono: 'The crowd was horrified […] they hated everything we stood for, and when I jumped up on the pier and began whipping on the fish with the war club, nobody even smiled' (p. 190). The allusion to the murder of Cook is blatant. By clubbing the fish, Thompson is symbolically killing a native. Throughout, *The Curse of Lono* links the Hawaiians symbolically to fish, invoking the stereotype of the noble savage, or non-white who can lose him/herself in ecstatic oneness with nature. At the end of the novel, Thompson describes his friendship with Mitch Kamahili, who believes that the fish in the bay are his family (p. 202). Sometimes, when drunk and stoned, Mitch dives into the water, swimming out into the ocean 'with the atavistic grace of some mammal finally remembering where it really wanted to be' (p. 203).

Moreover, Thompson is, at this point, Lono himself. He is thus reversing the earlier murder of Cook/Lono, taking the form of the returned colonizer, Cook's descendant, wreaking vengeance. It is not surprising that the crowd reacts in horror. Thompson follows this up with a photograph of himself with the fish, signed 'Lono' and captioned by hand, 'We killed like champions' (p. 192).

The caption anticipates Thompson's coverage of the Grenada invasion in 1984, the year after *The Curse of Lono* appeared in book form. Thompson assessed Grenada as 'one of those low-risk, high-gain, cost-plus operations that every West Point graduate dreams of. […] Bash the buggers silly; bomb the insane; walk heavy, talk wild, and kick ass in every direction' (*KF*, p. 209). As in *The Curse of Lono*, he uses the imagery of animal extermination: 'We have seen America's interests threatened in the Caribbean basin, and we have crushed that threat like a roach' (*KF*, p. 212).[16] *The Curse of Lono*'s violence is carried out symbolically, on the bodies of fish. Nevertheless, Thompson invites the reader to make connections between tourism and imperialism, and between the natives' clubbing of Cook and Thompson's clubbing of the marlin. In a telling aside, he leaves the reader in no doubt as to the strategic importance of the Hawaiian Islands: they are 'our only real base in the Pacific' and had the English not been so imprudent as to give them away, they 'might have controlled the whole Pacific for the next two hundred years' (*CL*, p. 111).

In another allusion to the harder side of US colonialism, Thompson invents an alter ego, Gene Skinner, who meets him at the airport (p. 33). Skinner is essentially a meaner, nastier, more outspoken version of Thompson's usual persona. The claimed link between them goes back to Thompson's 1975 trip to Vietnam to cover the fall of Saigon for *Rolling Stone*. Skinner is a stereotype of the shady operator, the intelligence agent-cum-smuggler: 'When I knew him in Saigon he was working for the CIA, flying helicopters for Air America and making what some people who knew him said was more than $20,000 a week in the opium business' (p. 34). Thompson described Skinner as 'a new character for the

---

16 Thompson reworked these ideas in 'Polo is My Life', where Genghis Khan's Mongol horsemen use animals as vehicles rather than victims. Again, there is an implied metaphor for American military might: 'The Mongols were merciless brutes with no sense of humour. They rode powerful horses at top speed and trampled anything that got in their way. Nothing could stop them. In time they conquered the whole world' (*PL*, p. 47).

Eighties. It is a brutal attitude – anti-humanist. [...] a character to fit the times' (C, p. 54).

The text ends with Thompson ensconced in the historic Hawaiian sanctuary of City of Refuge, armed with a bullhorn that only he knows how to use; he has put duct tape over the on-off volume switch, a ruse which, of course, fools the low-tech natives. He shouts across the rocks to order ice cubes: 'I uttered one final wavering burst of oriental gibberish, then tossed the bullhorn aside' (p. 202). The bullhorn is a metonym for Thompson's awkward relationship with Hawaii. He wants to write about the islands (he is busy getting through typewriter paper, hacking out letters and drafts) and adopt a voice that is his own, and yet he travesties the speech of the natives. He comes across as a stiff, alienated stranger; a parody of a tourist ordering a waiter about in pidgin: 'ALOHA! ICE CUBES MAHALO' (p. 201). Thompson seeks authenticity, but knows that his work will verge ambiguously on recycling old orientalist tropes and colonial plots: 'they're waiting for me out there by the parking lot, but the natives won't let them come any closer. They killed me once [as Lono], and they're not about to do it again' (p. 197).

The Curse of Lono thus demonstrates the underrated sophistication of Thompson's best later work. It is a self-ironic, reflexive reworking of *Fear and Loathing in Las Vegas* for the era of globalization, by an author who knew he had become trapped by his own brand. As well as enacting some of Thompson's anxieties about celebrity, it updates *Vegas* in order to use the Gonzo formula to anticipate a newly emerging world: that of post-Cold War American neo-colonialism, encapsulated by the increasingly rapid spread of US business and tourism. Thompson intercuts his text with excerpts from Hough and others to create complex juxtapositions that deepen his story, give it intertextual roots and situate it historically. As he did throughout his Gonzo writing, he positions himself ambiguously in the narrative as both observer and participant; thus, he is complicit in the neo-colonial politics of tourism even has he pours scorn upon them.

6 Conclusion: 'The Place of Definitions'

The modern nation state, a product of the Enlightenment, created its citizens as subjects. Michel Foucault argues that in the eighteenth century, the time of the Founding Fathers, the newly democratic nations, such as the USA, positioned themselves, in effect, as substitutes for the church:

> It was a question no longer of leading people to their salvation in the next world but, rather, ensuring it in this world. And in this context, the word 'salvation' takes on different meanings: health, well-being (that is, sufficient wealth, standard of living), security, protection against accidents. (Foucault, 2002, p. 334)

The state, as modelled here, is not inimical to personal freedom. On the contrary, it promotes an *image* of the individual as autonomous, and even offers a limited degree of *actual* autonomy, as a means of creating the subjectivity of its citizens on its own terms. The modern state was developed as 'a very sophisticated structure in which individuals can be integrated, under one condition: that this individuality would be shaped in a new form, and submitted to a set of very specific patterns' (Foucault, 2002, p. 334).

The post-Enlightenment nation state's capacity to nurture individuality created a philosophical problem for Thompson. Was he, by acting out his individualist beliefs, merely conforming to a prefabricated construct of American personal freedom that the state already endorsed and indeed regarded as central to itself? Foucault defines three forms of power that categorize the individual and make him or her a subject in the dual sense of something not only ruled from above, but also motivated by a consciousness of its own autonomy: these are 'domination (ethnic, social and religious)' economic exploitation and 'that which ties the individual to himself and submits him to others in this way' (Foucault, 2002, p. 331). He calls this last form 'the submission of subjectivity' (p. 332). Resistance to this last form of power must involve 'a struggle for a new subjectivity' outside the formulations offered by the state (p. 332). Foucault's account is more optimistic than Althusser's construction of ideology as all-pervading and constitutive of the subject (see Chapter 3). In Foucault's view, the

Conclusion: 'The Place of Definitions' 153

subject, though continually interpellated by the state and inevitably shaped by power relations, can potentially reconstruct itself on dissident lines.

The ambiguity of Thompson's self-fashioning, and of the evolving personas in his work, originates in the tension between the two possibilities of framing his subjectivity inside and outside the constructions offered by the state. Edgework offered a possible way out of this dilemma. If drug use or dangerous driving could create a liminal zone between safety and annihilation (see Chapter 4), then Thompson's desire to traverse the edge so often – or at least, write *as if* he were doing so – can be explained. Existence on the edge offered a defiant posture of resistance and a very real threat of crashing or overdosing; it also ensured that the subject was mobile, in transition between safety and insanity or death. Thus Thompson, as an edgeworker, could never be pinned down to a manufactured role, even one as superficially anti-statist as that of the stoned freak, rugged frontiersman or motorcycle outlaw. The threat of subjective dissolution was too strong for that.

I have argued throughout this book that Thompson adhered to the Founding Fathers' ideals of liberty; that he regarded the Constitution and its amendments, especially the fourth, as almost sacred; but that he believed that fraudulent, exploitative self-promoters like Nixon had travestied them, and corrupted the country from the top down. Fundamentally, Thompson was not a revolutionary; instead, he wanted to return the Republic to its original template. The problem with this thesis is that, although broadly true, it limits Thompson to a state-defined identity; that of a reincarnated patriot of 1776, a troublemaker of the Boston Tea Party variety, resisting the attempts of a cowardly, mendacious empire to impose an unfair set of laws upon him.

What if, instead of this, Thompson's search for autonomy by means of the lodge, the frontier or through edgework represented an attempt to construct a new subjectivity along the lines specified by Foucault? Foucault suggests how problematic this exercise might be:

> Maybe the target nowadays is not to discover what we are but to refuse what we are. We have to imagine and to build up what we could be to get rid of this kind of political 'double bind,' which is the simultaneous individualization and totalization of modern power structures. [… This will] liberate us both from the state and from the type of individualization linked to the state. (Foucault, 2002, p. 336).

Thompson felt this problem keenly. He resisted state interpellation, but was at risk of defining himself on the establishment's terms as an outsider whose very identity was shaped by dissidence. He baited Nixon mercilessly, but was also well aware that he depended on him for much of his best writing. His obituary of the deceased ex-president opens, 'Richard Nixon is gone now, and I am poorer for it' (*BS*, p. 239). This admits to exactly the sort of co-dependency that the state fosters in order to maintain existing power structures. Thompson knew this. He engaged with politics not only in order to control his environment, meaning to carve out a territory relatively free of official interference, but also to allow himself unhindered access to the one space where he could best attempt to build a new subjectivity free from the models offered by the state.

This space was the page. It was in his writing – and especially, *during* his writing – that Thompson was most free to enjoy himself and realize himself. As he told William McKeen in 1990, 'I haven't found a drug yet that can get you anywhere near as high as sitting at a desk writing, trying to imagine a story no matter how bizarre it is' (*C*, p. 97). This is how a key paradox can be resolved: that of Thompson's faith in the realization of an authentic self, set against his expression of this through a proliferation of fictional personas and through a Gonzo style that challenges the reader to assess how much – or more often, how little – of the outrageous farrago of images on the page is true.

In the final analysis, Gonzo was not performance art. It was not excessive drinking, illicit drug use, dangerous driving, shooting guns, or painting 'Fuck the Pope' on boats (McKeen, 2008, pp. 152–3). It was, instead, a discourse, a phenomenon of language. Thus, Thompson's identity in his work is not to be discovered in the antics of Raoul Duke, Gene Skinner, Yail Bloor, Dr Gonzo, the 'Thompson' on the page and all his other characters, however hilarious they are, but in the words that create them; in the flow of sentences, the metaphors, the rhythms and patterns of meaning.

This explains Thompson's faith in the unrevised first draft, his notorious tardiness and his tendency to leave the page blank until as late as possible before an approaching deadline, upon which he would begin to write manically: 'I don't say this with any pride, but I really couldn't imagine writing without a desperate deadline' (*C*, p. 156). Thompson was at his most self-assured when composing spontaneously: 'I know when I'm hitting it. I know when I'm on. I can usually tell because the copy's clean' (p. 158). This came out of his intuitive sense that he was most able to fulfil himself during the act of writing. From a young age, Thompson had wanted to be a novelist, and had literally copied the actions of other writers: he had typed out pages of Fitzgerald and Hemingway word for word, only to discover that Gonzo, the style that he branded as his own authentic literary mode, emerged not from the careful absorption of canonical models, but from the serendipitous combination of desperation, tiredness and an imminent deadline, when

Conclusion: 'The Place of Definitions' 155

he sent his unedited copy to *Scanlan's* for 'The Kentucky Derby is Decadent and Depraved' (see Chapter 1).

Not all his subsequent Gonzo work followed this template. Writing a story in real time, preferably as events actually occurred, remained an ideal that Thompson aimed for but rarely achieved. Even 'The Kentucky Derby' began and ended with long drafted sections. The notebook-based middle section – in fact, only eighteen paragraphs – reads as if crammed in by Thompson afterwards, as the result of a conscious decision to pad out his material in order to meet his deadline. He even signalled this section with a clear cue to the reader: 'taken as a whole, with sporadic memory flashes, the notes seem to tell the story. To wit:' (*GSH*, p. 38).

Thompson's problematic model of seemingly spontaneous reporting constructed after the event has canonical antecedents. In 1798, just after the birth of the USA as an independent nation, the English Romantic poet William Wordsworth, who sympathized strongly with the Founding Fathers' ideals, famously claimed that poetry was 'the spontaneous overflow of powerful feelings' but also that it 'takes its origin from emotion recollected in tranquillity' (Wordsworth, 2006, p. 273). This implies a strong creative tension between the spontaneity of the original feeling and the degree of distance required for tranquil recollection. Substitute 'deadline-induced chaos' for 'tranquillity' and we have an approximation of Thompson's model.

Wordsworth was neither a journalist nor a recreational drug user, and his writing was vastly different from Thompson's. Nevertheless, Gonzo might be read as Romanticism updated for the twentieth-century world of Nixon, LSD and television. Beneath his self-criticism and his streetwise cynicism, Thompson adhered to the Romantic template of the visionary capable of 'the unaccountable flight of spontaneous genius' (Berlin, 1999, p. 6). This inspired composer could, at least in theory, demonstrate the possibilities available to the human race through fulfilling his own potential: 'In [Wordsworth's poem] *Tintern Abbey* mankind is seen to be inherently capable of redemption through an act of self-realization' (Wu, 1998, p. xxxiii). Thus in creating Gonzo as a vehicle for his individualist, humanist project, Thompson had allowed himself to inherit something of the sensibility of the late eighteenth century, the period of Thomas Jefferson and Tom Paine, a time when the 'fashionableness of humanitarian sympathy was part of the ground-swell of radical political feeling' (Day, 1996, p. 12).

Thompson cherished the image of writing as improvised music; initially, this may have been because of the fashionable associations of jazz or rock, or the Beat generation's veneration of the unedited first draft, but Thompson also appreciated that his craft, like a musician's, was best expressed at the moment of performance, and who he was, or was in the process of becoming – that is, his authentic self – was best realized at this moment. As he wrote as early as 1958, 'you can either impose yourself on reality and *then* write about it, or you can impose yourself on reality *by* writing' (*PH*, p. 130: emphasis in original). Thompson divided writers into 'the action men and the thought men' (p. 129). He put Rabelais, Hemingway and Fitzgerald into the first category; Joyce, Proust and Pound were in the second. Thompson's method of putting himself through an experience and then writing it up would suggest he was an action man: *Hell's Angels* and *Fear and Loathing in Las Vegas* set a precedent for the rest of his work in this respect.

However, Thompson did not simply impose himself on reality and then record this on the page: he created himself in and through his fictions. Thus, he was most himself *when* writing. Indeed, nearly all of his readers knew him only through his work. Thompson became Duke, the man melded into the persona: the writing became as real as, or more real than, the original experience. Despite the subjective basis of most of Thompson's journalism, his temperamental preference for the action men, his political activism and the gregarious surface of his social life, Thompson was also a thought man, or one whose principal means of imposing himself on reality was by writing itself: 'The most overriding of all human desires is the need to amount to something. [...] As Faulkner says, writing is his way of saying "Kilroy was here," of imposing himself, however briefly, on reality' (*PH*, p. 128).

Like the transcendentalists who came before him, Thompson sought to make history rather than be made by it. The blank page offered Thompson the widest and most fertile uncharted space he could ever know, a *terra incognita* that, unlike the long-vanished geographical frontier, could never be fenced off, subdivided and neutralized by a state-imposed 'closure of the map' (Bey, 2003, p. 100). Although not physically dangerous, composition always posed the risk of *literary* death through failure or burnout. It was, then, a form of edgework: together the typewriter and the page created a liminal zone between achievement and oblivion.

In my first chapter, I argued that Thompson was what Claude Lévi-Strauss termed a *bricoleur*, or an improviser who used ready-made materials. It was through his engagement with powerful master narratives and outside agencies – myth, ideology, the state, hallucinogenic drugs – that Thomspon created his *bricolage*, found the edge and defined himself. Without an antagonist or without danger, Thompson was a lesser writer. This is why, as I argued in the chapter on the American Dream, it is much easier to discover what Thompson was *against* than what he stood *for*. The Dream proved impossible to define, hence his failure to complete the contracted book for Random House.

Instead, rather like Raoul Duke at the Old Psychiatrist's Club, Thompson wandered through the rubble that remained after the several seismic shocks to the Dream that occurred on and between Pearl Harbor and 9/11. These two rents in the fabric of the American world picture happened almost at the beginning and end of Thompson's life, and framed his adult awareness of the world. Between World War II and the War on Terror came Vietnam, the conflict that produced 'Dance of the Doomed' and informed several of Thompson's major works. Vietnam confirmed his intuition that America had become what the Founding Fathers had despised; an imperialist superpower. The war consolidated Thompson's anti-colonial sensibility, which had been catalysed during his early travels in South America while working for the *National Observer* and his residence in Puerto Rico that spawned *The Rum Diary*.

Like the USA, Thompson wrote himself into being: his work was his Declaration of Independence. On the page, he constructed his own Republic: not Plato's utopian state, but a divided nation that had lost its core values and was in the grip of at worst evil and at best incompetent politicians who sought to lure people away from the individualist frontier spirit that had originally driven the Union. The Gonzo Republic that Thompson created was not a realist portrait of the banal surface of America but was a trenchant dissection that exposed its often cancerous innards; a malevolent, grotesque subterranean world of predatory leaders, swine-like officials, greedheads and desperate freaks.

All this was brought to light by a cartoon persona, Duke/Skinner/Thompson, whose outrageous insubstantiality and deliberate lack of psychological depth were evidence of Thompson's refusal to steer towards the sirens of mimesis. By forging himself as an anti-realist, hyperbolic, manic anti-hero in his writing, Thompson posed the problem of human authenticity in twentieth-century USA. Could a thinking American citizen be anything more than a paper figure, a cartoon, in a nation that encouraged mendacity, shallowness and ignorance?

The answer was that a deeper sense of self *was* possible, but only through perceiving the sinister work of the greedheads and swine for what it was, even to the extent of admitting one's complicity in the whole business. Thompson and Steadman looking in the mirror at the Kentucky Derby, or Duke and Gonzo stumbling upon the rubble of the Old Psychiatrist's Club, symbolize the problem of selfhood and the state as Thompson saw it: when the Republic was ruined and corrupted, he knew that he was tainted by it and left without a national Dream. But through *writing* about the loss, Thompson could begin to set out for the most open frontier he knew he would ever find, to steer towards 'the place of definitions' (*HA*, p. 323).

Appendix I   Thompson on Film

The 'Thompson' who appears in the various film adaptations and documentaries is as protean as the Duke/Thompson/Skinner persona in the fiction. The filmic record is dominated by the readings, acting and voice-over work of Johnny Depp (see *Fear and Loathing in Las Vegas* and *Gonzo* especially), though Bill Murray deserves credit for his early portrayal of Thompson in *Where the Buffalo Roam*. Several significant commentators recur in interviews across several documentaries, like the historian Douglas Brinkley, now literary executor of the Hunter S. Thompson estate, and Thompson's first and second wives, Sondi Wright (formerly Sandy Thompson) and Anita Thompson. The film-maker Wayne Ewing, a personal friend of Thompson, has made a prolific and valuable record of the author's life and times, and all his DVDs are available from his website (see Appendix 2). Below, I have not attempted the futile task of imposing an overall interpretation on the film record; instead, I have simply highlighted some significant points of each film for the interested student or researcher.

Wayne Ewing, *Animals, Whores and Dialogue: Breakfast with Hunter 2* (2010)

The title of this sequel to *Breakfast with Hunter* comes from Thompson, who had taped the words 'Animals, Whores, Dialogue, Electricity' above the keys of his electric typewriter, as a reminder to add these ingredients to his writing whenever possible. Wayne Ewing's film has the same fly-on-the-wall style as *Breakfast with Hunter* and includes additional footage from many of the same events covered in the earlier documentary. Ewing has clearly used some material here that he did not have room to include in *Breakfast with Hunter*, but the later film is an equally important record of a significant writer; both documentaries afford insight into Thompson's private life and his public persona.

Most importantly, *Animals, Whores and Dialogue* focuses closely on Thompson's writing process. We see him composing in the kitchen at Owl Farm. Warren Zevon reads back to him on the speaker phone his freshly minted column denouncing George W. Bush and his crew: 'I piss down the throats of these Nazis' (*KF*, p. 67). We see Thompson attempting to write in the presence of Ewing, his wife Anita and others; at one point, exasperated, he tells them all to shut up so he can think. The slow deliberation of Thompson's working life comes across here, establishing a stark contrast to the pace of his Gonzo prose when read on the page. The difficulties of editing *The Proud Highway* are discussed; we see the cover photograph that was finally used, among several alternatives. Thompson wryly considers as a money-spinner a self-help book entitled *Dr Thompson's Guide to Physical Fitness*.

There are several readings of Thompson's prose by his friends, including 'the legacy of the big machine' sequence from *Hell's Angels* and sections of 'Strange Rumblings in Aztlán'. The film concludes with a poignant memorial party held by Thompson's widow Anita and some close friends at Owl Farm on 18 July 2005, which would have been his sixty-eighth birthday.

Alex Gibney, *Gonzo: The Life and Work of Dr. Hunter S. Thompson* (2009)

Gibney's documentary begins with the off-screen voices of interviewees commenting on Thompson's alleged decline – 'He lost that Gonzo edge'; 'I think he just had run out of juice' – while the camera shows us around his workplace, the kitchen at Owl Farm. We cut to scenes of the devastation in New York after 9/11, and of US troops fighting Islamic guerrillas, over the text of Thompson's column (read here by Johnny Depp) that accurately forecast a quasi-religious war in Iraq or Afghanistan (see Chapter 3). As one of the commentators in voiceover points out, to get Thompson motivated to reach his full height in his later years required a metaphorical 'kick in the groin'. The atrocities of 9/11 provided this stimulus.

We cut to Depp reading Thompson's account of edgework through fast motorcycle riding, from the end of *Hell's Angels* (see Chapter 4). A psychedelic moving montage of photos of the young Thompson plays over his comment that the edge cannot be explained honestly, as the only ones who know it have gone over. We see important 1960s footage including Thompson appearing on *To Tell the Truth*, a TV panel game show where contestants strive to identify the true candidate who is presented to them along with two fakes. The climactic line is 'Will the real Hunter Thompson please stand up?' – a query that might serve as a heading to a study of his various personas.

Gonzo then switches to a chronological, biographical narrative that it sustains throughout. There are some particularly interesting points made along the way by various friends and associates interviewed as talking heads, as well as some fascinating original footage.

A commercial for Thompson's 1970 Freak Power campaign plays, announcing in voiceover against a shot of Thompson riding his motorcycle on a high mountain road, 'The only thing against him is he's a visionary. He wants too pure a world'. In a film of a campaign debate with the incumbent sheriff, Thompson says the term freak 'is a very honourable designation and I'm proud of it'. Speaking at a press conference immediately after his defeat, Thompson claims he now knows that 'the American Dream really is fucked' (the last word, though bleeped out, is obvious). Despite the ironic origins of the concept of Freak Power (see Chapter 3), Thompson's personal commitment to his candidacy comes across clearly here.

Ralph Steadman points out that it was his and Thompson's chemistry that really 'made Gonzo possible'. Steadman had not tried drugs until Thompson gave him psilocybin after he landed in the USA, and this inflamed his satirical imagination. Or, as Sondi Wright (formerly Sandy Thompson) puts it, Thompson gives Steadman hallucinogenics and he simply 'loses it'; his style becomes much less conventional as a result. A film follows of a seemingly stoned Steadman, drawing manically.

The documentary's account of the origins of *Fear and Loathing in Las Vegas* replays original audio recordings made by Thompson during his 1971 visits to Las Vegas, now available on *The Gonzo Tapes*, a boxed set of audio CDs intended to complement the Gibney documentary. Thompson, speaking to Oscar Zeta Acosta on the tape, calls their white car 'Moby Dick', suggesting that he was already assessing the literary precedents for their actions. The taco stand scene, where Duke and Gonzo ask after the American Dream, is reconstructed using actors, in a sequence that feels like an out-take from the Gilliam movie.

Thompson's *Rolling Stone* colleague Tim Crouse points out how on the campaign trail in 1972, Thompson 'couldn't resist – ever – trying to shock the squares' when reporting, by making false claims about going to the toilet to shoot drugs, for instance. He seems to have borrowed this technique from the Hell's Angels, whose games, such as male-on-male kissing in public, were designed both to show class to the squares and to generate publicity (see Chapters 2 and 4).

Senator Gary Hart, former manager of the McGovern presidential campaign, argues that Thompson's rejection of McGovern over his appointment of Thomas Eagleton as running mate was 'infantile', because Thompson could not recognize the necessity for McGovern to make a peace offering to traditional conservative Democrats. Though here Thompson comes across as a fascinating and valuable commentator, he also seems politically immature in some respects, because he followed his convictions into unrealistic places.

In an extended interview, Douglas Brinkley makes the fascinating revelation that a 300-page Gonzo manuscript of Thompson's visit to the National Rifle Association headquarters exists. Thompson was allegedly firing guns into the walls, and generally intimidating the NRA staff, whose views on gun ownership had Thompson's full support but whose Republican politics he despised.

Jann Wenner, alluding to Joseph Conrad, notes that Thompson identified with Richard Nixon's 'darkness'. Wenner sees Thompson's failure to report on the Ali-Foreman fight, which was held in Zaire in October 1974, as the 'beginning of [Thompson's] decline'; Wenner notes that Thompson never showed up at the ring because he believed the fight would be a humiliating defeat for the underdog, his hero Ali, when in fact it was one of the sporting upsets of the century. For the first time, it seemed, Thompson conspicuously failed to grasp the *zeitgeist*: this suggests that perhaps his astute commentary on 9/11 was a return to form rather than evidence that Thompson's antennae had always been perfectly tuned.

Sondi Wright expresses her forthright view of her ex-husband's suicide: 'He wasn't on top. He was nowhere near on top'. She sees him as a desperate and lonely man. In her view, killing himself was 'just the opposite' of a courageous step, because the dark world of the early twenty-first century needs a Thompson on top form.

William Hicklin, *Hunter S. Thompson – Final 24: His final hours* (2006)

A documentary about the last day in Thompson's life, interspersed with biographical flashbacks. Part of a series on celebrity deaths, it features actors playing Thompson and his immediate family. Sondi Wright, Thompson's biographer Peter O. Whitmer and the family friends Michael Cleverly and Ben Fee are interviewed, along with Alan Rinzler, Thompson's former editor at *Rolling Stone*. Many of the flashback scenes are close imitations of those in the Terry Gilliam film of *Vegas*, and the off-screen narrator (Danny Wallace) often reads close paraphrases of passages in Thompson's work; neither Gilliam's original film footage nor Thompson's original words are used. Nevertheless, as the narrator rightly says, Thompson's 'lasting legacy will be his writing'; thus the documentary sensibly concentrates on his career as much as his final hours. Although this film is of interest, Alex Gibney's *Gonzo* handles Thompson's life and work in greater depth, and Wayne Ewing's *Breakfast with Hunter* and *Animals, Whores and Dialogue* offer intimate footage of the real Thompson rather than an actor.

Wayne Ewing, *Free Lisl: Fear & Loathing in Denver* (2006)

This documentary concerns the campaign to free Lisl Auman, a young woman from Colorado who was convicted of the murder of a police officer, despite being handcuffed in another officer's car, some distance away from events, at the time of the killing. Auman's conviction occurred under the felony murder law, which meant she could be charged with the crime, even though it was known she did not perform the actual killing, provided she could be proved to have aided the killer. The film argues that the police lied in court to imply that Auman had given the murderer his gun: the killer had shot himself dead at the scene, and so a scapegoat was needed to assuage police anger and satisfy public opinion.

Having read and liked *Fear and Loathing in Las Vegas*, Auman wrote to Thompson from jail. Using his media and legal contacts and his by then powerful internet presence, Thompson took on her case as his 'last hurrah'; in a terrible coincidence, he committed suicide only months before Auman's eventual release. The film interviews Auman and her parents as well as lawyers, journalists and others associated with the campaign. There is extensive coverage of the original 'Free Lisl' rally at which Thompson, Douglas Brinkley, Warren Zevon and others spoke and performed. Overall this is a significant film about a miscarriage of justice, but quite appropriately, Thompson's part is minor. In the end, although the Colorado Supreme Court eventually found in Auman's favour, they did so by challenging the basis of the original judge's instructions to the jury, thus allowing the highly questionable felony murder law to remain intact.

Tom Thurman, *Buy the Ticket, Take the Ride: Hunter S. Thompson on Film* (2006)

This documentary offers an overview of the films *When the Buffalo Roam* and *Fear and Loathing in Las Vegas*. As in Gibney's *Gonzo*, we see a series of talking heads offering their views and reminiscences of Thompson in the opening sequence: unlike Gibney's film, which superimposes the talking heads over montages and animations, Thurman uses a split screen; as the heads talk in one half, a sequence of Thompson's book covers appears in the other.

There are a number of informative interviews with Thompson's friends, allies and commentators. Ralph Steadman refers to the development of Gonzo during the preparation for 'The Kentucky Derby is Decadent and Depraved': Thompson 'provoked a situation in order to get a reaction, and once he got a reaction he knew where he was'. Douglas Brinkley accurately sums up Thompson's outsider position as that of 'an old-fashioned anarchist. He did not believe in institutions,' including the institutions of the counterculture. Tom Wolfe draws attention to the connection between Thompson and Mark Twain, arguing that Twain produced a nineteenth-century form of Gonzo journalism in works such as *The Innocents Abroad*.

Nick Nolte, the off-screen narrator, argues for the importance of *Where the Buffalo Roam*, not as a movie in its own right, but for the way it established Thompson 'as a bona fide pop culture icon, an action figure for the underground'. The film acted to build 'the foundation of a cult' around him. Bill Murray and Peter Boyle are praised for their individual work, but the picture as a whole is viewed as a failure.

Several of the main players on Gilliam's *Fear and Loathing in Las Vegas* film are interviewed. Anita Thompson argues that the movie accurately represents her husband's lifestyle through its hectic 'constant action'. Laila Nabulsi, the producer (also Thompson's ex-girlfriend), compares her experience to 'Gonzo film-making', while Johnny Depp, who played Raoul Duke, concludes that he became Thompson's 'partner in crime [...] the surrogate Dr Gonzo'. We discover that Bill Murray, who played Thompson in *Where the Buffalo Roam*, phoned Depp before shooting began, to point out that, in Depp's words, 'If you're gonna play Hunter and he seeps into your skin, you will always find yourself becoming him at one time or another for the rest of your life'. Nabulsi remarks that she took particular amusement in making Depp and Benicio Del Toro, two acknowledged sex symbols, take on the physically unattractive parts of the bald, gangling Duke and the fat, slovenly Gonzo.

The conclusion to *Buy the Ticket, Take the Ride* explores how Thompson became trapped in his Gonzo persona, summarizing him concisely as 'a real man inside a booming franchise'. A youthful-looking Thompson is seen complaining to a BBC film crew in 1977 that 'the myth is mushrooming and getting more and more warped'. He reiterates the suggestion made in his 1974 essay on the Super Bowl (see Chapter 1) that he planned to 'kill off one life and start another one'. After discussing Thompson's suicide and the memorial service at Owl Farm, Nick Nolte's narration concludes positively: Thompson 'will continue to stand for possibility itself, and the more unlikely the better. He gave us a reason to continue – or at least a damn good alibi'.

Wayne Ewing, *When I Die: a Documentary on the Raising of the Gonzo Memorial* (2005)

This detailed account of the site preparation for Thompson's memorial service at Owl Farm includes discussions of the technical and legal difficulties involved in creating the rocket, topped with a giant Gonzo fist, that was to shoot Thompson's ashes into the sky on the night of 20 August 2005. Anita Thompson and many of her husband's friends are interviewed, as are the special events team, loaned by Thompson's friend Johnny Depp. It was Depp's funds that enabled the service to happen as specified in Thompson's will. The film concludes with a documentary recording of the service itself and shows the reactions of the guests.

Wayne Ewing, *Breakfast with Hunter* (2004)

An important documentary filmed from 1996 to 1998. Using appropriately Thompson-like *bricolage*, it combines fly-on-the-wall reportage with some very useful original footage. For instance, we see excerpts from a Thames TV documentary of the 1970 Freak Power election for sheriff of Aspen, featuring an off-screen British narrator with an upper-class accent (then very common on UK television) who refers to the incumbent Carol Whitmire as the 'good guy' and Thompson as the 'bad guy', adopting a tone of sceptical caution about the Freak Power bid.

Breakfast with Hunter has two main narrative threads: first, the legal process in 1996–97 following a DUI charge made against Thompson on the night of an important local election. Thompson asserts that the charge is trumped up; it represents police harassment condoned by the local establishment who are trying to stymie his anti-development campaign in Aspen. We see the build-up to the initial hearing, with suggestions of police lies, and Thompson's disappointment when his attempt to have the court suppress the police evidence goes against him, meaning he will have to go to trial. As he had done in his 1990 sexual assault and drug possession case, he refused to enter into a plea bargain and thus risked a much longer sentence (see *Songs of the Doomed*).

The second main storyline is the preparation for the *Fear and Loathing in Las Vegas* movie. Terry Gilliam, Johnny Depp, Benicio Del Toro (who played the attorney) and the producer Laila Nabulsi all feature, plus the original director Alex Cox. One of the most revealing sequences follows the extensive argument between Thompson, Cox and the original screenwriter over the proposed *Fear and Loathing in Las Vegas* screenplay. Thompson has not read the script, to Cox's obvious frustration. Nevertheless, he objects vehemently to Cox's proposal to film the 'high and beautiful wave' speech as a cartoon, with an animated image of Duke surfing on a wave. Cox's defence of the proposal is to point out that the book has been associated with cartoons ever since Steadman's original drawings appeared. Thompson will have no truck with this and speaks to Nabulsi's answering machine to threaten 'war' if the proposed scene goes ahead. A short excerpt from this argument scene appears in Gibney's *Gonzo*.

In the previous scene of the documentary, the coming argument is anticipated when Johnny Depp, before a theatre audience in Louisville, reads out the Raoul Duke speech from *Vegas* that Cox had wanted to render in cartoon form: the point seems to be to suggest the way in which the scene *should* be done, although Depp's rendering is not at all close to that he gives in the eventual film as Raoul Duke. Instead, Depp is seen chewing gum throughout, perhaps as a way of simulating Thompson's characteristic mumbling, and is accompanied by a mournful solo piano. Gilliam's version abandoned the gum-chewing and used original footage of outdoor hippie gatherings to simulate Duke's flashbacks to the 1960s, with the Youngbloods' song 'Get Together' a call for hippie solidarity, superimposed on the soundtrack as Depp gives the speech in voiceover.

We see Thompson, Benicio Del Toro and Laila Nabulsi in a Hollywood hotel suite watching Wayne Ewing's original film of the argument with Cox, the footage that will eventually find its way into Ewing's DVD. This creates an uncanny effect, as the viewer gets to watch Thompson watching himself in the film that he/she has just seen. It is as if Thompson has kicked the viewer out and replaced them. Thompson and friends agree that a new director is needed, but acknowledge that they have little time. The tightness of Johnny Depp's schedule suggests the very real possibility that they may miss him and therefore may have to cast a different actor as Duke.

Depp, however, remained available and even went so far as to live with Thompson at Owl Farm to prepare for the role. We learn that many of the clothes Depp wore in the movie were borrowed from Thompson's wardrobe. We see Depp and Thompson bonding over guns at Owl Farm. Depp, who at this point was self-consciously working himself into the mannerisms and mindset of Thompson/Duke, adopts Thompson's distinctive two-handed shooting stance with a powerful-looking pistol that sports a long sight. The posture and weapon both found their way into the desert scene in the Gilliam film where Duke, about to return to Las Vegas for the District Attorneys' Convention, takes out his frustrations through blasting at rocks and lizards.

A late scene lets us onto the set of the *Vegas* movie, now in production. Thompson is present for the courtroom/cage sequence where Lucy takes the witness stand in a white dress and tells the court what Duke and Gonzo allegedly did to her. We also see the shooting of the reflexive scene in the Matrix club where the real Thompson appears on camera and Depp/Duke glances at him, astonished (see below). Ewing's documentary here offers valuable insights into Gilliam's and Depp's creative process. The documentary concludes with footage of the premiere of the Gilliam film in May 1998: a clearly relieved and pleased Thompson celebrates with Depp and Del Toro.

Terry Gilliam, *Fear and Loathing in Las Vegas* (1998)

Terry Gilliam's work is the most significant adaptation of Thompson's fiction so far. Although the plot is very close to that of the novel, Gilliam is not afraid to depart from the book on the level of style to create his own interpretation. The movie opens with an ironically deployed showbiz number, 'My Favourite Things' from *The Sound of Music*, playing over newsreel footage of anti-Vietnam War protests from the Johnson presidency. The film's title appears in red on a black background in Ralph Steadman's familiar Gonzo font, then drips away like blood, revealing the novel's epigraph from Dr Johnson: 'He who makes a beast of himself gets rid of the pain of being a man'. Thus the dangerous scrapes of the protagonists are put in the context of the far more destructive actions of the American government, especially in South-East Asia.

There are reflexive references to the book throughout: the hitchhiker picked up by Duke (Johnny Depp) and Gonzo (Benicio Del Toro) is wearing a Ralph Steadman-designed Mickey Mouse top, a variant on the Mickey-Mouse-with-swastika t-shirt he sports in the original Steadman illustration (*LV*, p. 7). The "electric snake" that is seen by Duke after they have checked in at the Mint Hotel (*LV*, p. 27) is now no longer a neon sign outside their hotel room window, but a US Air Force bomber seen on footage of the Vietnam War on the TV screen; the bomber comes out of the screen and covers the wall, either due to Duke's acid hallucinations or because the TV is projecting it onto the wallpaper.

As in the book, Duke and Gonzo try to bluff their way into a Debbie Reynolds concert, but now Gonzo adds the lurid claim that he 'used to romp with her'. Reynolds and her band are heard off-screen performing a crass showbiz arrangement of 'Sergeant Pepper's Lonely Hearts Club Band', as they do in the book; Duke and Gonzo, hysterical with stoned laughter, are thrown out of the theatre by the bouncer. The reference to the Circus-Circus as the 'Sixth Reich' is repeated from the book, as is the machine that projects your image over downtown Las Vegas for 99 cents; unfortunately we don't see the effects of the machine but hear a barker extolling them.

The real Hunter S. Thompson appears in a non-speaking role when Duke recalls the mid-1960s in San Francisco. Walking through the Matrix nightclub when Jefferson Airplane are performing, Duke sees Thompson sitting at a table and, in an uncanny moment, recognizes himself – 'holy fuck'. Thus the film presents us with a complex ontological game: we see an actor playing the persona of an author, meeting the flesh-and-blood author playing himself, or adopting the role of himself. Thus, both Depp *and* Thompson are playing at being Duke *and* Thompson: the film's playfulness exposes Thompson's original questioning of the role of the author (see Chapter 1). As *Buy the Ticket, Take the Ride* argues, Depp is a postmodernist actor who can foreground the sources of his work without parody; he is 'able to be ironic in a role without mocking the person he is playing'.

Homosexual desire is introduced explicitly to the film in an improvised departure from the script when the highway patrolman (Gary Busey) asks Duke for a kiss, as he is lonely. We don't see the kiss, but cut to Duke driving away, thinking (in voiceover) 'I felt raped'.

Thompson had had an acrimonious dispute with the original director Alex Cox over his proposal to render the 'crest of a high and beautiful wave' speech as a cartoon (see *Breakfast with Hunter* above). Not surprisingly, then, Gilliam's interpretation eschews cartoons and is punctuated by live-action effects. The patrons of the Mint Hotel bar in the registration scene turn into a pack of vicious lizards that are busy eating, fighting and copulating. Duke's paranoid fantasy of being arraigned for the statutory rape of Lucy is rendered as a courtroom sequence against a black background, with Lucy on a towering witness-stand above them. Duke and Gonzo appear in convicts' uniforms, in a cage and in chains. When Duke is high on adrenochrome, he sees Gonzo turn into a buffalo-devil-woman, with horns, fur and breasts. Gonzo also has predatory, cat-like eyes as he tries to serve Duke cocaine on the point of his hunting knife.

Duke wakes up after the adrenochrome binge next to a copy of *The Death Ship* by B. Traven: this is possibly an allusion to the complexity of the relationship between Thompson's life and his persona, because the pseudonymous Traven, like Thompson, wrote semi-autobiographical novels with radical political content, but his true identity was never discovered and remains the subject of controversy.

The attorney leaves. Duke, now alone, plays back his audio tape of the events of last night. The tape cues a series of flashbacks by Duke, rendered on screen, including the scene where the two men (clothed in the film, although naked in the book) fool the hapless maid Alice into thinking they are undercover cops; the sequence where Gonzo baits the redneck tourists at the stoplight; and a new scene, not in the novel, where Duke and Gonzo appear to be trying to wreck their hired Cadillac convertible in a supermarket car park. The tape snarls up, and in trying to repair it, Duke finds Gonzo's hunting-knife. The blade has blood on it. This triggers Duke's recollection of the North Vegas Coffee Lounge, and Gonzo's intimidation of the waitress there, in a sequence that closely matches the book.

Duke comes out of the flashback in his flooded hotel suite. We see him typing while Depp reads the main anti-Leary speech from the book in voiceover (see *LV*, pp. 178–9). As Depp gets near the end of the speech the room diminishes until, with the camera trained on it from above, it forms a square of light against a black background. Thus, Gilliam's positioning of Thompson's anti-Leary speech gives it much greater prominence than in the original.

Art Linson, *Where the Buffalo Roam* (1980)

Although valuable as a document of how Thompson was perceived at the time, this film has dated badly. It tends to rely on slapstick to support the strong but isolated performances of the lead actors, Bill Murray as Thompson and Peter Boyle as the attorney who is mysteriously turned into a Bulgarian called Laszlo. The script fails to capture the darkness or anger of Thompson's best writing. Consequently, the protagonists' actions come across as pranks rather than anything subversive, let alone as emerging from existential unease or a sense of complicity in the failure of the American Dream. The film totally avoids edgework; although sometimes vibrantly comic, it never generates a sense of peril. Even a potentially dangerous gun-running sequence is turned into a vehicle for pratfalls when an over-enthusiastic guerrilla gets hold of a Kalashnikov and starts spraying bullets around at random. The whole script was 'heavy-handed comedy. [...] a cheap cartoon' (McKeen, 2008, p. 267).

Thompson's actions appear arbitrary. About to abandon his assignment and run off to see Laszlo's secret hideout, he gives his Super Bowl tickets and hotel suite keys to a randomly chosen man in the street (although the man is black, possibly suggesting the protagonist's solidarity with the Brothers in their struggle against the Man). The unnamed black man starts a party with his friends and hotel staff in the suite. When Thompson's infuriated editor rings up asking where his overdue copy is, the man mistakes the name 'Hunter' for a request to go hunting and angrily dismisses it, slamming down the phone. Two hotel employees are sent to quell the noise: instead, in what is supposed to be a carnivalesque moment, they enter the spirit of the party and are seen smoking pot and enjoying themselves. Earlier, Thompson plays football in the same hotel room with members of the hotel staff. His attorney wears a Nixon mask in the restaurant. In each case, the film's only devices seem to be slapstick and/or rudimentary social criticism.

There are, however, some allusions to *Fear and Loathing in Las Vegas*. In a somewhat puerile early scene, we discover that Thompson has secreted a student nurse called 'Cookie' in his room, and is feeding her pills as they dance to disco music; the episode is presumably derived from the attorney's treatment of Lucy in *Vegas*. Cookie screams and thinks Laszlo is a bat when he appears at their window, in a clear reference to the opening of Thompson's novel. There is a poor imitation of the hitchhiker scene in *Vegas* when Thompson and Laszlo pick up a hitchhiker and make threatening remarks to him: Gilliam's film does this scene far better, as it sticks closer to the book.

One of the stronger scenes depicts an accidental meeting between Thompson and Richard Nixon in a men's room. Nixon is played by a professional lookalike. Thompson entertains the urinating Nixon with a speech in which he divides the country into two groups; the powerful but warped 'screwheads' of the establishment and the hopelessly victimized 'doomed' who are their subjects. Nixon zips up his fly and pronounces his verdict: 'Fuck the doomed'. The toilet scene was Murray's idea, and it gives him a better vehicle than the rest of the movie for his energetic, verbose Thompson persona.

Near the end, Thompson and Laszlo reach a peak of revolutionary subversion when they let off a fire extinguisher on Nixon's campaign plane; in an act of breathtakingly dangerous anarchy, they manage to hit Nixon in the face with foam. This comes after a gulling scene in which Thompson has given LSD to a self-important stuffed shirt of a reporter who identifies himself as 'Harris from the *Post*'. The drug is coded through the playing of the Beatles' 'Lucy in the Sky with Diamonds' on the soundtrack over unfunny scenes of Harris grinning beatifically and trying to force his way into the pilot's seat to fly the plane. Harris is later discovered singing to himself in the airplane toilet with his clothes dishevelled.

The penultimate scene offers a stronger image. Nixon's plane takes off, leaving Thompson and Laszlo adrift on the tarmac, with Laszlo's papers outlining his plans for a rural "paradise" blowing everywhere. This mocks the hippie dream of the original Duke and Gonzo quite effectively, and also questions Thompson's ideal of the lodge.

The final scene has Thompson back home writing at Owl Farm, where he started the film. He claims, 'It never got weird enough for me'. This is a much stronger piece of writing than the rest of the script, because Thompson wrote the text himself (Whitmer, 1993, p. 252). Overall, the film is worth seeing for Murray's and Boyle's performances and for the highlights of the toilet sequence and the final Owl Farm speech, but there are many tedious lows to negotiate in between.

Appendix II The Gonzo Net

The internet is a protean entity: it is quite likely that by the time these words are published, at least some of the information below will be out of date. Nevertheless, Thompson's estate, critics and fans offer an invaluable Web presence. I have tried to sketch some of the more significant sites below.

myspace.com/the_gonzo_way

Anita Thompson's site on myspace, including links to Thompson's early writing and a 30-minute video of Anita's appearance at Cody's Bookstore in Berkeley on ForA TV.

owlfarmblog.com

Anita Thompson's blog about life on Owl Farm, with regular entries linking to Thompson's writings plus the Gonzo Store and PlantTrees4Life.com. Earlier blog entries are archived here.

GonzoStore.com

A retail outlet run by the Hunter S. Thompson Estate for all things Gonzo, including clothing, jewellery and books.

totallygonzo.org

A site by and for the worldwide Hunter S. Thompson community, including links to Gonzo writing, Gonzo art and members of the Gonzo tribe. At the time of writing, several of the pages were still under construction, but the site allowed a link to some invaluable rare Thompson articles in facsimile.

myspace.com/hunterthompsonfilms

Wayne Ewing's myspace site, from which his films can be ordered. There are brief trailers and overviews of the films. As of 2010, there are four Thompson DVDs available (see Appendix I): *Breakfast With Hunter*; *Animals, Whores and Dialogue*; *When I Die*; and *Free Lisl*.

ralphsteadman.com

Dedicated to Ralph Steadman and all of his art, including his work with and for Thompson. It is also a retail outlet for Steadman's art and merchandise.

hstforbeginners.com

Accessible from hstbooks.org, this offers the opinions of several contributors, including Wayne Ewing and William McKeen, on the most salient points of Thompson's work, how best to approach it, and how to avoid slavish imitation if you are a writer.

hstbooks.org

Maintained by Marty Flynn, a highly knowledgeable collector of Thompson's books, this site offers an exhaustive index of his writings, as well as links to related sites.

www.rollingstone.com

Home page of *Rolling Stone* magazine. Includes online access to the *Rolling Stone* archive, but a subscription is required.

Bibliography

Entries are followed by abbreviations where used.

Works by Hunter S. Thompson

i. Books

(1967), *Hell's Angels*. London: Penguin. *(HA)*
(1980), *The Great Shark Hunt: Strange Tales from a Strange Time*. London: Picador. *(GSH)*
(1988), *Generation of Swine: Tales of Shame and Degradation in the '80s: Gonzo Papers, vol. 2*. New York: Summit. *(GS)*
(1991), *Songs of the Doomed: More Notes on the Death of the American Dream: Gonzo Papers, vol. 3*. London: Pan. *(SD)*
(1993), *Fear and Loathing in Las Vegas: A Savage Journey to the Heart of the American Dream*. London: Harper Collins. *(LV)*
(1995), *Better than Sex: Confessions of a Political Junkie: Gonzo Papers, vol. 4*. London: Black Swan. *(BS)*
(1998), *The Proud Highway: Saga of a Desperate Southern Gentleman 1955–1967*, Douglas Brinkley (ed.). London: Bloomsbury. *(PH)*
(1999), *The Rum Diary*. London: Bloomsbury. *(RD)*
(2000), *Fear and Loathing in America: The Brutal Odyssey of an Outlaw Journalist 1968–1976*, Douglas Brinkley (ed.). London: Bloomsbury. *(FLA)*
(2003), *Kingdom of Fear: Loathsome Secrets of a Star-Crossed Child in the Final Days of the American Century*. London: Penguin. *(KF)*
(2004), *Hey Rube: Blood Sport, the Bush Doctrine, and the Downward Spiral of Dumbness*. New York: Simon & Schuster. *(HR)*
(2005a), *The Curse of Lono*, co-author Ralph Steadman. Hong Kong: Taschen. *(CL)*
(2005b), *Fear and Loathing on the Campaign Trail '72*. London: Harper Collins. *(CT)*
(2008), *Conversations with Hunter S. Thompson*, Beef Torrey and Kevin Simonson (eds). Jackson: University Press of Mississippi. *(C)*
(2009), *Interviews with Hunter S. Thompson: Ancient Gonzo Wisdom*, Anita Thompson (ed.). London: Pan Macmillan. *(AGW)*
(2012), *The Mutineer: Rants, Ravings, and Missives from the Mountaintop 1977–2005*, Douglas Brinkley (ed.). New York: Simon & Schuster.

ii. Articles

(1967), 'Why boys will be girls', *Pageant*, August, pp. 94–101. (*WB*)
(1985), 'Dance of the doomed', *Rolling Stone*, 9 May, 47, pp. 50–9, pp. 90–93. (*DD*)
(1990), 'There were no rules, fear was unknown, and sleep was out of the question. . . .', foreword to Paul Perry and Ken Babbs, *On the Bus: The Complete Guide to the Legendary Trip of Ken Kesey and the Merry Pranksters and the Birth of the Counterculture*. London: Plexus, pp. xv–xvi.
(1992), 'Back in the early days, everything was so painful that we couldn't stand it; that's why we had to do drugs', *Rolling Stone*, 11 June, pp. 46–8.
(1994), 'Polo is my life: fear and loathing in horse country ', *Rolling Stone*, 15 December, pp. 44–57, pp. 109–11. (*PL*)
(1997), 'The shootist: a short tale of extreme precision and no fear', *Rolling Stone*, 18 September, p. 54. (*TS*)
(1999), 'Hey rube! I love you. Eerie reflections on fuel, madness & music'. *Rolling Stone*, 13 May, pp. 39–40. (*LY*)
(2004), 'The fun-hogs in the passing lane: fear and loathing campaign 2004', *Rolling Stone*, 11 November, pp. 58–61. (*FH*)

iii. Recordings

(1996), *Fear and Loathing in Las Vegas by Hunter S. Thompson*. No city: Margaritaville Records.
(2008), *The Gonzo Tapes: The Life and Work of Dr. Hunter S. Thompson*. Los Angeles: Shout! Factory.

Works about Hunter S. Thompson

i. Books

Banco, Lindsey Michael (2008), *Psychedelic Trips: Travel and Drugs in Contemporary Literature*. Unpublished PhD thesis. Kingston, Ontario, Canada: Queen's University.
—(2010), *Travel and Drugs in Twentieth-Century Literature*. New York: Routledge.
Bingley, Will and Anthony Hope-Smith (2010), *Gonzo: A Graphic Biography of Hunter S. Thompson*, foreword by Alan Rinzler. London: SelfMadeHero.
Carroll, E. Jean (2005), *Hunter: The Strange and Savage Life of Hunter S. Thompson*. London: Simon & Schuster.
Cleverly, Michael and Bob Braudis (2008), *The Kitchen Readings: Untold Stories of Hunter S. Thompson*. New York: Harper Collins.
Cowan, Jay (2009), *Hunter S. Thompson: An Insider's View of Deranged, Depraved, Drugged Out Brilliance*. Guilford, Connecticut: Lyons Press.
DeKoven, Marianne (2004), *Utopia Limited: The Sixties and the Emergence of the Postmodern*. Durham, NC: Duke University Press.

Hellmann, John (1981), *Fables of Fact: The New Journalism as New Fiction*. Urbana: University of Illinois Press.
Klinkowitz, Jerome (1977), *The Life of Fiction*. Urbana: University of Illinois Press.
McKeen, William (1991), *Hunter S. Thompson*. Boston: Twayne.
—(2008), *Outlaw Journalist: The Life and Times of Hunter S. Thompson*. London: Aurum Press.
Perry, Paul (2009), *Fear and Loathing: The Strange and Terrible Saga of Hunter S. Thompson*. London: Plexus.
Steadman, Ralph (2006), *The Joke's Over: Bruised Memories: Gonzo, Hunter S. Thompson and Me*. Orlando: Harcourt.
Thompson, Anita (2007), *The Gonzo Way: A Celebration of Dr. Hunter S. Thompson*. Golden, Colorado: Fulcrum.
Weingarten, Marc (2006), *The Gang That Wouldn't Write Straight: Wolfe, Thompson, Didion, and the New Journalism Revolution*. New York: Crown.
Wenner, Jann and Corey Semyour (2007), *Gonzo: the Life of Hunter S. Thompson*, with introduction by Johnny Depp. London: Sphere.
Whitmer, Peter O. (1993), *When the Going Gets Weird: The Twisted Life and Times of Hunter S. Thompson: A Very Unauthorized Biography*. New York: Hyperion.
Whitmer, Peter O. and Bruce Van Wyngarden (2007), *Aquarius Revisited: Seven Who Created the Sixties Counterculture that Changed America*. New York: Citadel Press.

ii. Articles and Book Chapters

Bridgstock, Martin (1989), 'The twilit fringe – anthropology and modern horror fiction'. *Journal of Popular Culture* 23: 3 (Winter), pp. 115–23.
Brinkley, Douglas (2005), 'Contentment was not enough: the final days at Owl Farm'. *Rolling Stone*, 24 March, pp. 36–42.
—(2006), 'A savage journey'. *Rolling Stone*, 18 May, p. 214.
Bruce-Novoa (1979), 'Fear and loathing on the buffalo trail'. *MELUS* 6: 4 (Winter), pp. 39–50.
Conrad, Harold (2008), 'Fear and loathing in Hunter Thompson' in Beef Torrey and Kevin Simonson (eds), *Conversations with Hunter S. Thompson*. Jackson: University Press of Mississippi, pp. 57–67.
Depp, Johnny (2005), 'A pair of deviant bookends'. *Rolling Stone*, 24 March, pp. 48–9.
Gilmore, Mikal (2005), 'The last outlaw'. *Rolling Stone*, 24 March, pp. 44–7.
Grassian, Daniel (2000), 'The half-baked cultural detective: *Fear and Loathing in Las Vegas* as postmodern noir'. *Popular Culture Review* 11: 2, pp. 99–111.
Green, James (1975), 'Gonzo'. *Journal of Popular Culture* 9: 1 (Summer), pp. 204–10.
Hirst, Martin (2004), 'What is Gonzo? The etymology of an urban legend'. *UQ*, Eprint edition 2004-01-19, pp. 1–16.
Jarnow, Jesse (2008), 'Man of action: Hunter S. Thompson keeps moving' in Beef Torrey and Kevin Simonson (eds), *Conversations with Hunter S. Thompson*. Jackson: University Press of Mississippi, pp. 195–204.

Landreth, Elizabeth (1975), 'There shall be no night: Las Vegas'. *Journal of Popular Culture* 9: 1 (Summer), pp. 197–203.
Lyng, Stephen (1990), 'Edgework: a social psychological analysis of voluntary risk taking'. *The American Journal of Sociology* 95: 4 (January), pp. 851–86.
Sickels, Robert C. (2000), 'A countercultural Gatsby: Hunter S. Thompson's *Fear and Loathing in Las Vegas*, the death of the American dream and the rise of Las Vegas, USA'. *Popular Culture Review* 11: 1, pp. 61–73.
Tamony, Peter (1983), 'Gonzo'. *American Speech*, 58: 1 (Spring), pp. 73–5.
Thompson, Juan (2005), 'My father'. *Rolling Stone*, 24 March, p. 72.
Wenner, Jann S. (2005), 'My brother in arms'. *Rolling Stone*, 24 March, pp. 33–4.
Wilson, Rob (1991), 'Theory's imaginal other: American encounters with North Korea and Japan'. *Boundary 2* 18: 3, 'Japan in the World' (Autumn), pp. 220–41.

iii. Films

Ewing, Wayne (dir.) (2004), *Breakfast with Hunter*. Wayne Ewing Films, Inc. & Gonzo International.
—(2005), *When I Die: a Documentary on the Raising of the Gonzo Memorial*. Wayne Ewing Films, Inc.
—(2006), *Free Lisl: Fear & Loathing in Denver*. Wayne Ewing Films, Inc.
—(2010), *Animals, Whores & Dialogue*, Wayne Ewing Films, Inc., The Estate of Hunter S. Thompson.
Gibney, Alex (dir.) (2009), *Gonzo: The Life and Work of Dr. Hunter S. Thompson*. Magnolia Pictures.
Gilliam, Terry (dir.) (1998), *Fear and Loathing in Las Vegas*. Universal Studios.
Hicklin, William (dir.) (2006), *Hunter S. Thompson – Final 24: His Final Hours*. MVD Visual.
Linson, Art (dir.) (1980), *Where the Buffalo Roam*. Universal Pictures.
Thurman, Tom (dir.) (2006), *Buy the Ticket, Take the Ride: Hunter S. Thompson on Film*. FBN Motion Pictures.

iv. Recordings.

(1998), *Fear and Loathing in Las Vegas: Music from the Motion Picture*. Los Angeles: Geffen Records.

Other Works

Holy Bible, Authorized King James Version. Oxford: Oxford University Press.
Abrams, Richard M. (2008), *America Transformed: Sixty Years of Revolutionary Change, 1941–2001*. New York: Cambridge University Press.
Acosta, Oscar Zeta (1989a), *The Autobiography of a Brown Buffalo*. New York: Vintage.
—(1989b), *The Revolt of the Cockroach People*. New York: Vintage.

Bibliography

Adams, James Truslow (1945), *The Epic of America*. London: Routledge.
Allen, Donald (ed.) (1999), *New American Poetry 1945–1960*. Berkeley: University of California Press.
Alt, John (1982), 'Popular culture and mass consumption: the motorcycle as cultural commodity'. *Journal of Popular Culture* 15: 4 (Spring), pp. 129–41.
Althusser, Louis (1981), 'Ideology and ideological state apparatuses: notes towards an investigation' in *Lenin and Philosophy and Other Essays*, trans. Ben Brewster. New York: Monthly Review Press, pp. 85–126.
Anderson, Benedict (1983), *Imagined Communities: Reflections on the Origin and Spread of Nationalism*. London: Verso.
Annesley, James (2006), *Fictions of Globalization*. London: Continuum.
Arnold, Vivien (1976), 'The image of the freeway'. *JAE* 30: 1 *Teaching the Landscape* (September), pp. 28–30.
Bakhtin, Mikhail (1981), *The Dialogic Imagination: Four Essays*, trans. Caryl Emerson and Michael Holquist. Austin: University of Texas Press.
—(1984), *Rabelais and His World*, trans. Hélène Iswolsky. Bloomington: Indiana University Press.
Barger, Ralph 'Sonny' (2001), *Hell's Angel: The Life and Times of Sonny Barger and the Hell's Angels Motorcycle Club*. London: Fourth Estate.
Barthes, Roland (1977), *Image Music Text*, trans. Stephen Heath. London: Fontana.
Baudrillard, Jean (1994), *Simulacra and Simulation*, trans. Sheila Faria Glaser. Ann Arbor: University of Michigan Press.
—(1995), *The Gulf War Did Not Take Place*, trans. Paul Patton. Sydney: Power Publications.
—(2003), *The Spirit of Terrorism and Other Essays*, trans. Chris Turner. London: Verso.
Beckett, Samuel (2000), *Waiting for Godot*. London: Faber.
Berlin, Isaiah (1999), *The Roots of Romanticism*, Henry Hardy (ed.) London: Chatto & Windus.
Bey, Hakim (2003), *T. A. Z.: The Temporary Autonomous Zone, Ontological Anarchism, Poetic Terrorism* (second edition). New York: Autonomedia.
—(1994), *Immediatism: Essays by Hakim Bey*. Edinburgh: AK Press.
Bhabha, Homi K. (1994), *The Location of Culture*. London: Routledge.
—(ed.) (1990), *Nation and Narration*. London: Routledge.
—(2004), 'Foreword: framing Fanon by Homi K. Bhabha' in Fanon, Frantz, *The Wretched of the Earth*, trans. Richard Philcox, with commentary by Jean-Paul Sartre and Homi K. Bhabha. New York: Grove Press, pp. vii–xli.
Boon, Marcus (2002), *The Road of Excess: A History of Writers on Drugs*. Cambridge, MA and London: Harvard University Press.
Bredahl, A. Carl. (1981), 'An exploration of power: Tom Wolfe's acid test'. *Critique* 23: 2 (Winter), pp. 67–84.
Brown, Travis Jr. (1976), 'On an aesthetic of highway speed'. *Journal of American Esthetics*, 30: 1 (September), pp. 25–7.

Budd, Louis J. (1995), 'Mark Twain as an American icon' in Forrest G. Robinson (ed.), *The Cambridge Companion to Mark Twain*. Cambridge: Cambridge University Press, pp. 1–26.
Burroughs, William S. (1977), *Junky*. London: Penguin.
—(2005), *Naked Lunch: The Restored Text*, James Grauerholz and Barry Miles (eds). London: Harper Collins.
Bush, Clive (1977), *The Dream of Reason: American Consciousness and Cultural Achievement from Independence to the Civil War*. London: Edward Arnold.
Butler, Judith (1990), *Gender Trouble: Feminism and the Subversion of Identity*. London: Routledge.
Calvino, Italo (1989), *The Literature Machine*, trans. Patrick Creagh. London: Picador.
Capote, Truman (2009), *In Cold Blood: A True Account of a Multiple Murder And Its Consequences*. London: Penguin.
Carrigan, Tim, Bob Connell, and John Lee (2002), 'Toward a new sociology of masculinity', in Rachel Adams and David Sivran (eds), *The Masculinity Studies Reader*. Oxford: Blackwell, pp. 99–118.
Carroll, Lewis (1998), *Alice's Adventures in Wonderland and Through the Looking-Glass*. London: Penguin.
Carter, James M. (2008), *Inventing Vietnam: The United States and State Building, 1954–1968*. Cambridge: Cambridge University Press.
Carter, Jimmy (1976), 'To establish justice in a sinful world: excerpts from Jimmy Carter's law day speech, May 4th 1974'. *Rolling Stone*, 16 December, 72.
Cervantes, Miguel (2003), *Don Quixote*, edited and trans. John Rutherford. London: Penguin.
Chandler, John M. (1971), *Life, Liberty and the Pursuit of Happiness: A Social History of the United States of America in Documents*. Oxford: Oxford University Press.
Conrad, Joseph (1990), *Heart of Darkness and Other Tales*, Cedric Watts (ed.). Oxford: Oxford University Press.
Cooper, Ken (1992), '"Zero pays the house": the Las Vegas novel and atomic roulette'. *Contemporary Literature* 33: 3 (Autumn), pp. 528–44.
Cox, Peter (2007), 'Globalisation of what? Power, knowledge and neocolonialism', in Anne Boran and Peter Cox (eds), *Implications of Globalisation*. Chester: Chester Academic Press, pp. 88–110.
Crouse, Timothy (1974), *The Boys on the Bus*. New York: Ballantine.
Davenport-Hines, Richard (2002), *The Pursuit of Oblivion: A Social History of Drugs*. London: Phoenix.
Day, Aidan (1996), *Romanticism*. London: Routledge.
Debord, Guy (2009), *Society of the Spectacle*, trans. Ken Knabb. Eastbourne: Soul Bay Press.
DeGroot, Gerrard J. (2008), *The Sixties Unplugged: A Kaleidoscopic History of a Disorderly Decade*. Cambridge, MA and London: Harvard University Press.

Deleuze, Gilles and Félix Guattari (1984), *Anti-Oedipus: Capitalism and Schizophrenia*, trans. Robert Hurley, Mark Seem, and Helen R. Lane. London: Athlone Press.

—(1988), *A Thousand Plateaus: Capitalism and Schizophrenia*, trans. Brian Massumi. London: Athlone Press.

Dennis, Everette E. and William L. Rivers (2011), *Other Voices: The New Journalism in America*. New Brunswick: Transaction.

Denton, Sally and Roger Morris (2002), *The Money and the Power: The Making of Las Vegas and its Hold on America, 1947–2000*. London: Pimlico.

De Quincey, Thomas (1971), *Confessions of an English Opium Eater*, Alethea Hayter (ed.). Harmondsworth: Penguin.

Derrida, Jacques (1978), *Writing and Difference*, trans. Alan Bass. London: Routledge.

—(1995), 'The rhetoric of drugs', in Derrida, Jacques, *Points... Interviews 1974–1994*, Elisabeth Weber (ed.), trans. Michael Israel. Stanford: Stanford University Press, pp. 228–54.

Didion, Joan (2006), *We Tell Ourselves Stories in Order to Live: Collected Nonfiction*. New York: Everyman's Library.

Eliot, T. S. (1974), *Collected Poems 1909–1962*. London: Faber.

Emerson, Ralph Waldo (1984), *Essays*, Sherman Paul (ed.). London: Dent.

Fanon, Frantz (2004), *The Wretched of the Earth*, trans. Richard Philcox, with commentary by Jean-Paul Sartre and Homi K. Bhabha. New York: Grove Press.

Fitzgerald, F. Scott (1991), *The Great Gatsby*, Matthew J. Bruccoli (ed.). London: Scribners.

Fleming, Carole, Emma Hemmingway, Gillian Moore, and Dave Welford (2006), *An Introduction to Journalism*. London: Sage.

Foucault, Michel (2000), *Essential Works of Foucault 1954–1984, Volume 2: Aesthetics*, James D. Faubion (ed.), trans. Robert Hurley and others. London: Penguin.

—(2002), *Essential Works of Foucault 1954–1984, Volume 3: Power*, James D. Faubion (ed.), trans. Robert Hurley and others. London: Penguin.

Franklin, Bob, Martin Hamer, Mark Hanna, Marie Kinsey, and John E. Richardson (2005), *Key Concepts in Journalism Studies*. London: Sage.

Garton Ash, Timothy (2010), 'To bear true witness to history's tragedy and triumph is a sacred trust.' *The Guardian*, 11 March, 31.

Giddens, Anthony (1999), *Runaway World: How Globalisation is Reshaping Our Lives*. London: Profile.

Ginsberg, Allen (1959), *Howl and Other Poems*, introduction by William Carlos Williams. San Francisco: City Lights.

'Gonzo. Specialty definition'. http://www.websters-online-dictionary.org/definition/gonzo accessed 15.2.10

Greene, Graham (2005), *The Quiet American*. London: Vintage.

Hamill, Pete (2004), 'Introduction', in Twain, Mark, *The Best Short Stories of Mark Twain*, Lawrence I. Berkove (ed.). New York: Random House, pp. xi–xxv.

Harcup, Tony (2004), *Journalism: Principles and Practice*. London: Sage.

Hardt, Michael and Antonio Negri (2001), *Empire*. Cambridge, MA and London: Harvard University Press.
Held, David and Anthony McGrew (2003), 'The great globalization debate: an introduction', in David Held and Anthony McGrew (eds), *The Global Transformations Reader* (second edition). Cambridge: Polity Press. pp. 1–50.
Hemingway, Ernest (1967), *By-line: Selected Articles and Dispatches of Four Decades*, William White (ed.). New York: Scribner's.
—(2004a), *Fiesta: The Sun Also Rises*. London: Arrow.
—(2004b), *The Old Man and the Sea*. London: Arrow.
Hofstadter, Richard, William Miller, and Daniel Aaron (1964), *The Structure of American History*. Eaglewood Cliffs, NJ: Prentice-Hall.
Hollinger, David A. and Charles Capper (eds) (2006), *The American Intellectual Tradition, Volume 1: 1630–1865* (fifth edition). New York, Oxford: Oxford University Press.
Hopkins, Jerry and Danny Sugerman (1980), *No One Here Gets Out Alive*. London: Plexus.
Hoskyns, Barney (1997), *Beneath the Diamond Sky: Haight-Ashbury, 1965–1970*. New York: Simon & Schuster.
Huxley, Aldous (1959), *The Doors of Perception and Heaven and Hell*. Harmondsworth: Penguin.
—(1999), *Moksha: Aldous Huxley's Classic Writings on Psychedelics and the Visionary Experience*, Michael Horowitz and Cynthia Palmer (eds). Rochester: Park Street Press.
Jowett, Garth S. (2010), 'The selling of the Pentagon'. http://www.museum.tv/eotvsection.php?entrycode = sellingofth. Accessed 17 September.
Kafka, Franz (1961), *Metamorphosis and Other Stories*, trans. Willa and Edwin Muir. Harmondsworth: Penguin.
Kaplan, Justin (1970), *Mr Clemens and Mark Twain*. Harmondsworth: Penguin.
Kearns, Doris (1976), *Lyndon Johnson and the American Dream*. London: Andre Deutsch,.
Kerouac, Jack (1991), *On the Road*. London: Penguin.
—(2006), *Big Sur*. London: Harper Perennial.
Kierkegaard, Søren (2005), *Fear and Trembling*, trans. Alastair Hannay. London: Penguin.
King, Stephen (1981), *Danse Macabre*. London: MacDonald Future.
Klein, Naomi (2001), *No Logo*. London: Flamingo.
Kurlansky, Mark (2005), *1968: The Year that Rocked the World*. London: Vintage.
Lamb, Christopher (1990), 'Changing with the times: The world according to "Doonesbury"'. *Journal of Popular Culture* 23: 4 (Spring), pp. 113–29.
Larsen, Lars Bang (n. d.), 'When the light falls: notes on ecstasy and corruption'. in Lisa Mark (ed.), *Ecstasy: In and About Altered States*. Cambridge, MA and London: MIT Press, pp. 176–85.

Leary, Timothy (1990), *Flashbacks: A Personal and Cultural History of an Era: An Autobiography*. New York: Tarcher/Putnam.
—(1995), *High Priest*. Second Edition. Berkeley: Ronin.
—(1998), *The Politics of Ecstasy*. Berkeley: Ronin.
Leary, Timothy, Ralph Metzner, and Richard Alpert (1995), *The Psychedelic Experience: A Manual Based on the Tibetan Book of the Dead*. New York: Citadel Press.
Legrain, Philippe (2003), *Open World: The Truth About Globalisation*. London: Abacus.
Lenson, David (1995), *On Drugs*. Minneapolis: University of Minnesota Press.
Lévi-Strauss, Claude (1972), *The Savage Mind*. London: Weidenfeld and Nicolson.
Logevall, Fredrik (2001), *The Origins of the Vietnam War*. Harlow: Pearson.
Lois, Jennifer (2001), 'Peaks and valleys: the gendered emotional culture of edgework'. *Gender and Society* 15: 3 (June), pp. 381–406.
Loomba, Ania (2005), *Colonialism/Postcolonialism* (second edition). London: Routledge.
Mailer, Norman (1968), *The Armies of the Night: History as a Novel; The Novel as History*. London: Weidenfeld and Nicolson.
—(1998), 'The white negro: superficial reflections on the hipster' in Mailer, Norman, *The Time of Our Time*. London: Abacus, pp. 211–30.
Mankiewicz, Frank (1973), *Perfectly Clear: Nixon from Whittier to Watergate*. New York: Quadrangle.
Marcuse, Herbert (1964), *One Dimensional Man*. London: Sphere.
—(1969), *Eros and Civilization: A Philosophical Enquiry into Freud with a New Preface by the Author*. London: Sphere.
Marwick, Arthur (1999), *The Sixties*. Oxford: Oxford University Press.
Marx, Karl and Friedrich Engels (1992), *The Communist Manifesto*, David McLellan (ed.). Oxford: Oxford University Press.
Melville, Herman (1986), *Moby-Dick*, Harold Beaver (ed.). Harmondsworth: Penguin.
Mencken, H. L. (1925) ,'To expose a fool'. *American Mercury*, October, pp. 158–60. http://purple.niagara.edu/chambers/mencken.html. Accessed 15 February 2010.
Miles, Barry (2000), *Ginsberg: A Biography*. London: Virgin.
—(2004), *Hippie*. London: Cassell.
Miller, Henry (1994), *Tropic of Cancer*. New York: Grove Press.
—(2007), *The World of Sex*. London: Oneworld Classics.
Morgan, Ted (1991), *Literary Outlaw: The Life and Times of William S. Burroughs*. London: Bodley Head.
Myerson, Joel (ed.) (1995), *The Cambridge Companion to Henry David Thoreau*. Cambridge: Cambridge University Press.
Nederveen Pieterse, Jan (2004), *Globalization and Culture: Global Mélange*. Lanham: Rowman & Littlefield.

Osterhammel, Jürgen and Niels P. Petersson (2005), *Globalization: A Short History*, trans. Dona Geyer. Princeton: Princeton University Press.

Paine, Thomas (1969), *Rights of Man*. London: Penguin.

Partridge, Christopher (2003), 'Sacred chemicals: psychedelic drugs and mystical experience', in Christopher Partridge and Theodore Gabriel (eds), *Mysticisms East and West: Studies in Mystical Experience*. Carlisle: Paternoster Press, pp. 96–131.

Perry, Paul and Ken Babbs (1990), *On the Bus: The Complete Guide to the Legendary Trip of Ken Kesey and the Merry Pranksters and the Birth of the Counterculture*. London: Plexus.

Pinchbeck, Daniel (2003), 'Ten years of therapy in one night'. *The Guardian Weekend*, 20 September, pp. 30–2.

Porte, Joel (1999), 'Introduction: representing America – the Emerson legacy', in Joel Porte and Saundra Morris (eds), *The Cambridge Companion to Ralph Waldo Emerson*. Cambridge: Cambridge University Press, pp. 1–12.

Rand, Ayn (2007), *The Fountainhead*. London: Penguin.

Reynolds, David (2009), *America, Empire of Liberty: A New History*. London: Allen Lane.

Robinson, David M. (1999), 'Transcendentalism and its times', in Joel Porte and Saundra Morris (eds), *The Cambridge Companion to Ralph Waldo Emerson*. Cambridge: Cambridge University Press, pp. 13–24.

Rolling Stone, Cover to Cover: Forty Years of Rolling Stone Magazine on 3 Searchable DVD-ROMS. Every Issue, Every Page 1967–May 2007. No city: Bondi Digital Publishing, 2008. (RS)

Rorabaugh, William J. (2002), *Kennedy and the Promise of the Sixties*. Cambridge: Cambridge University Press.

Roszak, Theodore (1971), *The Making of a Counter Culture: Reflections on the Technocratic Society and Its Youthful Opposition*. London: Faber.

Said, Edward W. (1991), *The World, The Text, and the Critic*. London: Vintage.

—(1995), *Orientalism: Western Conceptions of the Orient*. Harmondsworth: Penguin.

Sartre, Jean-Paul (2004), 'Preface by Jean-Paul Sartre' in Fanon, Frantz (ed.). *The Wretched of the Earth*, trans. Richard Philcox, commentary by Jean-Paul Sartre and Homi K. Bhabha. New York: Grove Press, pp. xliii–lxii.

Saunders, Nicholas, Anja Saunders, and Michelle Pauli (2000), *In Search of the Ultimate High: Spiritual Experience Through Psychoactives*. London: Rider.

Sedgwick, Eve Kosofsky (1985), *Between Men: English Literature and Male Homosocial Desire*. New York: Columbia University Press.

—(1994), *Epistemology of the Closet*. Harmondsworth: Penguin.

Shapiro, Harry (2003), *Waiting for the Man: The Story of Drugs and Popular Music*. London: Helter Skelter.

Stavans, Ilan (1995), 'The Latin phallus'. *Transition* 65, pp. 48–68.

Stempel, Daniel (2007), 'Fear and loathing in academe: gonzo scholarship and the war against tourism'. *Philosophy and Literature* 31: 1 (April), pp. 95–110.

Stevens, Jay (1993), *Storming Heaven: LSD and the American Dream*. London: Harper Collins.
Stiglitz, Joseph E. (2002), *Globalization and Its Discontents*. London: Penguin.
Tamony, Peter (1970), 'The hell's angels: their naming'. *Western Folklore* 29: 3 (July), pp. 199–203.
Thoreau, Henry David (1992), *Walden and Resistance to Civil Government* (second edition), William Rossi (ed.). New York, London: Norton.
Trudeau, Garry B. (1992), *Action Figure! The Life and Times of Doonesbury's Uncle Duke*. Kansas City: Andrews and McMeel.
Turner, Frederick Jackson (1963), *The Significance of the Frontier in American History*, Harold P. Simonson (ed.). New York: Frederick Ungar.
Twain, Mark (1966), *The Innocents Abroad*. New York: Signet.
—(2004), *The Best Short Stories of Mark Twain*, Lawrence I. Berkove (ed.). New York : Random House.
Venn, Couze (2006), *The Postcolonial Challenge: Towards Alternative Worlds*. London: Sage.
Watts, Alan W. (1957), *The Way of Zen*. London: Thames and Hudson.
White, Theodore H. (1982), *America in Search of Itself: The Making of the President, 1956–1980*. New York: Harper & Row.
Wolfe, Thomas (1972), *The Web and the Rock*. Harmondsworth: Penguin.
Wolfe, Tom (1996), *The Electric Kool-Aid Acid Test*. London: Black Swan.
—(1981), *The Kandy-Kolored Tangerine-Flake Streamline Baby*. London: Picador.
Wolfe, Tom and E. W. Johnson (eds) (1996), *The New Journalism*. London: Picador.
Wordsworth, William (2006), 'Preface to *Lyrical Ballads*', in Stephen Greenblatt et al. (eds), *The Norton Anthology of English Literature* (eighth edition), volume 2. New York: Norton. pp. 262–74.
Wright, Esmond (1996), *A History of the United States of America. Volume Three. The American Dream: from Reconstruction to Reagan*. Cambridge, MA.: Blackwell.
Wu, Duncan (1998), 'Introduction'. *Romanticism: An Anthology* (second edition). Oxford: Blackwell. pp. xxx–xxxvii
Zizek, Slavoj (2002), *Welcome to the Desert of the Real! Five Essays on September 11 and Related Dates*. London: Verso.

Index

1960s, *see* sixties
9/11 (11 September 2001)   2, 15, 92–4, 95, 157, 159, 161

acid tests   54–5, 64–5, 66
Acosta, Oscar Zeta   11, 48, 117, 126, 135–8, 160
Adams, James Truslow   97–8
adrenochrome   167
Agnew, Spiro   34, 50, 53, 62, 88, 136
alcohol   2, 8, 9, 15, 41, 47, 55, 60, 62, 67, 82, 126, 133–5
Alger, Horatio   97–100, 108, 139
Ali, Muhammed   141, 161
Alice in Wonderland (Carroll)   84
Alsop, Joe   99
Altamont (festival)   62
Althusser, Louis   79, 126–7, 152
American Dream, the   10, 18, 31, 50, 53, 66, 70, 78, 84, 87, 96, 97–123, 127, 133, 139, 156, 160, 168
American frontier, *see* frontier, the
amphetamine   11, 25, 27, 34, 41, 42, 48, 57, 83, 86, 147
Anderson, Benedict   124, 141
Animals, Whores and Dialogue (Ewing)   158–9
Arendt, Hannah   99
Armies of the Night, The (Mailer)   12–13
Aspen, Colorado   4–6, 13, 71, 74–7, 93, 135, 138, 164
atheism   5, 57
author function   19–24, 147: *see also* Foucault, Michel
'Author's Note' to *The Great Shark Hunt* (Thompson)   21–3

Bakhtin, Mikhail   78, 134
Banco, Lindsey Michael   57, 149
Barger, Ralph 'Sonny'   66–7, 120
Baudrillard, Jean   10, 73–4, 85, 94, 95
Beat Generation   33–5, 71, 100, 155
Beatles, The   54, 169
Beckett, Samuel   31, 108
Better Than Sex: Confessions of a Political Junkie (Thompson)   14, 28, 89–92
Bey, Hakim   18, 43, 63, 73, 88, 92, 110, 156
Big Sur, California   110–1, 118
Bin Laden, Osama   15, 92–4
blacks/blackness   42, 62, 71–2, 125–6, 128, 134, 136, 138, 140, 168
Black Power   71–2, 125
Bloor, Yail (character)   25, 154
Borges, Jorge Luis   38
Boyle, Peter   163, 168–9
Breakfast with Hunter (Ewing)   164–6
bricolage   28–32, 91, 156, 164
Brinkley, Douglas   14, 16, 18, 19, 40, 86, 91, 101, 133, 158, 161, 162
Brown Power   138
Bruce-Novoa   105, 137
Bryan, William Jennings   37
Buchanan, Pat   6
Burroughs, William S.   35, 71, 78, 87–8, 100, 116, 143
Busey, Gary   167
Bush, George (senior)   40, 89
Bush, George W. (junior)   2, 89, 158
Butler, Judith   119, 126–7
Buy the Ticket, Take the Ride: Hunter S. Thompson on Film (Thurman)   162–3

Index

California 10, 31, 64, 65, 82, 100, 110, 112, 123, 136
Calvino, Italo 7–8
Carmichael, Stokeley 72
capitalism 29, 34, 43, 49–55, 62, 64, 73–6, 85, 92, 99, 100, 103, 115–6, 128, 139
Cardoso, Bill 17
Caroll, E. Jean 8, 19, 45, 154
Carter, Jimmy 14, 79, 83, 89
Céline, Louis-Ferdinand 12
Chancellor, John 83
Chicanos 11, 48, 117, 126, 135–8
civil rights struggle 5, 72, 125, 127
Clinton, Bill 40, 89–92
cocaine 26, 27, 167
colonialism 124–51
Coleridge, Samuel Taylor 46
commodity fetishism 120
communism/communists 58, 83, 85, 101, 142–3
Conrad, Joseph 67–8, 86, 102, 148, 161
Constitution (US) 6, 85, 87, 95, 101, 153
consumerism 15, 54, 57, 73, 100
Cook, James 146–51
counterculture 5–7, 12, 42–69, 88, 100, 104, 163
Cowan, Jay 8, 16, 29, 36, 40, 45–6
Cox, Alex 164–5, 167
Crouse, Timothy 80–3, 117, 160
Curse of Lono, The (Thompson) 14, 15, 73, 117–8, 119, 126, 144–51

'Dance of the Doomed' (Thompson) 135, 141–4, 157
Davis, Al 23
De Quincey, Thomas 26, 46
Debord, Guy 10, 72–3
Declaration of Independence (US) 6, 95, 157
DeKoven, Marianne 47, 49–53, 57, 58, 103, 108, 113, 116, 138
Del Toro, Benicio 163–6

Deleuze, Gilles 28–32, 63, 68–9
Democratic Party 5, 13, 40, 70, 74, 79–81, 83, 109, 160
Democratic Party Convention, Chicago 1968 70–1, 74–5, 122
Depp, Johnny 32, 158–69
Derrida, Jacques 28–9, 54
Dexedrine 48
Didion, Joan 42
Don Quixote (Cervantes) 11, 108
Doonesbury 19, 25
drugs, *see* entries for individual substances
Duke, Raoul (character) 7, 11, 19, 25, 27–32, 36, 38, 39, 47–63, 69, 83, 91, 95–100, 103–5, 113–23, 138–41, 149, 154, 156–60, 163–9
Dylan, Bob 112, 131

Eagleton, Thomas 160
ecstasy 51–62
edge, the 27–8, 36, 68, 76, 106–9, 110, 113, 119–23, 153, 156, 159
edgework 17, 27, 61, 66, 68, 73, 76, 94, 106–9, 110, 121, 153, 156, 159, 168
Eglin Air Force Base, Florida 9
Eisenhower, Dwight 79, 99, 104, 107
Electric Kool-Aid Acid Test, The (Wolfe) 65, 68, 101
Eliot, T. S. 33, 104
Elko, Nevada (conference) 109
Emerson, Ralph Waldo 3–5, 16, 32
espn.com 14
ether 34, 103–4
Ewing, Wayne 158–9, 162, 163–6, 170

Fanon, Frantz 127–32, 143–4
fascism 54, 101
Faulkner, William 17, 156
FBI 1–2, 4, 38
'fear and loathing' (phrase) 34, 50, 53, 59, 101–2, 105, 113, 126–7, 136
'Fear and Loathing at the Super Bowl' (Thompson) 22–4, 25, 73, 163

Index   185

Fear and Loathing in America
   (Thompson)   6, 7, 10–11, 13, 16,
   26, 42, 47–8, 70–1, 76, 89, 95, 97,
   102, 104, 109, 112, 125–6, 133,
   135–8
Fear and Loathing in Las Vegas
   (Gilliam)   158, 163, 164–8
Fear and Loathing in Las Vegas
   (Thompson)   7, 10–11, 17, 21,
   25–32, 35, 38, 44, 45–63, 66, 69,
   83–4, 87, 91, 97, 100, 105–8, 113,
   115–18, 122–3, 126, 137–41, 145,
   147, 148–51, 156
   American Dream in   11, 31, 50,
      53, 103–5, 108–9
   District Attorneys' Confer-
      ence   11, 30–2, 115–6
   drugs in   30–1, 45–63, 66, 69,
      83, 87, 103–4, 113, 120–1, 137–9,
      166–7
   gender in   113–17, 119–21
   Leary, Timothy in   31, 44–7, 51,
      53–63, 65–6, 87, 168
   opening paragraph   27–8
   origins of   11, 48, 137
   protagonists, *see* Duke, Raoul
      and Gonzo, Dr
   race/racism in   137–41
   relationship to Thompson's
      life   7, 10–12, 15, 48, 55–6,
      103–4, 126, 137–41
*Fear and Loathing on the Campaign
   Trail '72* (Thompson)   13–14,
   26–8, 80–4, 90, 117, 122, 160
   magazine version   80
   metaphors   80–4
   opening paragraph   26–8
   protagonist   26–8
'Fear and Loathing in Limbo:
   The Scum Also Rises'
   (Thompson)   14, 85–8
'First Visit With Mescalito'
   (Thompson)   122–3
Fitzgerald, F. Scott   9, 102–3, 154,
   156
five Ws   22–3, 131

Ford, Gerald   14, 84, 86, 89
Foucault, Michel   19–24, 126–7,
   147, 152–3
Fouding Fathers   6, 16, 80, 99, 101,
   152–5, 157
Fourth Amendment   90, 153
Freak Power   5, 13, 71–5, 76–7,
   79, 88–9, 92, 95, 107, 125,127,
   160, 164
Free Lisl: Fear & Loathing in Denver
   (Ewing)   162
frontier, the   35, 63, 66, 69, 78, 94,
   105, 107, 109–10, 120–3, 153, 156–7

Geiger, Bob   125
gender   112–21
gender performativity   119–21, 127
Generation of Swine
   (Thompson)   7, 14, 40–1
Genet, Jean   71
Gibney, Alex   159–61, 162, 164
Gilliam, Terry   160, 161, 163–6,
   166–8, 169
Ginsberg, Allen   33–4, 36, 71, 100
globalization   93, 95, 123, 144–51
Goldwater, Barry   87, 101, 126
*Gonzo: The Life and Work of Dr
   Hunter S. Thompson* (Gibney), *see*
   Gibney, Alex
Gonzo journalism   10–11, 16–19,
   105, 108, 129, 130, 163
Gonzo (definition)   10, 16–19
Gonzo, Dr (character)   11, 25–6,
   30–1, 34, 36, 47–63, 83, 97, 104, 108,
   113–21, 126, 138–40, 154, 157, 160,
   164, 166–9
Gonzo Tapes, The
   (Thompson)   160
Great Gatsby, The (Fitzgerald)   38,
   102–3, 108
Greak Shark Hunt, The
   (Thompson)   11, 14, 17, 21–4,
   25–6, 37–8, 43–4, 73, 85–8
   'Author's Note'   21–3
   'Fear and Loathing at the Super
      Bowl'   22–4, 25, 73, 163

'Fear and Loathing in Limbo: The Scum Also Rises' 14, 85–8
'Fear and Loathing in Washington: The Boys in the Bag' 109
'The Great Shark Hunt' 25–6
Great Society, The 44, 98
Greene, Graham 135
Grenada, US invasion of 150
grotesque 54, 77–9, 82, 84, 95, 157
Guinea Worm (image) 77–8, 96
Guattari, Félix 28–32, 63, 68–9
Gulf War (1990–91) 89

Haig, Alexander 23
Haight-Ashbury, San Francisco 42–4, 48, 50, 52, 55–8, 61, 63, 69, 111, 113
hashish 46: *see also* marijuana
Hawaii 144–51
Hell's Angels (bikers) 10, 42, 51, 52, 62, 63–9, 106, 115–7, 119–21, 160
Hell's Angels (Thompson) 10, 12, 13, 63–9, 73, 97, 106, 116, 119–21, 156, 159
  ending 88, 106
  gender in 115–21
  war machine 63, 68–9
Hemingway, Ernest 9, 16, 36–8, 133–5, 145–6, 154, 156
heroin 42, 58, 62, 78, 81, 141
Hey Rube (Thompson) 14, 92–4
Hicklin, William 161
hippies 5, 42–4, 48–52, 58, 62–3, 75–6, 98, 100, 111–2, 113, 122
Hitler, Adolf 48, 84, 142
Hoffman, Abbie 72, 74
Holmes, John Clellon 34
homosexuality 78, 117–9, 167
homosocial desire 119–21
Hoover, J. Edgar 89
hotels 11, 21–2, 27, 38, 40, 50, 57, 59–60, 70, 86, 118, 120–1, 122–3, 131, 138, 140, 142, 165, 166–8
humanism 5–7, 16, 67, 85, 95, 104, 115–6, 125–30, 132, 136, 151, 155

Humphrey, Hubert 82–3, 122
Hunter S. Thompson – Final 24: His final hours (Hicklin) 161
Huxley, Aldous 32, 46, 48, 56, 59–62
hyperreality 10, 73–4, 84–9, 93–4: *see also* Baudrillard, Jean

ibogaine 80–4, 90, 96
ideology 2, 6, 43, 66–7, 71–5, 79, 87, 105, 109, 116, 127–30, 152–3, 156
ideological state apparatus 79
imperialism 6, 15, 127–32, 150, 157
individualism 3, 16, 22, 37, 43, 46–7, 67, 80–1, 88, 99, 103, 105, 109–10, 126, 128, 152, 155, 157
Industrial Workers of the World, The (Wobblies) 67
inverted pyramid, *see* five Ws

Jarnow, Jesse 18
Jefferson, Thomas 5–6, 18, 155: *see also* Founding Fathers
Jefferson Airplane 61, 166
Jefferson County Jail 8
'Jimmy Carter and the Great Leap of Faith' (Thompson) 83
Johnson, Dr Samuel 7, 166
Johnson, Lyndon B. 6, 44, 46, 98, 107, 142, 166
Joke's Over, The (Steadman) 146–8
journalism (Thompson) 8, 9–30, 36–40, 43–4, 70–1, 80–9, 90, 92–4, 111, 129–32, 135–7, 141–4, 145, 154–5
Joyce, James 156

Kafka, Franz 60
Kandy-Kolored Tangerine-Flake Streamline Baby, The (Wolfe) 57–8
Kemp, Paul (character) 118, 133–5
Kennedy, John F. 14, 77, 89, 100–2, 104–5

Index

'Kentucky Derby is Decadent and Depraved, The' (Thompson) 10–12, 17, 40, 119, 130–1, 148, 155, 157, 162
Kerouac, Jack 34–6, 100, 104, 111
Kesey, Ken 7, 51, 54, 64–5, 111
King, Martin Luther Jr. 72
Kingdom of Fear (Thompson) 1–2, 5, 36, 79, 115, 150, 159
Kissinger, Henry 84, 89

La Honda, California 54, 64–6
Laos 140–4
Larsen, Lars Bang 51–5
Las Vegas, Nevada 11, 27, 29, 31–2, 34, 47–62, 116, 120, 123, 137–41, 160, 165–6
Latin America 129–35
Leary Timothy 5, 31, 44–7, 51, 53–66, 77, 82, 87, 98, 168
Lennon, John 139
Lenson, David 46–7
Lévi-Strauss, Claude 28–32, 156
liberalism 49, 130
Linson, Art 168–9
lodge, the 35, 109–12, 113, 122–3, 135–6, 153, 169
Los Angeles, California 10, 48, 108, 122, 135–7, 138
Louisville, Kentucky 1, 8–9, 165
Lowenstein, Allard K. 71
LSD 5, 25, 27, 31, 41, 42, 45–63, 64–6, 67, 75–6, 82–3, 88, 106, 113, 115, 155, 169
'Lucy in the Sky with Diamonds' 169
Lyng, Stephen 106–9

Mackin, Cassie 117
Mafia, the 49
Mailer, Norman 12–13, 71, 72, 110
Malcolm X 125–6
Manson Family 31
Marcuse, Herbert 52–3, 55
marijuana 26, 33, 42, 143

Marxism 64, 85, 101, 125–32
McGovern, George 13–14, 79–84, 160
McKeen, William 8, 9, 15–17, 19, 25, 36–8, 43, 48, 67, 91, 97, 110–1, 113–4, 118, 121, 124, 143–4, 154, 168, 171
Melville, Herman 108
Mencken, H. L. 36–7
Merry Pranksters 51, 52, 64–6, 106
mescaline 27, 30, 46, 59, 74, 90, 123, 136
metaphor 3, 35, 44, 48, 55, 58, 63, 76–7, 82–4, 87–8, 112, 139, 150
Miller, Henry 110–1
Mint 400 Motorcycle Race 11, 130, 138
Mitchell, Jim and Artie 114
modernism 33, 49–52, 72
Morrison, Jim 62
motorcyle gangs, *see* Hell's Angels
Murray, Bill 25, 158, 163, 168–9
Muskie, Edmund 81–3, 90, 96

Nabulsi, Laila 163–5
Naked Lunch (Burroughs) 71, 78, 88, 143
Nation (magazine) 10
National Observer 9, 129, 130–2, 157
National Rifle Association 161
Naziism 54, 63, 120, 159
New Journalism (movement) 12, 50
New Journalism, The (anthology) 12
New York City, N. Y. 15, 33, 72, 74, 134, 159
New York Times 43–4, 181
Nixon, Richard M. 5–7, 11, 13–14, 23, 29, 32, 37, 39, 48, 50, 53, 62, 70–96, 102–4, 107, 109, 117, 122, 127, 141, 153–5, 161, 168–80

objectivity 10, 15–18, 22, 29, 54, 64, 67, 80–2, 87, 104, 118, 124–32

O'Farrell Theatre, San Francisco 114–5
One Flew Over the Cuckoo's Nest (Kesey) 65
Othello (Shakespeare) 137–41
Outlaw Journalist (McKeen) 8: see also McKeen, William
Owl Farm 4–5, 42, 45, 92, 95, 112–3, 135, 158–9, 163–4, 165, 169, 170

Pageant (magazine) 113
Paine, Thomas 6, 155
Pearl Harbor 144, 157
Perot, Ross 40, 91–2
Perry, Paul 8, 145
Peru 129–30
Plato 157
Playboy 25, 38, 47, 53
'Polo is My Life' (Thompson) 150
pornography 19, 114–5
postcolonialism 124–51
postmodernism 32, 49–53, 73–4, 138, 167
Pound, Ezra 33, 156
Prince Jellyfish (Thompson) 133
Proud Highway, The (Thompson) 2, 3, 6, 9, 13, 34, 43, 54, 57, 89, 101–2, 110–2, 118, 125–6, 128–9, 135, 156
Proust, Marcel 156
psychedelics (drugs), *see* LSD, mescaline
psychedelic sport 106–7
psychedelic (term) 42–69, 106–7, 159
Puerto Rico 118–9, 133–5, 157

Rabelais, François 78, 82, 90, 96, 102, 156
race, racism 124–51: *see also* blacks/blackness, Black Power, Brown Power, Chicanos, civil rights struggle
Rand, Ayn 3, 114
Random House 10, 48, 97, 104–5, 108, 156

Reagan, Ronald 111, 115, 147
Republican Party 5, 6, 23, 40, 74, 79, 91, 101, 127, 161
Revelation, Book of 23–4, 40–1
Reynolds, Debbie 50, 54
Rolling Stone (magazine) 7, 11, 13–16, 19, 25, 43, 45, 48, 62, 80–9, 90, 91, 109, 135, 136, 141–4, 150, 160, 171
Romanticism 155
Rorabaugh, W. J. 99, 104
Roszak, Theodore 5, 50–1, 53–5, 77
Rubin, Jerry 72, 75
Rum Diary, The (Thompson) 110, 118, 126, 133–5, 157
Rumsfeld, Donald 2

Sabonis-Chafee, Terry 70
Said, Edward 130, 141
Saigon 77–8, 135, 141–4, 150: *see also* Vietnam War
Salazar, Ruben 11, 48, 135–7
San Francisco, California 9, 31, 35, 42–4, 47–9, 55, 61, 107, 111, 113–4, 135, 166
Sartre, Jean-Paul 85, 127–30, 143
satire 10, 17, 22, 39, 41, 55, 78, 80, 82, 88, 96, 125, 131, 138
Scanlan's Monthly 10, 17, 95–6, 155
'Scum Also Rises, The' (Thompson) 14, 85–9
Seconal 62
Sedgwick, Eve Kosofsky 118–9
Selling of the Pentagon, The (documentary) 140–1
Semonin, Paul 101, 127–8
'Sergeant Pepper's Lonely Hearts Club Band' 54, 166
sexuality 32, 47, 53, 55, 57, 60, 72, 112–21, 126, 134–5, 163, 164, 167: *see also* homosexuality
Sickels, Robert C. 31, 49, 58, 98–9, 103
Silberman, Jim 48, 97
simulation, *see* Baudrillard, Jean
Situationists 72–3

Index

sixties (decade) 5, 9, 12, 14, 33, 35, 41, 42–69, 70–2, 98–100, 104–5, 113–4, 118, 123, 130–5, 137, 144, 147, 165
Skinner, Gene (character) 150–1, 154, 157
slavery 16, 115
Slick, Grace 61
Songs of the Doomed (Thompson) 14, 28, 105, 141–4, 164
Sound of Music, The 166
Southern, Terry 71
speed (drug), *see* amphetamine
Sports Illustrated 11
sport/sports journalism 9, 14, 22–4, 77, 96, 106–7, 117, 131, 145, 161
Steadman, Ralph 7, 8, 21, 26, 84, 88, 91, 119, 138, 145–8, 157, 160, 162, 164, 166, 171
'Strange Rumblings in Aztlán' (Thompson) 10–11, 48, 135–7, 138, 159
subjectivity 4, 12–13, 18–19, 29, 36–9, 46, 79–80, 103, 120, 123, 124–37, 146, 152–7
Super Bowl 22–5, 27, 73, 163, 168

Talese, Gay 12
television 32, 71–4, 78, 81, 88–92, 99, 104, 136, 140–1, 155, 159, 164, 166
temporary autonomous zone 42–4, 48, 64, 73
Thompson, Anita (second wife) 2, 16, 114, 158–9, 163–4, 170
Thompson, Hunter Stockton, life of:
  Aspen sheriff election, *see* Freak Power
  biographies of 8, 15–16
  career 8–16
  childhood 1–2, 8–9
  crimes of 1–4, 8–9
  early journalism 9–10, 16–17, 43–4, 70, 111, 113, 122–3, 129–32
  homosexuality, attitude to 118

humanism 5–7, 16, 67, 85, 95, 104, 115–6, 125–30, 132, 136, 151, 155
individualism 3, 16, 22, 37, 43, 46–7, 67, 80–1, 88, 99, 103, 105, 109–10, 126, 128, 152, 155, 157
marriages, *see* Thompson, Anita and Thompson, Sandy
military service 9
money 9, 146–7
politics 1–7, 13–15, 17–18, 70–96, 99–105, 124–51, 152–7
race, attitude to 122–51
self-fashioning 1–8, 15–16, 19–32, 45–7, 68–9, 73, 79–80, 87, 94–6, 99, 106–12, 152–7
suicide 15–16, 21, 144, 161–3
travels abroad 9, 129–35, 141–51
women, attitude to 112–20
Thompson, Hunter Stockton, writing of:
  authorship 19–32
  commerical pressures on 9, 146–8
  deadlines 2, 17, 27, 40, 86, 110, 122, 154–5
  drafts 11, 29, 68, 134, 151, 154–6
  editing of 11, 29–30, 91, 108, 155, 159
  fantasy in 24, 31, 38, 54, 80–4, 90, 116, 120, 123, 142–3, 167
  'fear and loathing' (phrase) 34, 50, 53, 59, 101–2, 105, 113, 126–7, 136
  gender in 112–20
  Gonzo, gonzo journalism, *see* separate entries
  grotesque in 54, 77–9, 82, 84, 95, 157
  improvisation 16–19, 28–32, 36, 155–6
  masculinity in, *see* gender in
  metaphors 3, 35, 44, 48, 55, 58, 63, 76–7, 82–4, 86–8, 112, 139, 150
  metonymy 47, 54, 68, 97, 116, 134–5, 151
  music and 18–19, 36, 40, 45, 61, 64, 155–6

persona in 8, 12–13, 15, 19–32, 68–9, 87, 96, 103–4, 116–8, 130, 145–8, 150, 156–8, 163, 167
politics in 1–7, 13–15, 17–18, 70–96, 99–105, 124–51, 152–7
protagonists, *see* individual entries
satire, *see* satire
sexism in 112–20
structure 17–18, 21–4, 28–41, 57–9, 80–2, 86–9, 91–2, 108, 124–6, 143–4
style 10, 13–15, 16–19, 24, 26, 33, 36, 37, 65, 82, 87, 105, 107–8, 124–5, 130, 147, 154–5
subjectivism, *see* self-fashioning, subjectivity
works of, *see* individual entries
writing methods of 9–15, 16–24, 27, 28–41, 48, 68, 73, 77, 86–7, 91, 96, 103, 105, 106–7, 122, 137–8, 146–8, 151, 152–7
Thompson, Juan (son) 9, 16
Thompson, Sandy (first wife) 9, 45, 110, 112–14, 158, 160
Thoreau, Henry David 3–7, 16, 20, 32, 77, 111–2
Thurman, Tom 162–3
Time (magazine) 43
To Tell the Truth 159
transcendentalism 4–6, 55, 112, 156
Trudeau, Garry, *see Doonesbury*
Turner, Frederick Jackson, *see* frontier, the
Twain, Mark 36, 38–40, 148, 163

'Uncle Duke', *see Doonesbury*

Venn, Couze 126–7
Vietnam (travels to) 135, 141–4, 150: *see also* Vietnam War

Vietnam War 4, 5, 15, 32, 53, 58, 66, 69, 70, 77, 84, 123, 135, 136, 140–4, 150, 157, 166
Vonnegut, Kurt 38

War on Drugs, the 62
War on Terror, the 2, 15, 92–4, 95, 157
Washington, D. C. 89
Watergate scandal 14, 77, 84–9, 93, 102, 109
Wenner, Jann 7, 16, 62, 83, 90, 144, 161
When I Die: a Documentary on the Raising of the Gonzo Memorial (Ewing) 163–4
Where the Buffalo Roam (Linson) 168–9
Whitmer, Peter O. 139, 161
'Why Anti-Gringo Winds Often Blow South of the Border' (Thompson) 130–2
Wolfe, Thomas (novelist) 101
Wolfe, Tom (New Journalist) 12–13, 57–8, 65–6, 68, 101, 106, 163
Woodstock (festival) 49, 54
Woody Creek, Colorado 4, 89, 91, 112
Wordsworth, William 155
World War Two 1, 63, 157: *see also* Pearl Harbor
Wright, Sondi, *see* Thompson, Sandy

Yippies (Youth International Party) 72–5

Zevon, Warren 158–9, 162
Ziegler, Ron 87–8
Zizek, Slavoj 95

www.ingramcontent.com/pod-product-compliance
Lightning Source LLC
Chambersburg PA
CBHW061832300426
44115CB00013B/2342